Fodors 92 Santa Fe, Taos, Albuquerque

Ron Butler

To my daughter, Alexandra.
They'll love you in Santa Fe.

Fodor's Travel Publications, Inc.
New York and London

Fodor's Santa Fe, Taos, Albuquerque

Editor: Edie Jarolim
Editorial Contributors: Robert Blake, David Low, Marcy Pritchard, Melissa Rivers, Julie Tomasz
Art Director: Fabrizio LaRocca
Cartographer: David Lindroth
Illustrator: Karl Tanner
Cover Photograph: Jean M. Berg

Design: Vignelli Associates

About the Author

Ron Butler, who is based in Tucson, Arizona, has held editorial staff positions on *Esquire*, *True*, and *Penthouse* magazines. His articles have appeared in such publications as *Travel & Leisure*, *Travel Holiday*, and *Ladies Home Journal*, and his books include *Esquire's Guide to Modern Etiquette* (Lippincott) and *The Best of the Old West* (Texas Monthly Press).

Special Sales

Fodor's Travel Publications are available at special discounts for bulk purchases (100 copies or more) for sales promotions or premiums. Special editions, including personalized covers, excerpts of existing guides, and corporate imprints, can be created in large quantities for special needs. For more information, write to Special Marketing, Fodor's Travel Publications, 201 E. 50th Street, New York, NY 10022, or call 1-800-800-3246. Inquiries from the United Kingdom should be sent to Fodor's Travel Publications, 20 Vauxhall Bridge Road, London, England SW1V 2SA.

Contents

Maps

Foreword

Travel writers never truly appreciate the diligence and support of regional state and city tourist offices until they've returned from the trail, so to speak, and in hindsight recall all the help and assistance they've received. So I wish particularly to thank Don Laine of the Taos County Chamber of Commerce, Wadine Gibbons of the Santa Fe Convention and Visitors Bureau, and Sharon Maloof of the State of New Mexico Economic Development and Tourism Department. Also a special thanks to Jean Culberson of the Santa Fe Real Estate Agency who, finding me in front of her office momentarily lost and confused, invited me in, let me use her phone, gave me a cup of coffee, and sent me on my way.

While every care has been taken to ensure the accuracy of the information in this guide, the passage of time will always bring change, and consequently the publisher cannot accept responsibility for errors that may occur.

All prices and opening times quoted here are based on information supplied to us at press time. Hours and admission fees may change, however, and the prudent traveler will avoid inconvenience by calling ahead.

Fodor's wants to hear about your travel experiences, both pleasant and unpleasant. When a hotel or restaurant fails to live up to its billing, let us know and we will investigate the complaint and revise our entries where the facts warrant it.

Send your letters to the editors of Fodor's Travel Publications, 201 E. 50th Street, New York, NY 10022.

Highlights'92 and Fodor's Choice

Highlights '92

The recession, which put such a kibosh on foreign travel, has proved a boon to domestic destinations, with New Mexico reaping a harvest of new visitors. To be sure, the budgets of individual travelers are still showing the strain—domestic travelers are more likely to arrive by privately owned vehicles than by air, and from nearer than farther states. But come they do.

The depressed dollar has also produced a greater influx of foreign travelers who tend to stay longer and spend more. To make sure visitors from other countries experience all of the state's marvels, in 1991 the U.S. House Appropriations Subcommittee on Rural Development awarded New Mexico State University's Hospitality and Tourism Service Program a $230,000 grant to attract foreign tourism to southern New Mexico. Meanwhile, a U.S. Department of Commerce study ranked both Albuquerque and Santa Fe second nationally (behind Philadelphia) as historical, cultural, and minority centers, praising them for "capitalizing on their Hispanic and Native American heritage by devising events that enhance their appeal."

Art in the Land of Enchantment remains a major attraction. Last summer ('91), New York artist Ronald Sherr received the $250,000 Hubbard Art Award for Excellence at Ruidoso's prestigious 2nd Annual Hubbard Art Award Show for his 44-by-28-inch oil and gold leaf painting entitled *Portrait of Elaine*. R.C. Hubbard announced that the recession forced him to cancel the 1992 awards because of the year-long postponement of his new $15 million, 207-room Sierra Blanca Radisson Resort Hotel in Ruidoso (on the way to Carlsbad Caverns) where the prestigious art event was to have taken place. Nineteen hundred ninety-three is also the target date for the unveiling of Hubbard's new $1.5 million, 40,000-square-foot Hubbard Museum of the Horse in Ruidoso, the new home of the Ann Stradling Museum of the Horse collection, which recently moved from Patagonia, Arizona.

Also in transition is the campus museum of Santa Fe's Institute of American Indian Arts, open to the public since 1972. Holding the largest collection of contemporary Native American art in the United States—including painting and photography along with traditional crafts—the museum will reopen during the summer of 1992 as an expanded state-of-the-art facility in the renovated former Federal post office, a block east of Santa Fe's historic plaza. Its new location is expected to increase annual visitation from 30,000 to more than 200,000.

The popular Santa Fe Railroad exhibit (47 paintings from the company's 600-painting collection, along with other extensive railroad memorabilia) wound down at Santa Fe's Museum of Fine Art at the end of 1991. It is expected to go on tour throughout the state, although plans have not yet been formalized. Called "Creating Images of the Southwest: The Santa Fe Railway Collection," the exhibit includes archival photographs and an exquisite place setting from an antique railroad dining car.

Also new for 1992 is the Hurd Ranch Guest Homes, adobe casitas in historic San Patricio, 20 miles east of Ruidoso. The rentals, adjacent to the Hurd-La Rinconada gallery, are part of the sprawling compound belonging to one of America's leading art dynasties. Owner-artist Michael Hurd is the son of the late legendary artist Peter Hurd and Henriette Wyeth, of the famed painting Wyeths. Rentals are available on a weekly basis only (for information, contact Hurd Ranch Guest Homes, Box 100, San Patricio, NM 88348, tel. 505/653–4331).

Good food remains another strong incentive for visiting New Mexico. Santa Fe's trendy Coyote Cafe has won numerous accolades, the most recent of them being the James Beard Awards nomination as the Best Southwestern Restaurant. At the same time, owner-chef Mark Miller was inducted into the prestigious Fine Dining Hall of Fame during the National Restaurant Association Convention in Chicago. Success breeds success. In November 1991, Miller opened a Coyote Cafe clone called the Red Sage in Washington, D.C.

Fodor's Choice

No two people will agree on what makes a perfect vacation, but it can be fun and helpful to know what others think. We hope you'll have a chance to experience some of Fodor's Choices yourself while visiting New Mexico. For detailed information on individual entries, see the relevant sections of this guidebook.

Lodging

Inn of the Governors, Santa Fe (*Expensive*)

La Posada de Santa Fe, Santa Fe (*Expensive*)

Inn of the Animal Tracks, Santa Fe (*Moderate*)

Taos Inn, Taos (*Expensive*)

Hotel La Fonda de Taos, Taos (*Moderate*)

Las Palomas de Taos/The Mabel Dodge Luhan House, Taos (*Moderate*)

Hyatt Regency Albuquerque, Albuquerque (*Expensive*)

La Posada de Albuquerque, Albuquerque (*Expensive*)

Elaine's, A Bed and Breakfast, Albuquerque (*Moderate*)

Scenic Drives

The High Road to Taos (the old road linking Santa Fe and Taos)

The Enchanted Circle (90-mile loop from Taos through canyon and alpine country, with a few colorful mining towns thrown in)

Route 66, America's most nostalgic highway, includes a colorful stretch that now constitutes Albuquerque's Central Avenue

Turquoise Trail (the old route between Albuquerque and Santa Fe)

Historic Buildings

Museum of Fine Art, Santa Fe

Palace of the Governors, Santa Fe

Santuario de Chimayo, Chimayo

San Francisco de Asis Church, Ranchos de Taos

Taos Pueblo, Taos

Ernie Pyle Memorial Library, Albuquerque

Romantic Sites

Any spot beside the road under a cottonwood tree during chile-harvesting season (August–September), where enterprising farmers have set up tumble drier–like roasting machines to roast bagfuls of freshly picked chiles for sale to passing motorists.

Santa Fe at Christmastime, with *farolitos* glowing everywhere

Taos Book Shop, Taos (many serious romances, as in books, have begun in bookstores)

Courtyard in the Millicent Rogers Museum with the Indian maiden statue by R.C. Gorman

Outdoor hot tubs at Ten Thousand Waves, Santa Fe

Puye Cliff Dwellings, Santa Clara Pueblo, near Santa Fe

Taste Treats

Hatch chiles

Sopaipillas, the light fluffy pastry bread served warm with honey during spicy Mexican meals to help neutralize the hotness

Indian fry bread (American cousin of *sopaipillas*, available at the pueblos and wherever Native American food is featured)

Chilaquilese con chorizo (warm cheese dip with bits of Mexican sausage and chile)

Blue corn tortillas

Red chile burritos

Green chile salsa

Restaurants

The Compound, Santa Fe (*Expensive*)

La Tertulia, Santa Fe (*Moderate*)

Restaurante Rancho de Chimayo, Chimayo (*Inexpensive*)

El Patio de Taos (when Elizabeth Taylor visited famed Taos artist R.C. Gorman, he brought her here for dinner) (*Expensive*)

Andy's La Fiesta Restaurant, Ranchos de Taos (*Moderate*)

Casa Vieja, Albuquerque (*Expensive*)

Antiquity Restaurant, Albuquerque (*Moderate*)

New Mexico

World Time Zones

| +12 | +13 | | | -9 | | | | -5 | -4 | -3 | | 25 |

Numbers below vertical bands relate each zone to Greenwich Mean Time (0 hrs.).
Local times frequently differ from these general indications,
as indicated by light-face numbers on map.

+11   +12 -   -11   -10   -9   -8   -7   -6   -5   -4   -3   -2

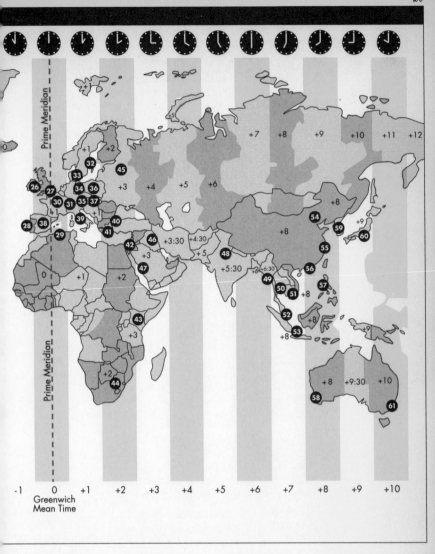

Introduction

I t was winter, a good 25 years ago, when I first visited New Mexico. I was traveling with Gerta, the beautiful young German woman who was not yet my wife. We headed out from Tucson with the famous Southwestern artist Ted DeGrazia and his wife, Marion, in De Grazia's big Mercedes. DeGrazia wanted to sketch and paint Christmas ceremonial dances at the various pueblos. A fanatic about color, he was also looking for a red blanket of a certain shade. He'd been searching for months and he was sure he'd find it in New Mexico.

I don't recall where we stayed in Santa Fe, our first stop, but I remember being surprised at how shocked DeGrazia was when he learned that Gerta and I would be sharing the same room, even though we weren't married. I guess it just wasn't done in those days. I also recall that we shopped under the portals at the Palace of the Governors on the Santa Fe Plaza; I still have the inlaid turquoise and silver cuff links I bought there. I understand cuff links are coming back.

We went on to Taos, where we paid a perhaps-too-early-in-the-morning visit to the writer Frank Waters, a friend of DeGrazia's. I had a copy of Waters's *The Man Who Killed the Deer* that I was hoping to have autographed. Unannounced visits are quite common in the West, but ours couldn't have been more badly timed. Waters was just sitting down to breakfast and obviously having a tiff with his wife. Our arrival—"paying homage to the great writer" was his wife's ironic phrase, I think—set her off. A plate of scrambled eggs went flying across the kitchen, smashing into the wall. We could still hear the shouting as we got into the car. I never did get the book signed.

On Christmas Eve, we headed out to the services at the Taos Pueblo. There was a huge crowd and no room to sit; we squeezed into the church balcony. A tall, powerfully built Indian standing next to me lit a cigarette. I told him he shouldn't smoke in church. He told me we were in an "Indian place" and he'd smoke if he wanted to. I wasn't about to argue. After the priest said Mass, two Indian deer dancers, bedecked in deerskins and antlers, came thumping down the center of the church aisle, rattles shaking, chanting; they were followed by others and then by a buffalo dancer. DeGrazia sketched away.

At the Nambe Pueblo, where we went next, we were surprised to discover the same priest saying Mass. In fact, this priest was at every pueblo we visited that night, eventually saying "midnight" Mass at two in the morning at Santa Clara. Somewhere along the way we got arrested. Driving down a long dirt road to one of the pueblos, we picked up an Indian who was going in the same direction. He was quite young and quite drunk, and it was the latter condition that found all four of us being led to the office of the tribal governor—who was apparently also a judge.

It was a serious offense, we were told, bringing alcohol into the pueblo. We hadn't, but because the intoxicated Indian was with us, it was assumed that we had contributed to his condition. For a while it looked as though we were going to spend Christmas Eve in jail, but then DeGrazia had a brainstorm. He opened his wallet and slowly laid out a string of credit cards, all gleaming plastic and bright colors. The governor-judge picked up each card and studied it carefully, running his finger over the embossed lettering. What message they transmitted, we don't know, but they did the trick. The cards were returned, and we were promptly released.

It was late and everyone was exhausted, but DeGrazia wanted to press on. An impressionist artist, he painted Indians with stylistic brilliance in a dazzling palette of colors. For the moment, however, he was making only quick pencil sketches. The more tired he was, he explained, the more blurred everything became, and only the most important details stood out. He worked best in that dreamlike state.

Before visiting the pueblos, Gerta and I had noticed a blanket in the window of the local J. C. Penney's. It was red, a terrible color red, a red that reminded us a bit of Campbell's tomato soup. We bought it, had it gift wrapped, and gave it to DeGrazia on Christmas morning. He seemed touched when he opened the box; it was just the color he was looking for, he said, trying to keep a straight face. How did we ever find it?

DeGrazia died in 1982. He had planned to move to Santa Fe and build a studio there at the base of the Sangre de Cristo Mountains, but that never came to pass. The city has expanded since that first visit and has changed, as have we all. Yet, like DeGrazia, I find New Mexico's spiritual pull at times overwhelming. And the impressions it leaves— especially after I go too long without sleep—are the most vivid of anywhere I've been.

Recently I was driving north from Carlsbad, alone, when I pulled up in front of the Inn of the Mountain Gods, centerpiece of the sprawling Mescalero Indian Reservation in the southern part of the state. Midway between Alamogordo and Roswell in Lincoln County, the reservation is home to more than 2,500 Mescalero Apaches, and the inn is Apache owned and run. The idea of vacationing for a few days on an Indian reservation appealed to me. I wanted to read, write, and relax away from it all. In the back of my mind were thoughts of hogans, tepees, and lazy curls of smoke rising from smoldering camp fires.

These visions dissipated when a pleasant young man in jeans and a white shirt said, "Good morning, sir," as he unloaded my bags and then drove my car to an adjacent parking lot. Valet parking? I could have been in Beverly Hills.

But once inside, I knew I had come to the right place. The canyon-size lobby was dominated by a three-story-high copper-sheathed fireplace. Beyond, the glass-paneled walls looked out onto Mescalero Lake, and beyond the lake, the slender tips of ponderosa pine speared a bank of low-hanging clouds, all framed by a wall of jagged mountains. Indian paintings, artifacts, and wall hangings were displayed throughout the lobby. Even before I signed in I found myself pricing turquoise jewelry at a display case.

Three miles northeast is the town of Ruidoso, home of the Ruidoso Racetrack. On Labor Day, the track's All-American Quarter Horse Futurity offers as much as $3 million in prize money; it's billed as the nation's richest purse. The town itself is small, one of those places where people still give directions by the number of bumps in the road. In addition to its shops and antique stores, downtown Ruidoso has a number of saloons where the racetrack grooms, stable boys, and tipsters congregate. I stopped into one of these bars one night wearing a suit, and the bartender asked me if I was a doctor.

On the north, east, and west Ruidoso is bordered by Lincoln National Forest. In 1950, after a devastating forest fire was brought under control there, firefighters found a small, badly burned bear cub clinging to a tree. Nurtured back to health, the cub was later flown to the Washington, D.C., zoo. He was named Smokey, and became the symbol for the nation's campaign to prevent forest fires.

When I checked out of the hotel several days later, loaded down with Indian rugs, bracelets, pottery, images of another way of life, I felt ready once again to face the rigors of city, traffic, and deadlines.

Extolling the glories of an area of which one is particularly fond invariably leaves one with a sense of misgiving. I can't help but wonder to what extent I'm contributing to changing the things that I value. With a statewide population of about 1½ million, New Mexico isn't exactly being overrun. But a new runway is proposed for the Taos Municipal Airport, capable of handling scheduled commercial aircraft. And I just heard that the Inn of the Mountain Gods was installing a hundred slot machines in its lobby. "I don't know why I paint Indians," DeGrazia once wrote to me. "Maybe I'm afraid that the Indians are going to vanish and I want to be around them to fill my eyes."

1 Essential Information

Before You Go

Centers of art, rural Spanish villages, Indian pueblos, ghost towns, prehistoric ruins, mining towns, space age laboratories, historical sites, desert wilderness, canyons that plunge deep into the earth and mountains that soar to the heavens, New Mexico is as much a state of mind as it is a state of grace, the ancient, Indian spiritual Land of Enchantment. The state is large and diverse, with a population of less than 1½ million. It all awaits. *"Nos vemos,"* they say. "We'll see you soon."

Visitor Information

A detailed 164-page *New Mexico Vacation Guide* is available free from the **New Mexico Tourism and Travel Division** (Joseph M. Montoya Bldg., 1100 St. Francis Dr., Santa Fe 87503, tel. 505/827–0291 or 800/545–2070). It covers the state section by section (northwest, north central, northeast, central, southeast, and south), profiling cities and attractions, from the great outdoors to art and cultural events, with maps, activity calendars, and other useful information.

To find out about outdoor pursuits, contact the **USDA Forest Service, Southwestern Region** (Public Affairs Office, 517 Gold Ave., SW, Albuquerque 87102, tel. 505/842–3292). For information about New Mexico's Native Americans, contact the **Indian Pueblo Cultural Center** (2401 12th St., NW, Albuquerque 87102, tel. 505/843–7270).

The New Mexico Tourism and Travel Division operates seven Welcome Centers, staffed from 8 AM to 5 PM daily, which provide information, maps, and brochures. They offer clean rest rooms, drinking water, picnic tables, public telephones, and plenty of parking space. They are located on I–10 at the New Mexico/Texas line, 5 miles south of Anthony; at the intersection of U.S. Highways 64/84 and 17 at Chama, near the Colorado line; on I–40 at the New Mexico/Texas line, 40 miles east of Tucumcari; on I–10 just west of Lordsburg, 22 miles east of the New Mexico/Arizona border; in Raton at 1100 Clayton Road; in Gallup at 701 E. Montoya Boulevard; and on I–25, 15 miles south of Santa Fe on the road to Albuquerque.

Tour Groups

If you're interested in learning about New Mexico's fascinating history—tales of ancient Native American civilizations, Spanish conquistadores, cattle barons, and homesteaders—as well as in seeing the state's modern artists and cities, then you may want to consider an escorted tour. Creative itineraries abound, hitting the traditional tourist spots along with out-of-the-way places you may not be able to get to on your own. They also tend to save you money on air fare and hotels. If group travel is not your style, consider an independent package. Here, too, creativity abounds. You can design your own itinerary by stringing together mini hotel packages in various cities, taking a self-drive tour, or whipping up a unique combination of all the above.

When evaluating any tour, be sure to find out exactly what expenses are included (particularly tips, taxes, and service charges; side trips; additional meals; and entertainment); ratings of all hotels on the itinerary and the facilities they offer; cancellation policies for both you and the tour operator; and, if you are traveling alone, the cost of a single supplement.

Listed below is a sampling of operators and packages to give you an idea of what is available. For additional resources, contact your travel agent or the New Mexico Tourism and Travel Division. Most tour operators request that bookings be made through a travel agent—there is no additional charge for doing so.

General-Interest Tours
Maupintour (Box 807, Lawrence, KS 66044, tel. 913/843–1211 or 800/255–4266) provides a solid but quick overview of the state, hitting the top tourist spots in eight days. An 11-day "Rockies Rail Adventure" winds through Albuquerque, Santa Fe, and Taos before heading to Colorado. A 12-day tour exploring the Indian lands of the Southwest also is available.

Tauck Tours (11 Wilton Rd., Westport, CT 06881, tel. 203/226–6911 or 800/468–2825) offers an eight-day tour of the "land of enchantment," featuring Carlsbad Caverns, Albuquerque, Santa Fe, and Taos. There's an optional hot-air balloon ride too.

Several of the West Coast itineraries offered by **Domenico Tours** (751 Broadway, Bayonne, NJ 07002, tel. 201/823–8687 or 800/554–TOUR) include stops in New Mexico.

Special-Interest Tours
Adventure
American Wilderness Experience (Box 1486, Boulder, CO 80306, tel. 303/494–2992) includes llama treks into New Mexico's Pecos and Gila Wilderness areas among its many hiking, kayaking, horseback riding, and backpacking trips worldwide.

Rocky Mountain Tours (1323 Paseo de Peralta, Santa Fe 87501, tel. 505/984–1684) offers custom tours for preorganized groups, as well as tours to American Indian country and rafting trips on the Rio Grande and Rio Charma.

Ecological/Nature
Is it possible to go on vacation today, experience the outdoors, and do the environment some good? Of course. Here's a sampling of some trips that offer the chance to help scientists on research projects in New Mexico (or around the world). Others are less hands on, but a portion of the trip is donated to environmental causes. Either way, such a vacation enables you not only to escape to the outdoors, but also to make a contribution to conservation.

The Archaeological Conservancy (415 Orchard Dr., Santa Fe 87501, tel. 505/982–3278), a national nonprofit preservation organization, features archaeologist-led tours of prehistoric sites and contemporary American Indian villages of New Mexico.

Earthwatch (680 Mount Auburn, Box 403N, Watertown, MA 02272, tel. 617/926–8200) sponsors more than 100 scientific expeditions around the world. Research projects vary each year, but frequently include New Mexico destinations.

National Audubon Society (950 Third Ave., New York, NY 10022, tel. 212/546–9140), whose trips comply with a seven-point code of environmental-travel ethics, runs about 24 domestic and international natural- and cultural-history outings a year that occasionally include New Mexico.

The Sierra Club (Sierra Club Outings, 730 Polk St., San Francisco, CA 94109, tel. 415/923–5630) offers both service trips (surveys of cultural sites in Chaco Culture National Historic

Park, for example) and adventure trips (base-camp expeditions in the Pecos Wilderness)—all led by experienced volunteers.

Victor Emanuel Nature Tours (Box 33008, Austin, TX 78764, tel. 512/328–5221) has 150 birding and natural-history trips worldwide (including the American Southwest) and donates a portion of its money to various conservation organizations.

Rafting, Canoeing, Kayaking   **Los Rios River Runners, Inc.** (100 E. San Francisco St., Santa Fe 87501, tel. 505/986–6565 or 800/338–6877, fax 505/986–0214) schedules half-day, full-day, and overnight trips on the Rio Grande and the Rio Charma, including the world-famous "Taos Box."

New Wave Rafting Company (Rte. 5, Box 302A, Santa Fe 87501, tel. 505/984–1444 or 505/455–2633) offers half-day, full-day, and overnight rafting expeditions that depart daily from Santa Fe Plaza.

Rio Bravo River Tours (1412 Cerrillos Rd., Santa Fe 87501, tel. 505/988–1153 or 800/451–0708) features family-oriented rafting trips navigated by experienced guides.

Package Deals for Independent Travelers

United Vacations (tel. 800/328–6877) and **American Airlines Fly AAway Vacations** (tel. 817/355–1234 or 800/433–7300) both have fly/drive packages that combine special rental car and hotel rates in Albuquerque, Santa Fe, and Taos. American also offers three-night, air-inclusive ski packages to New Mexico. **Continental's Grand Destinations** (tel. 800/634–5555) four- and seven-night ski packages to Taos and Big Sky include lift tickets and round-trip air transportation.

Tips for British Travelers

Tourist Information   The U.S. Travel and Tourism Administration (22 Sackville St., London W1X 2EA, tel. 071/439–7433) has information and brochures.

Passports and Visas   You will need a valid 10-year passport to enter the United States (cost £15 for a standard 32-page passport, £30 for a 94-page passport). Application forms are available from most travel agents and major post offices and from the **Passport Office** (Clive House, 70 Petty France, London SW1H 9HD, tel. 071/279–3434 for recorded information, or 071/279–4000). You do not need a visa if you are visiting on business or pleasure; are staying fewer than 90 days; have a return ticket or onward ticket; are traveling with a major airline (in effect, any airline that flies from the United Kingdom to the United States); and complete visa waiver 1791, which is supplied either at the airport of departure or on the plane. If you fail to comply with any of these requirements or are entering the United States by land, you will need a visa. Apply to a travel agent or the **United States Embassy Visa and Immigration Department** (5 Upper Grosvenor St., London W1A 2JB, tel. 071/499–3443 for a recorded message, or 071/499–7010). Visa applications to the U.S. Embassy must be made by mail, not in person. Visas can be given only to holders of 10-year passports, although visas in expired passports remain valid. If you think you may stay longer than three months, you must apply for a visa before you travel.

Customs Entering the United States, a visitor 21 or over can bring in 200 cigarettes or 50 cigars or 2 kilograms smoking tobacco, 1 liter of alcohol, and duty-free gifts to a value of $100. You may not bring in meat or meat products, seeds, plants, or fruit. Returning to the United Kingdom, a traveler 17 or over can take home (1) 200 cigarettes, 100 cigarillos, 50 cigars, or 250 grams of tobacco; (2) one liter of alcohol over 22% volume, two liters of alcohol under 22% volume, or two liters of fortified or sparkling wine; (3) two liters of still table wine; (4) no more than 50 liters of beer or 25 mechanical lighters; (5) 60 cc of perfume and 250 ml of toilet water; (6) other goods to a value of £32.

Insurance The **Association of British Insurers** (Aldermary House, 10-15 Queen St., London EC4N 1TT, tel. 071/248–4477) gives free general advice on all aspects of holiday insurance. **Europ Assistance** (252 High St., Croydon, Surrey CR0 1NF, tel. 081/680–1234) is a proved leader in the holiday insurance field.

Tour Operators **American Express Holidays** (Portland House, Stag Place, London SW1E 5BZ, tel. 071/834–9744) offers many touring options in the Southwest, providing itineraries and arrangements for fly/drive holidays, motorcoach tours, and motor-home rentals.

Speedbird Holidays (Pacific House, Hazelwick Ave., Three Bridges, Crawley, West Sussex RH10 1NP, tel. 0293/611611) has a 17-day "Southwestern Horizons" coach tour that includes the Grand Canyon, Albuquerque, Santa Fe, Taos, Mesa Verde, and Utah's canyon lands.

Airlines and Airfares The major airport in New Mexico is in Albuquerque. Flying time varies considerably with the airline and length of stopover in various hub cities; approximate flying time from London to Albuquerque via New York is 14½ hours.

When to Go

The best time to go to New Mexico is purely a matter of personal preference. If you're interested in a particular sport, activity, or special event, go when that's available, and don't worry too much about the weather. Most ceremonial dances at the Indian pueblos occur in the summer, early fall, Christmas, and Easter. The majority of other major events are geared to the traditionally heavy tourist season of July and August; the Santa Fe Opera, Chamber Music Festival, and Indian and Spanish markets all take place during those two months. The Santa Fe Fiesta and New Mexico State Fair in Albuquerque are held in September, and the Albuquerque International Hot Air Balloon Fiesta is in October.

The relatively cool climates of Santa Fe and Taos are also a lure in summer, as is the skiing in the Taos area in winter. Christmas is a wonderful time to be in New Mexico, not only because of Native American ceremonials, but also for the Spanish religious folk plays, special foods, and musical events. Hotel rates are generally highest during the peak summer season, but fluctuate less than do those in most major resort areas. If you plan to come in July or August, be sure to make reservations in advance. You can pretty much avoid the tourist crowds by coming during the shoulder seasons, spring and fall. Spring weather is unpredictable; sudden storms may come up. October is one of the best months to visit: the air is crisp, colors are brilliant, and whole mountainsides become tumbling cascades of red and gold.

Climate What follows are average daily maximum and minimum temperatures for Santa Fe and Albuquerque.

Santa Fe	Jan.	39F	4C	May	68F	20C	Sept.	73F	23C
		19	− 7		42	6		48	9
	Feb.	42F	6C	June	78F	26C	Oct.	62F	17C
		23	− 5		51	11		37	3
	Mar.	51F	11C	July	80F	27C	Nov.	50F	10C
		28	− 2		57	14		28	− 2
	Apr.	59F	15C	Aug.	78F	26C	Dec.	39F	4C
		35	2		55	13		19	− 7

Albuquerque	Jan.	46F	8C	May	78F	26C	Sept.	84F	29C
		24	− 4		51	11		57	14
	Feb.	53F	12C	June	89F	32C	Oct.	71F	22C
		28	− 2		60	16		44	7
	Mar.	60F	16C	July	91F	33C	Nov.	57F	14C
		33	1		64	18		32	0
	Apr.	69F	21C	Aug.	89F	32C	Dec.	48F	9C
		42	6		64	18		26	− 3

See also the What to Pack section, below, for more information on the climate in New Mexico.

Current weather information for more than 750 cities around the world may be obtained by calling **WeatherTrak** information service at 900/370–8728 (cost: 95¢ per minute). A taped message will tell you to dial the three-digit access code for the destination in which you're interested. The code is either the area code (in the United States) or the first three letters of the foreign city. For a list of all access codes, send a stamped, self-addressed envelope to Cities (9B Terrace Way, Greensboro, NC 27403). For more information, call 800/247–3282.

A similar service operated by American Express can be accessed by dialing 900/WEATHER (900/932–8437). As well as supplying a three-day weather forecast for 600 cities worldwide, this service provides international travel information and time and day. The cost is 75¢ per minute.

Festivals and Seasonal Events

January **Indian New Year's Celebrations,** all pueblos. Comanche, deer, and other traditional dances, including the Turtle Dance (the men's traditional animal dance), are performed at the Taos Pueblo. For information, call 505/758–8626.

February **Winterfestival,** Santa Fe. The annual celebration of winter takes place over four days in late February, both in town and on the slopes of the Santa Fe Ski Area. Events range from snow-sculpture competitions to downhill racing, including the Governor's Cup race. Hot-air ballooning, music, and drama are also featured. For additional information, call 505/983–5615.

March **Living History Weekend,** Columbus. The town of Columbus sits on the border of Mexico where a reenactment of the 1916 clash between American forces and Pancho Villa's Mexican soldiers takes place at Pancho Villa State Park early in March. There are tactical demonstrations, field-camp drills, authentic equipment and uniforms, all lots of fun. For information, call 505/928–2996.

April **Albuquerque Founder's Day,** Albuquerque. This mid-April event commemorates the April 23, 1706, founding of Albuquerque by Governor Francisco Cuervo y Valdes, whose costumed persona presides over the event. An auction and entertainment are part of the celebration at the Old Town Plaza. For information, call 505/243–3696.

May **Buzzard Days,** Carrizozo. Rattlesnake races and horseshoe competitions are held during the second weekend in May, not far from Trinity, the site of the first atom-bomb explosion. For information, call 505/648–2472.

Spring Festival of the Arts, Santa Fe. The annual spring arts festival, consisting of a citywide celebration of exhibits; demonstrations; lectures; tours; open studios; music, dance, and theater performances; and poster and book signings, is held for 10 days in mid-May. For information, contact Santa Fe Festival Foundation (1524 Paseo de Peralta, Santa Fe 87501, tel. 505/988–3924).

June **New Mexico Arts and Crafts Fair,** Albuquerque. On the last weekend in June the New Mexico State Fairgrounds is the setting of this annual crafts spectacular that brings together more than 200 artists and craftspeople to display their talents. Spanish, Native American, and other North American cultures are represented. There's food and entertainment aplenty. The State Fairgrounds is located on San Pedro Drive between Lomas and Central boulevards. For information, call 505/884–9043.

July **Rodeo de Santa Fe,** Santa Fe. A taste of the Old West comes to Santa Fe in mid-July, with calf roping, bull riding, and a traditional opening-day rodeo parade. World-champion rodeo participants come from all parts of the United States and Canada to this annual event, held since 1959. For information, call 505/982–4659 or 505/471–4300.

Spanish Market, Santa Fe. Held on the Plaza over the last full weekend in July, this festive gathering features Spanish arts, crafts, and good things to eat. You can smell the green-corn tamales and chocolate mole from blocks around. Many exhibitors are from remote villages, where outstanding handicrafts are produced. For more information, contact the Spanish Colonial Arts Society (Box 1611, Santa Fe 87501, tel. 505/983–4038).

August **Banjo and Fiddle Mini-Festival,** Santa Fe. The 18th annual toe-tapping, banjo, fiddle, guitar, mandolin, old-time band, and bluegrass mountain-music festival takes place for two days in late August, attracting big-name folk musicians and thousands of loyal fans to the Santa Fe Rodeo Grounds, where the event unwinds. For information, contact the Banjo and Fiddle Contest (Rte. 7, Box 115-BK, Santa Fe 87505, tel. 505/983–8315 or 505/982–9848).

Bat Flight Breakfast, Carlsbad. On the second Thursday of August each year, early risers gather at the entrance to Carlsbad Cavern to eat breakfast and to watch tens of thousands of bats, who've just been out for the night feeding on insects, fly back into the cave. For additional information, contact superintendent, Carlsbad Caverns National Park (3225 National Parks Hwy., Carlsbad 88220, tel. 505/785–2232).

Indian Market, Santa Fe. Indian arts, pottery, jewelry, blankets, and rugs are displayed and sold at the annual Indian Market on the Plaza in mid-August. Many of the town's more than 150 art galleries feature special group and individual shows of leading Native American artists. At least 800 artists and craftspeople are expected to attend this 70th annual market. For more information, contact Southwestern Association of Indian Affairs (SWAIA, Box 1964, Santa Fe 87501, tel. 505/983–5220).

September **Las Fiestas de Santa Fe,** Santa Fe. The city's biggest celebration begins the first Friday after Labor Day and commemorates the reconquest of Santa Fe from the San Juan Indians by Don Diego de Vargas in 1692. Parades, dancing, pageantry, ethnic foods, arts and crafts, fireworks, and the burning of *Zozobra* (Old Man Gloom) are all part of the fun. For more information, contact Las Fiestas de Santa Fe (Box 4516, Santa Fe 87505, tel. 505/988–7575).

New Mexico State Fair, Albuquerque. One of the nation's liveliest state fairs takes place in early through mid-September at the New Mexico State Fairgrounds (San Pedro Dr. between Lomas and Central Blvds.), with arts, crafts, livestock shows, entertainment, a midway, a rodeo, and living Early Spanish and Native American villages. For information, call 505/265–1791.

October **Fall Festival of the Arts,** Santa Fe. This annual 10-day fall arts festival generally begins during the first weekend in October and highlights New Mexico's finest painters, sculptors, ceramicists, weavers, and woodworkers. For information, contact Santa Fe Festival Foundation (1524 Paseo de Peralta, Santa Fe 87501, tel. 505/988–3924).

International Balloon Fiesta, Albuquerque. More than 600 hot-air balloons will participate in a mass ascension at sunrise during the first two weekends in October. This major event in the world of ballooning—you'll never see anything like it—takes place at Balloon Fiesta Park. For information, call 505/821–1000.

November **Arts and Crafts Fair,** Santa Fe. On the second Saturday of November, over 50 local and statewide artists offer folk dolls, Spanish colonial woodwork, *santos* (saint) carvings, *retablos* (religious paintings on tin or wood), wooden toys, fabric crafts, jewelry, and other handmade goods for sale in an annual charity event that takes place at the famous La Fonda Hotel. Proceeds from the rental of vendor space go to local charities; proceeds from the sale of objects go to the artists. Admission is free. For additional information, call 505/471–7873.

Indian National Finals Rodeo, Albuquerque. The big enchilada of Indian rodeo competition takes place at the New Mexico State Fairgrounds (San Pedro Dr., between Lomas and Central Blvds.) in the Tingley Coliseum in mid-November, with a powwow, ceremonial dances, and Native American arts and crafts. For information, call 505/265–1791.

December **Christmas Indian Dances,** various pueblos. The Spanish dance-drama *Los Machinas* is performed at Picuris and San Juan pueblos. There are also pine-torch processions at San Juan and

Taos pueblos (the Kachina Dance at Taos) and Basket, Buffalo, Deer, Harvest, Rainbow, and Turtle dances at Acoma, Cochiti, San Juan, Santa Clara, and Taos Indian pueblos. For information, call 505/843–7270.

Procession of the Virgin, Taos Pueblo. After vespers on Christmas Eve, the procession of the Virgin Mary takes place, with dancers and bonfires. For information, call 505/758–8626.

Christmas Season, Santa Fe. During the Christmas holidays the New Mexico capital is at its most festive and hospitable, with the incense of piñon smoke sweetening the air and the darkness of winter illuminated by thousands of *farolitos*, lunch sack–size paper bags weighted with sand and bearing a candle. (To clear a minor note of confusion, candles in a paper bag are called farolitos north of Albuquerque, and *luminarias* to the south and in neighboring Arizona.) A custom believed to have derived from the Chinese lanterns the conquistadores brought with them, the glowing farolitos are everywhere, lining walkways, doorways, rooftops, walls, window sills, and sometimes even gravesites with soft puddles of light. The songs of Christmas are sung around corner bonfires (*luminarias*, as the holiday bonfires are called in Santa Fe), and mugs of hot cider and melt-in-your-mouth Christmas cookies, *biscochitos*, are offered to all who pass by. With glowing lights reflected on the snow, Santa Fe is never lovelier. Numerous religious pageants and processions take place. Early in the month are 10 days of **Las Posadas** at San Miguel Mission (401 Old Santa Fe Tr., tel. 505/983–3974), during which the story of Mary and Joseph's journey to Bethlehem is reenacted. The **Feast Day of Our Lady of Guadalupe,** December 12, is grandly celebrated at Santuario de Guadalupe, and **Christmas at the Palace** resounds with hours of festive music emanating from the Palace of the Governors.

What to Pack

Clothing In New Mexico you can choose a climate by choosing an elevation or an area of this large state. Snowfall ranges from less than 2 inches annually in the lower Rio Grande Valley to as much as 300 inches in the mountains of the north-central region, the waning folds of the Rockies. Santa Fe has a relatively mild climate, even in the wintertime, despite some notable exceptions. Taos, higher up, is colder. Every part of the state receives at least 70 percent sunshine year-round. But typical of the Southwest, even when the days are warm, evenings and nights are chilly to cold. You should pack accordingly.

The areas of higher elevation are, of course, considerably cooler than are Carlsbad and other low-lying southern portions of the state. That means winter visitors should pack warm clothes—coats, parkas, and whatever else your body's thermostat and your ultimate destination dictate. Sweaters and jackets will also be needed for summer visitors because while days are warm, nights at the higher altitudes can be extremely chilly. And bring comfortable shoes; you're likely to be doing a lot of walking.

Socially, New Mexico is one of the most informal and laid-back areas of the country, which for many is much a part of its appeal. Conceivably no more than three or four restaurants in the entire state enforce a dress code, even for dinner meals, though men are likely to feel more comfortable wearing a jacket in the major hotel dining rooms, and women in tennis shoes may receive a look of stern disapproval from the maître d', if indeed there happens to be one.

The Western look, popular throughout the country a few years back when even New York Wall Streeters were wearing boots and 10-gallon hats, has, of course, never lost its appeal in the West. But what has changed is the corny, hokey part, when dressing "Western" meant wearing everything from bandannas to gunbelts. The look has become more subtle and refined. Western-style clothes are no longer a costume. They're being mixed with tweed jackets, for instance, for a more conservative, sophisticated image. Which is to say, you can dress Western with your boots and big belt buckles in even the best places in Santa Fe, Taos, Albuquerque, or Carlsbad, but if you come strolling through the lobby of the Eldorado Hotel looking like Hopalong Cassidy, you'll get some funny looks.

Miscellaneous Again, depending on where you're headed in New Mexico, you may find the sun strong, the air dry, and the wind hot and relentless. Bring skin moisturizers if dry skin's a problem, and sunglasses to protect your eyes from the glare of lakes or ski slopes (or to keep soot out of your eyes if you decide to ride the rails on the historic Cumbres & Toltec Scenic Steam Train). Film is expensive in many of the more popular tourist destinations, so shutterbugs should bring plenty. Proliferating quickie film-processing outlets, not to mention New Mexico's spectacular sights and scenery, tend to make most people shoot more than usual. If high altitude is a problem (it may cause headaches and dizziness), check with your doctor about special medication. You'll need good walking shoes or sneakers for prowling the ruins and the mesas and the miles and miles of museum corridors.

Carry-on Luggage Passengers aboard major U.S. carriers are usually limited to two carry-on bags. Bags stored under the seat must not exceed 9″ × 14″ × 22″. Bags hung in a closet can be no larger than 4″ × 23″ × 45″. The maximum dimensions for bags stored in an overhead bin are 10″ × 14″ × 36″. Any item that exceeds the specified dimensions will generally be rejected as a carry-on and handled as checked baggage. Keep in mind that an airline can adapt these rules to circumstances; on an especially crowded flight, you may be allowed to bring only one carry-on bag aboard.

In addition to the two carry-ons, passengers may also bring aboard a handbag; an overcoat or wrap; an umbrella; a camera; a reasonable amount of reading material; an infant bag; and crutches, braces, a cane, or other prosthetic devices upon which the passenger is dependent. Infant-child safety seats can also be brought aboard if parents have purchased a ticket for the child or if there is space in the cabin.

Checked Luggage Luggage allowances vary slightly among airlines. Many carriers allow three checked pieces; some allow only two. It is best to consult the airline before you go. In all cases, check-in luggage cannot weigh more than 70 pounds per piece or be larger than 62 inches (length plus width plus height).

Cash Machines

Virtually all U.S. banks belong to a network of ATMs (Automatic Teller Machines), which dispense cash 24 hours a day in cities throughout the country. There are some eight major networks in the United States, the largest of which are Cirrus, owned by MasterCard, and Plus, affiliated with Visa. Some banks belong to more than one network. Many banks issue cards automatically to their savings- or checking-account customers; in some cases customers must apply for them. Cards issued by Visa and MasterCard also may be used in the ATMs, but the fees are usually higher than the fees on the cards linked to personal bank accounts, which are generally minimal (or nonexistent). There is also a daily interest charge on credit-card "loans," even if monthly bills are paid on time. Each network has a toll-free number you can call to locate machines in a given city. The Cirrus number is 800/4–CIRRUS; the Plus number is 800/THE–PLUS. Check with your bank for information on fees and on the amount of cash you can withdraw on any given day. Express Cash allows American Express cardholders to withdraw up to $1,000 in a seven-day period (21 days overseas) from their personal checking accounts at ATMs worldwide. Gold-Card members can receive up to $2,500 in a seven-day period (21 days overseas). Express Cash is not a cash-advance service; only money already in the personal checking account you chose to link to your American Express card can be withdrawn. Every transaction carries a 2% fee, with a minimum charge of $2 and a maximum of $6. Call 800/CASH–NOW to receive an application to link your checking account with this system and to receive a PIN (personal identification number) at least three to four weeks before departure; also call this number to locate the nearest Express Cash machine.

Traveling with Film

If your camera is new, shoot and develop a few rolls before you leave home. Pack some lens tissue and an extra battery for your built-in light meter. Invest about $10 in a skylight filter; it will protect the lens and reduce haze.

Film doesn't like hot weather, so if you're driving in summer, don't store film in the glove compartment or on the shelf under the rear window. Put it behind the front seat on the floor, on the side opposite the exhaust pipe.

On a plane trip, never pack unprocessed film in check-in luggage; if your bags get X-rayed, your pictures could be damaged. Always carry undeveloped film with you through security and ask to have it inspected by hand. (It helps to keep your film in a plastic bag, ready for quick inspection.) Inspectors at American airports are required by law to honor requests for inspection by hand.

The newer scanning machines used in all U.S. airports are safe for anything from five to 500 scans, depending on the speed of your film. The effects are cumulative; you can put the same roll of film through several scans without worry. After five scans, though, you're asking for trouble. If your film gets fogged and you want an explanation, send it to the National Association of Photographic Manufacturers (550 Mamaroneck Ave., Harrison, NY 10528). It will try to determine what went wrong. The service is free.

Traveling with Children

Publications *Family Travel Times* is a newsletter published 10 times a year by TWYCH (Travel With Your Children, 80 Eighth Ave., New York, NY 10011, tel. 212/206–0688). A one-year subscription costs $35 and includes access to back issues. The organization also offers a free phone-in service that provides advice and information on specific destinations.

Great Vacations with Your Kids, by Dorothy Jordan and Marjorie Cohen, provides complete advice on planning your trip with children, from toddlers to teens. If unavailable at your local bookstore, write or call E. P. Dutton (375 Hudson St., New York, NY 10014, tel. 212/366–2000).

Kids and Teens in Flight, a useful brochure about children flying alone, is available from the U.S. Department of Transportation. To order a free copy, call 202/366–2220.

Getting There On domestic flights, children under two who are not occupying a seat travel free. Various discounts apply to children 2–12 years old, and up to 18 during special promotions, so check with your airline when making reservations.

Regulations about infant travel on airplanes are in the process of changing. Until they do, however, if you want to be sure your infant is secure, you must bring your own infant car seat and buy a separate ticket. Check with the airline in advance to be sure your seat meets the required standard. If possible, reserve a seat behind one of the plane's bulkheads, where there's usually more legroom and enough space to fit a bassinet (which is available from the airlines). The booklet *Child/Infant Safety Seats Acceptable for Use in Aircraft* is available from the Federal Aviation Administration (APA-200, 800 Independence Ave., SW, Washington, D.C. 20591, tel. 202/267–3479). If you opt to hold your baby on your lap, do so with the infant outside the seat belt, rather than inside it, so he or she doesn't get crushed in case of a sudden stop.

When reserving tickets, also ask about special children's meals or snacks. The February 1990 and 1992 issues of *Family Travel Times* include "TWYCH's Airline Guide," which contains a rundown of the children's services offered by 46 different airlines.

Getting Around On all Amtrak routes, children under age 2 ride free (provided
By Rail they don't occupy a seat), children 2–11 pay half price, and children 12 and over pay the full adult fare. For information on routes and reservations, call **Amtrak** (tel. 800/USA–RAIL).

By Bus On Greyhound/Trailways buses, one child under age 2 travels free on an adult's lap, and one child 2–4 pays 10% of the adult fare; children 5–11 pay half the adult price, and children 11 or older pay full fare. For further information, call **Greyhound/ Trailways** (tel. 800/752–4841).

Hotels At the **Best Western Hotels** in Albuquerque and Santa Fe (reservations 800/528–1234), children under 12 stay free in their parents' rooms. All **Holiday Inns** (reservations 800/465–4329) allow children 12 and under to stay free when sharing a room with their parents, and some offer "Family Plans" that provide the same privileges for children 18 and under. During holiday periods and on weekends, the new **Hyatt Hotel** in Albuquerque (tel. 505/842–1234, ext. 51) offers special games and activities—including classes in Southwestern cooking—for young guests. **Bishop's Lodge** in Santa Fe (tel. 505/983–6377) has a summer riding and horsemanship program for children.

Condominiums and Resorts **Campanilla Compound** (334 Otero St., Santa Fe 87501, tel. 505/988–7585) and **Pueblo Hermosa** (501 Rio Grande, Santa Fe 87501, tel. 505/984–2590) offer excellent facilities for families with children. In many cases, especially for larger families, resort accommodations work out to be much cheaper than hotels.

Adventure Holidays In the Southwest region, children's- and family-adventure holidays abound. **Santa Fe Adventures, Inc.** (Box 15086, Santa Fe 87506–5086, tel. 505/983–0111 or 800/766–5443) provides children 4 and older with half-day educational trips and activities, leaving parents free to relax and explore museums. A children's lunch is included. A separate Family Adventure Group offers hot-air ballooning, animal tracking, and overnight family backpacking trips. **Santa Fe Detours** (La Fonda Hotel, 100 E. San Francisco St., Santa Fe 87501, tel. 800/DETOURS) organizes children's wagon rides and safaris.

Baby-sitting Services Baby-sitters are available at many hotels and resorts. In Santa Fe, both **Enchanting Land Babysitting Service** (tel. 505/988–2718) and **The Kid Connection** (tel. 505/471–3100) offer reputable services. **Trudy's Discovery House** in Taos (tel. 505/758–1659) provides drop-in day care for visiting families.

Hints for Disabled Travelers

Most of the region's national parks and recreational areas have accessible visitors' centers, rest rooms, campsites, and trails, and more are being added every year. For information on accessible facilities at specific parks and sites in New Mexico, contact the **National Park Service, Southwest Region** (Box 728, Santa Fe 87504, tel. 505/988–6375).

All blind or disabled U.S. citizens and permanent residents are entitled to a free lifetime pass to all federally operated parks, monuments, historic sites, recreational areas, and wildlife refuges that charge entrance fees. The **Golden Access Passport,** which must be obtained in person from a federally operated park or recreational area, also provides a 50% discount on federal fees charged for facilities and services, such as camping, boat launching, and parking.

Getting Around By Rail **Amtrak** (tel. 800/USA–RAIL; TDD 800/523–6590) offers all handicapped passengers a 25% discount on regular fares (handicapped children ages 2–11 get a 25% discount on already lower children's fares). However, it is wise to check the price of excursion tickets first. Excursion tickets often work out to be much cheaper than handicapped discounts on regular tickets. All trains and all large stations have accessible toilets, although some of the region's smaller, unmanned stations do not. Reserve tickets 48 hours in advance to be sure of special seats, individually prepared meals, and wheelchair assistance. For a free copy of *Access Amtrak*, a guide to special services for elderly and handicapped travelers, write to Amtrak (Passenger Marketing, 600 Massachusetts Ave., NE, Washington, D.C. 20002).

By Bus Although Greyhound/Trailways buses have no special facilities for disabled passengers, an attendant can ride free if a written request is presented. For additional information contact **Greyhound/Trailways** (tel. 800/752–4841; TDD 800/345–3109).

By Car **Avis** (tel. 800/331–1212), **Hertz** (tel. 800/654–3131), and **National** (tel. 800/328–4567) can provide hand controls on some of their rental cars with advance notice.

Associations The **Information Center for Individuals with Disabilities** (Fort Point Pl., 1st floor, 27-43 Wormwood St., Boston, MA 02210, tel. 617/727–5540; TDD 617/727–5236) offers useful problem-solving assistance, including lists of travel agents who specialize in tours for disabled people.

Moss Rehabilitation Hospital Travel Information Service (1200 W. Tabor Rd., Philadelphia, PA 19141–3009, tel. 215/456–9600; TDD 215/456–9602) provides information on tourist sights, transportation, and accommodations in destinations around the world for a small fee.

Travel Industry and Disabled Exchange (TIDE, 5435 Donna Ave., Tarzana, CA 91356, tel. 818/368–5648) publishes a quarterly newsletter and a directory of travel agencies and tours that cater specifically to disabled people. The annual membership fee is $15.

Mobility International USA (Box 3551, Eugene, OR 97403, tel. 503/343–1284—voice and TDD) is an internationally affiliated organization. For a $20 annual fee, it coordinates exchange programs for disabled people around the world and offers information on accommodations and organized study programs.

The **Society for the Advancement of Travel for the Handicapped** (26 Court St., Penthouse Suite, Brooklyn, NY 11242, tel. 718/858–5483) provides information on access and lists of tour operators specializing in travel for disabled people. The annual membership costs $40, or $25 for students and seniors. Send $1 and a stamped, self-addressed envelope for information on a specific destination.

Publications *The Itinerary* (Box 2012, Bayonne, NJ 07002, tel. 201/858–3400) is a bimonthly travel magazine for disabled people. Call for a subscription ($10 for one year, $18 for two); it's not available in stores.

Twin Peaks Press (Box 129, Vancouver, WA 98666, tel. 206/694–2462 or 800/637–2256 for orders only) specializes in books for disabled people. *Travel for the Disabled*, by Helen Hecker, offers helpful hints, as well as a comprehensive list of guidebooks and facilities geared to disabled people. *Wheelchair Vagabond*, by John G. Nelson, contains valuable information for independent travelers who are planning extended trips in a car, van, or camper. Twin Peaks also offers a Traveling Nurse's Network, which provides registered nurses to accompany and assist disabled travelers.

Hints for Older Travelers

The **Golden Age Passport** is a free lifetime pass to all parks, monuments, and recreational areas run by the federal government. Permanent U.S. residents 62 or older may pick up the passport in person at any of the national parks that charge admission. The passport covers the entrance fee for the holder and anyone accompanying the holder in the same private vehicle. It also provides a 50% discount on camping, boat launching, and parking charges. Proof of age is required.

Getting Around
By Rail Amtrak (tel. 800/USA–RAIL) offers a 25% discount on all regular fares (not including excursion tickets) for all travelers 65 and older. For a free copy of *Access Amtrak,* a guide to its services for elderly and handicapped travelers, write to Amtrak (Passenger Marketing, 600 Massachusetts Ave., NE, Washington, D.C. 20002).

By Bus **Greyhound/Trailways** (tel. 800/752–4841) offers senior citizens (64 and older) a 10% reduction on regular fares Mondays through Thursdays and a 5% reduction on weekends.

Publications The *Senior Citizens Guide to Budget Travel in the United States and Canada,* by Paige Palmer, is available for $3.95, plus $1 for shipping, from Pilot Books (103 Cooper St., Babylon, NY 11702, tel. 516/422–2225), if you can't find it at your local bookstore.

The Discount Guide for Travelers Over 55, by Caroline and Walter Weintz, lists helpful addresses, package tours, reduced-rate car rentals, and so forth, in the United States and abroad. If unavailable from your local bookseller, send $7.95 plus $1.50 shipping and handling to NAL/Cash Sales (Bergenfield Order Dept., 120 Woodbine St., Bergenfield, NJ 07621, tel. 800/526–0275).

Associations **The American Association of Retired Persons** (AARP, 1909 K St., NW, Washington, D.C. 20049, tel. 202/662–4850) has two programs for independent travelers: (1) the Purchase Privilege Program, which offers discounts on hotels, airfare, car rentals, RV rentals, and sightseeing; and (2) the AARP Motoring Plan, provided by Amoco, which furnishes emergency road-service aid and trip-routing information for an annual fee of $33.95 per person or couple. AARP members must be 50 years or older; annual dues are $5 per person or couple.

If you plan to use an AARP or other senior-citizen identification card to obtain a reduced hotel rate, mention it at the time you make your reservation, rather than when you check out. At participating restaurants, show your card to the maître d' before you're seated, because discounts may be limited to certain menus, days, or hours. When renting a car, be sure to ask about special promotional rates that may offer greater savings than are available with your discount ID.

Elderhostel (75 Federal St., 3rd floor, Boston, MA 02110–1941, tel. 617/426–7788) is an innovative, educational program for people 60 and older. Participants live in dorms on some 1,200 campuses around the world. Mornings are devoted to lectures and seminars, afternoons to sightseeing and field trips. Fees for two- to three-week trips—including room, board, tuition, and round-trip transportation—range from $1,800 to $4,500.

Mature Outlook (6001 N. Clark St., Chicago, IL 60660, tel. 800/336–6330), a subsidiary of Sears Roebuck & Co., is a travel club for people over 50 that provides hotel and motel discounts and publishes a bimonthly newsletter. Annual membership is $9.95; there are 800,000 members currently. Instant membership is available at Sears stores and participating Holiday Inns.

National Council of Senior Citizens (925 15th St., NW, Washington, D.C. 20005, tel. 202/347–8800), a nonprofit advocacy group, has some 5,000 local clubs across the United States. Annual membership is $12 per person or couple. Members receive a monthly newspaper with travel information and an ID card for reduced-rate hotels and car rentals.

Saga International Holidays (120 Boylston St., Boston, MA 02116, tel. 800/343–0273) specializes in group travel for people over 60. A selection of variously priced tours allows you to choose the package that meets your needs.

September Days Club (tel. 800/241–5050) is run by the moderately priced Days Inns of America. The $12 annual membership fee for individuals or couples over 50 entitles them to reduced car rentals and to reductions of 15% to 50% at most of the chain's more than 350 motels.

Hotels   Hyatt Hotels (tel. 800/233–1234/Worldwide Reservations) are offering room discounts to guests 62 and over. These new rates offer 25% off regular room rates and are subject to availability, so be sure to request them when making reservations.

Further Reading

General Interest   Numerous books and novels have been written about or are set in New Mexico. A classic list of such books would surely include *Death Comes for the Archbishop*, by Willa Cather, a novel based on the life of Archbishop Jean Baptiste Lamy, who built, among other churches, the Cathedral of St. Francis in Santa Fe. *Wind Leaves No Shadow*, by Ruth Laughlin; *Miracle Hill*, by Barney Mitchell; *Navajos Have Five Fingers*, by T. D. Allen; *Santa Fe*, by Oliver La Farge; *New Mexico*, by Jack Schaefer; and *Star Over Adobe*, by Dorothy Pillsbury are all good choices as well. *Lautree*, by Norman Zollinger, is an entertaining mystery set in Albuquerque. Zollinger, who owns the Professor Book Center on Lomas Boulevard, NE, in Albuquerque, also wrote *Riders to Cibola*, which chronicles the conquistadores' search for the legendary Seven Cities of Gold. Albuquerque author Tony Hillerman, best-selling mystery writer whose plots frequently revolve around the exploits of Navajo detectives Joe Leaphorn and Jim Chee, received an Edgar Allan Poe Award from the Mystery Writers of America in 1974 for his book *Dance Hall of the Dead*. *The Wood Carvers of Cordova, New Mexico*, by Charles L. Briggs, is a prize-winning study of the making and selling of religious images in a northern New Mexico village. *Eliot Porter's Southwest* is the famed photographer's view of the Southwest in pure visual poetry, much of it focused around his Tesuque, New Mexico, home.

Indian Lore and   *The Man Who Killed the Deer*, by Frank Waters, is a classic of
Pueblo Life   Pueblo life. *Masked Gods*, by the same author, has an enthusiastic following in the Southwest that reaches cult proportions. J. J. Brody's profusely illustrated book *Anasazi and Pueblo Painting* has been described as an indispensable volume for art historians and students of Southwestern culture. *Mornings in Mexico*, by D. H. Lawrence, contains a number of essays pertaining to Taos and the Pueblo Indian ritual dances. *Pueblo Style and Regional Architecture*, edited by Nicholas C. Markovich, Wolfgang F. E. Preiser, and Fred G. Strum, covers the evolution of architecture in the Southwest, with particular emphasis on New Mexico. *Pueblos: Prehistoric Indian Cul-*

tures of the Southwest, by Sylvio Acatos, with photos by Maximilien Bruggman, presents a portrait of the life, history, art, and spirit of the peace-loving people who carved a civilization in the region. *Nacimientos: Nativity Scenes by Southwest Indian Artists,* by Guy and Doris Monthan, offers photographic details and written descriptions of ceramic nativity scenes produced by Pueblo Indians.

New Mexican Personalities

Billy the Kid made his mark, was killed, and is buried in New Mexico. *Billy the Kid: A Short and Violent Life,* by Robert M. Utley, a noted historian, is considered the definitive work on the notorious outlaw. *The Life of D. H. Lawrence,* by Keith Sagar, published in 1980, is a good biography of the world-renowned author so strongly associated with (and buried in) New Mexico. Taos is also Georgia O'Keeffe country, and her death in 1986 brought forth a wealth of books about the famous American artist. Among the best surely is *Georgia O'Keeffe: Arts and Letters,* published by the New York Graphic Society in conjunction with a retrospective exhibit of her work at the National Gallery of Art, Washington, D.C. Another is the reissue of the massive coffee-table book *Georgia O'Keeffe,* with text by the artist herself. *Portrait of an Artist: A Biography of Georgia O'Keeffe,* by Laurie Lisle, spans the artist's life and career. *Georgia O'Keeffe: Some Memories of Drawings,* edited by Doris Bry, is a collection of the artist's major drawings done between 1915 and 1963, with comments about each.

On Albuquerque, Santa Fe, and Taos

Albuquerque—A Narrative History by Marc Simmons is a fascinating look at the city's birth and development. *The Wingspread Collectors Guide to Santa Fe and Taos* and *The Wingspread Collectors Guide to Albuquerque and Corrales* (Wingspread, Box 13566-T, Albuquerque 87192) include useful information with high-quality color reproductions about art galleries, art, and crafts of the region; they also include listings and features of museums, hotels, restaurants, and historic sites. Photographers have long been attracted to the mystical beauty of Taos country. *Taos: A Pictorial History,* by John Sherman, contains numerous pages of black-and-white historical photographs of many of the major characters, events, and structures that have carved the backbone of Taos, as well as of Native Americans, Hispanics, and Anglo immigrants, with accompanying text and captions.

Arriving and Departing

By Plane

Airports and Airlines

The newly expanded and remodeled **Albuquerque International Airport** is the gateway to New Mexico. Car rentals, air taxis, and bus shuttles are readily available at the airport, which is 65 miles southwest of Santa Fe and 130 miles south of Taos. Airlines serving Albuquerque International Airport are **America West** (tel. 800/247–5692), **American** (tel. 800/433–7300), **Continental** (tel. 800/525–0280), **Delta** (tel. 800/221–1212), **Mesa Air** (tel. 800/637–2247), **Southwest** (tel. 800/531–5601), **TWA** (tel. 800/221–2000), **United** (tel. 800/241–6522), and **USAir** (tel. 800/428–4322).

Air-shuttle service via **Mesa Airlines** operates up to seven times a day between Albuquerque and Santa Fe; the flying time aboard the nine-passenger Cessna Caravan is 25 minutes, and the fare ranges from $79 to $110 for round-trip flights, depending on the time of day and the time of year, and half that for one-way flights. Interline buses at the airport link Mesa Airlines with all Albuquerque connections.

Smoking Smoking is banned on all routes within the 48 contiguous states, within the states of Hawaii and Alaska, to and from the U.S. Virgin Islands and Puerto Rico, and on flights of under six hours to and from Hawaii and Alaska. The rule applies to both U.S. and foreign carriers. On a flight where smoking is permitted, you can request a nonsmoking seat during check-in or when you book your ticket. If the airline tells you there are no seats available in the nonsmoking section on the day of the flight, insist on one: Department of Transportation regulations require carriers to find seats for all nonsmokers, provided they meet check-in-time restrictions.

Lost Luggage On domestic flights, airlines are responsible for up to $1,250 per passenger in lost or damaged property. If you're carrying valuables, either take them with you on the plane or purchase additional insurance for lost luggage.

Luggage Insurance Some airlines issue luggage insurance when you check in, but many do not. Insurance for lost, damaged, or stolen luggage is available through travel agents or directly through various insurance companies. Coverage for lost luggage is usually part of a comprehensive travel-insurance package that includes personal accident, trip cancellation, and sometimes default and bankruptcy. Two companies that issue luggage insurance are **Tele-Trip** (Box 31685, 3201 Farnam St., Omaha, NE 68131, tel. 800/228–9792), a subsidiary of Mutual of Omaha, and **The Travelers Corporation** (Ticket and Travel Dept., 1 Tower Sq., Hartford, CT 06183, tel. 203/277–0111 or 800/243–3174). Tele-Trip operates sales booths at airports, and also issues insurance through travel agents. The company will insure checked or hand luggage through its travel-insurance packages. Rates vary according to the length of the trip. The Travelers Corporation will insure checked or hand luggage at $500–$2,000 valuation per person, for a maximum of 180 days. Rates for one–five days for $500 valuation are $10; for 180 days, $85. Other companies with comprehensive policies include **Access America, Inc.**, a subsidiary of Blue Cross–Blue Shield (Box 11188, Richmond, VA 23230, tel. 800/334–7525 or 800/284–8300), and **Near Services** (450 Prairie Ave., Suite 101, Calumet City, IL 60409, tel. 708/868–6700 or 800/654–6700).

By Car

I–40 runs east/west across the middle of the state (Tucumcari, Albuquerque, Gallup); I–10 cuts across the southern part of the state from the Texas border at El Paso to the Arizona line, through Las Cruces, Deming, and Lordsburg; I–25 runs north from the state line at El Paso through Albuquerque and Santa Fe, then angles northeast to exit at the Colorado line near Raton.

U.S. highways connect all major cities and towns with a good network of paved roads. State roads go to the smaller towns; most of them are paved, two-lane thoroughfares. Roads on Indian lands are designated by wooden, arrow-shape signs; these, like roads in national forests, are usually not paved.

Technically, there may not be a lot of true desert in New Mexico, but there is a lot of high, dry, lonesome country. Keep your gas tank full and abide by the signs, and you shouldn't have any trouble.

Arroyos, dry washes or gullies, are bridged on major roads, but lesser roads often dip down through them. These can be a hazard during the rainy season of July, August, and September. If water is running through an arroyo, don't try to cross it, even if it looks shallow—it may have an axle-breaking hole in the middle. Just wait a little while, and it will drain off almost as quickly as it filled. If you stall in a running arroyo, get out of the car and onto high ground if possible. If you are in back country and in an off-road vehicle, never drive (or walk) in a dry arroyo bed if the sky is dark anywhere upstream. A sudden thunderstorm 15 miles away could send a raging flash flood down a wash that was perfectly dry a few minutes earlier.

Avoid unpaved roads in New Mexico, unless they are well graded and graveled, when they are wet. The soil has a lot of *caliche,* or clay, in it that gets very slick when mixed with water.

Car Rentals

If you're going on to Santa Fe or Taos from the Albuquerque Airport, it might be best to rent a car because there's so much spectacular scenery to see along the way. Car-rental services located at the airport are **Alamo** (tel. 800/327–9633), **American International** (tel. 800/527–0202), **Avis** (tel. 800/331–1212), **Budget** (tel. 800/527–0700), **Dollar** (tel. 800/421–6868), **General** (tel. 800/327–7607), **Hertz** (tel. 800/654–3131), **Major** (tel. 800/346–2567), **National** (tel. 800/328–4300), **PayLess** (tel. 800/541–1566), **Rent Rite** (tel. 800/243–7483), **Rich Ford** (tel. 800/331–3271), and **Thrifty** (tel. 800/367–2277).

By Bus

Frequent ground-shuttle service is also available between Albuquerque and Santa Fe via **Greyhound/Trailways** (tel. 505/471–0008); the cost is $11.13. Continuing on to Taos costs $10.50 more. **Shuttlejack** (tel. 800/452–2665) also offers bus service between Albuquerque and Santa Fe, $20 one-way, but doesn't go to Taos.

Staying in New Mexico

Shopping

Antiques Though the American West is still relatively young, antique shops and roadside museums dot the desert landscape with tiny pockets of nostalgia and treasured keepsakes. You'll find everything in New Mexico's antique shops, from early Mexican typewriters to period saddles, ceramic pots, farm tools, pioneer aviation equipment, and yellowed newspaper clippings about Kit Carson and D. H. Lawrence.

Art Santa Fe is the fine-arts capital of the Southwest, with over 150 galleries. Albuquerque and Taos are not far behind. Native American art, Western art, fine art, junk art—you'll find everything for sale in New Mexico, and in all media: sculptures, prints, posters, ceramics, etchings, drawings, photographs, and exquisite miniatures by such legendary names as Georgia O'Keeffe, R. C. Gorman, and artists of the Taos Society of Artists. Bring your checkbook.

Crafts Spanish families have lived in the Rio Grande valley for over 300 years. Handcrafted furniture, religious carvings and paintings, *santos* (representations of saints) and *retablos* (holy images painted on wood or tin), command high prices from collectors. Colorful hand-woven Hispanic textiles are much in demand. Indian blankets, rugs, kachina dolls, baskets, silver jewelry, turquoise, pottery, beadwork, ornamental shields, drums, and ceramics can be found almost everywhere in New Mexico, from the portals under the Palace of Governors on the historic Santa Fe Plaza to the Indian pueblos that range across the entire state. Expect to pay thousands of dollars for a rare 1930s kachina doll or just a few cents for hand-wrapped bundles of sage, juniper, sweet grass, and lavender that are used by Native Americans in healing ceremonies, gatherings, and daily cleansing of the home. Ignited like incense, this herbal combination gives off a sacred smoke; passing it once around the room is enough to change and charge the air.

Spices You'll find stands beside the road selling *chile ristras*, strings of crimson chiles to hang in your kitchen or beside the front door, and you'll find shops everywhere selling chile powder and other spices. You can generally smell them from the road; walk in, and your eyes begin to water, your mouth to salivate. For many, especially natives of the Southwest, *picante* is the purest, finest word in the Spanish language. It means hot—spicy hot. All around you, in boxes, bags, packets, jars, and cans, there's everything—salsas, chili pastes, powders, herbs, spices, peppers, barbecue sauce, and fiery potions in bottles that you must shake before using.

Sports and Outdoor Activities

Bicycling Albuquerque is a biker's paradise, with miles and miles of designated bike lanes and trails crisscrossing and skirting the city. Not only is Albuquerque's highly active Parks and Recreation Department aware of bikers' needs, but bike riding is heavily promoted as a means of cutting down on traffic congestion and subsequent air pollution, an ever-mounting problem in most major cities today. Santa Fe and Taos, because of hilly terrain and narrow, frequently congested downtown streets, are less hospitable to bikers. However, mountain biking is popular in both areas. With their low gears and knobby tires, mountain bikes open the back roads and trails to bike excursions of all kinds.

Cycling events featured throughout the year include the Santa Fe Century (50- or 100-mile recreational rides), the Sabusco Hill Climb (an annual race to the Santa Fe Ski Area), and the Tour de Los Alamos (road race and criterium). The U.S. Cycling Federation–sanctioned races are open to all U.S. citizens. Check with local bike shops, or for specifics contact the **Sangre de Cristo Cycling Club** (134 Romero St., Santa Fe 87501, tel. 505/984–1603).

Bird-watching New Mexico represents five of the seven ecological zones to be found in the world. Because of this, bird watchers have a won-

derful opportunity to spot birds migrating from the jungles of
South America to the tundra of the Arctic Circle. The **Bosque
del Apache National Wildlife Sanctuary** (Box 1246, Socorro
87801, tel. 505/835–1828), 90 miles south of Albuquerque, is the
winter home to thousands of migrating birds, including one of
only two wild flocks of the rare whooping crane.

Camping Looking for an escape from the desert heat and urban crowds?
New Mexico has over a million acres of remote, rugged wilderness areas, with hundreds of campgrounds, picnic areas, and
recreational sites, including the first designated wilderness
area in the nation, the Gila Wilderness, north of Silver City.
For information on New Mexico's five national forests and the
Kiowa National Grasslands (part of the Cibola National Forest), contact the **USDA Forest Service** (Southwest Regional Office, Public Affairs Office, 517 Gold Ave., SW, Albuquerque
87102, tel. 505/842–3292), **Carson National Forest** (Forest Service Bldg., 208 Cruz Alta Rd., Box 558, Taos 87571, tel. 505/
758–6200), **Cibola National Forest** (2113 Osuna Road, NE, Suite
A, Albuquerque 87113, tel. 505/761–4650), **Gila National Forest**
(2610 N. Silver St., Silver City 88061, tel. 505/388–8201), **Lincoln National Forest** (Federal Bldg., 11th and New York, Alamogordo 88310, tel. 505/437–6030), and **Santa Fe National
Forest** (1220 St. Francis Dr., Box 1689, Santa Fe 87504, tel. 505/
988–6940).

Canoeing, The choice is yours—a lazy glide along a serpentine waterway,
Kayaking, and past colorful mesas and soaring cliffs, or a heart-thumping ride
River Rafting through white-water rapids. **The Taos Box,** a 17-mile run
through the churning rapids of the upper **Rio Grande,** is one of
New Mexico's most exciting rafting experiences. Most of the
hard-core river rafting is done in the Taos area; the **Taos County Chamber of Commerce** (Drawer 1, Taos 87571, tel. 505/732–
3873 or 800/732–TAOS) can supply a list of local outfitters.
More leisurely trips can be had aboard the sightseeing crafts
that ply the **Pecos, Rio Charma,** and other of the state's meandering rivers. For statewide information concerning river recreational activities, contact the **New Mexico Department of
Economic Development and Tourism** (Joseph M. Montoya
Bldg., 1100 St. Francis Dr., Santa Fe 87503, tel. 505/827–0291
or 800/545–2040).

Fishing Spots for happy fishing include the **Rio Grande,** which tra-
verses New Mexico north to south, passing 30 miles west of
Santa Fe; **Abiquiu Lake,** 40 miles northwest of Santa Fe; **Heron
Lake,** 20 miles southwest of Chama via US 64 and NM 96; and
Blue Water Lake (closer to Albuquerque), also in the northwest, 28 miles west of Grants via NM 371. The **San Juan's**
high-quality-water regulations make for some of the best trout
fishing in the country. Six-thousand-acre **Heron Lake** offers
rainbow trout, lake trout, and kokanee salmon. Trout fisher-
men will also find their nirvana in the sparkling streams of the
Sangre de Cristo range, bordering Santa Fe. The **Pecos River**
and its tributaries offer excellent backcountry fishing.

Anyone over 12 must have a New Mexico fishing license. Including a trout-validation stamp, the license costs out-of-state visitors $25 per year. Temporary licenses may also be purchased.
Nearly 300 stores, in addition to game-and-fish offices, sell
fishing and hunting licenses.

Fishing on Indian reservations is not subject to regulations, but may require special permits; the **Indian Pueblo Cultural Center** (2401 12th Street, NW, Albuquerque 87102, tel. 505/843–7270) can provide further information.

Most major recreational areas offer boat and equipment rentals. For additional information, or to obtain copies of state fishing regulations and maps, contact the **New Mexico Game and Fish Department** (Villagra Bldg., 400 Galisteo St., Santa Fe 87503, tel. 505/827–7911). Another source of information is the **New Mexico Council of Outfitters and Guides** (160 Washington St., SE, No. 175, Albuquerque 87108, tel. 505/248–4461), representing independent guides and outfitters throughout the state.

Golfing   Golf isn't the first thing that comes to mind when New Mexico is mentioned, but the state has a respectable share of green turf, with over 60 courses, cool green oases amid the desert, offering recreation throughout the year. The dry climate here makes playing much more comfortable than in more humid states. There are excellent public courses in Albuquerque, Angel Fire, Las Vegas, Los Alamos, and Santa Fe; Taos will soon join the ranks with the opening of a new course in July 1992. **The Golf Association** (10035 Golf Course La., NW, Albuquerque 87114, tel. 505/897–0864) can provide a list of courses, along with details on the greens fees and hours for each club.

Hiking   Bring your walking shoes. Few states in the nation are as blessed with such a diverse network of designated and wilderness trails. New Mexico's air is clean and crisp, and its ever-changing terrain is aesthetically rewarding as well. The **State Parks and Recreational Division** (Energy, Minerals, and Natural Resources Department, 408 Galisteo St., Box 20003, Santa Fe 87503, tel. 505/827–0291) can provide further information and maps.

Hunting   The New Mexico Game and Fish Department has instituted many innovative game management and wildlife restoration programs. As a result, hunters have a diverse selection of wildlife to pursue. Mule deer and elk herds are sizable and steadily growing, and waterfowl and upland game bird hunting is excellent.

Head to the wide, windswept plains of eastern New Mexico for antelope. The mountainous backcountry still has a fairly sizable bear population. In addition, there are limited special hunts for barbary and bighorn sheep, oryx, javelina, and Siberian and Persian ibex.

Four Native American reservations conduct hunts in New Mexico separate from the regular state hunts: the Jicarilla and Mescalero Apaches, the Navajos, and the Zunis all have extensive landholdings in the state and offer the opportunity to hunt certain species when the regular state season is closed.

Out-of-state hunters must check with the New Mexico Game and Fish Department for the hunt dates in the area they plan to visit. General big-game hunting licenses are not available to nonresidents, but separate licenses may be bought for turkey and all big game. A general license for small game (squirrel, and birds other than turkey) is available to nonresidents for $51. Indian tribes have their own fee schedules. For more information, contact the **New Mexico Game and Fish Department**

(Villagra Bldg., 400 Galisteo St., Santa Fe 87503, tel. 505/827–7911). Licenses may be ordered by mail.

Skiing New Mexico offers slopes for everyone, from novice to daredevil, at its many world-class ski areas. Snowmaking equipment is available in most areas to ensure a long season, usually from Thanksgiving through Easter. Check with the **Bureau of Land Management** (224 Cruz Aulta Rd., Taos 87571, tel. 505/758–8851) and state park officials for advice on local snow and trail conditions and weather updates.

Downhill The major downhill ski areas in New Mexico include **Angel Fire Resort** (Drawer B, Angel Fire 87710, tel. 505/377–6401 or 800/633–7463), **Pajarito Mountain Ski Area** (Box 155, Los Alamos 87544, tel. 505/662–SNOW or 505/662–5725), **Red River Ski Area** (Box 900, Red River 87558, tel. 505/754–2382), **Sandia Peak Ski Area** (10 Tramway Loop, NE, Albuquerque 87122, tel. 505/296–9585 or 505/242–9052), **Santa Fe Ski Area** (1210 Louisa, Suite 10, Santa Fe 87501, tel. 505/982–4429), **Sipapu Lodge and Ski Area** (Rte. Box 29, Vadito 87579, tel. 505/587–2240), **Ski Apache** (Box 220, Ruidoso 88345, tel. 505/336–4356 or 505/336–4357), **Ski Cloudcroft** (Box 53, Cloudcroft 88317, tel. 505/682–2333 or 505/682–2733), and **Taos Ski Valley** (Box 90, Taos Ski Valley 87525, tel. 505/776–2291).

Cross-Country **Enchanted Forest** near Red River offers groomed trails in the state's best-known Nordic ski area. Head to the Sangre de Cristo Mountains for high-altitude terrain. There are also exciting cross-country trails north of Chama along the New Mexico–Colorado border, in the **Tularosa Mountains** in the Gila Wilderness, and to the south in the **Sacramento Mountains** adjacent to White Springs National Monument. The **Sandia** and **Manzano Mountains** near Albuquerque are easily accessible for skiers.

Tennis Tennis courts are almost as mandatory in today's hotels as swimming pools and color televisions, especially in the West, where there's room to spread out and breathe. In addition to hotel courts, numerous public courts are to be found in Albuquerque, Santa Fe, and Taos; check individual chapters for locations and specifics.

Spectator Sports

Horse Racing Horse racing with pari-mutuel betting is very popular in New Mexico. Following are the state's tracks and schedules: **Downs at Santa Fe** (tel. 505/471–3311), 5 miles south of Santa Fe, early June–Labor Day, Wed., Fri.–Sun., holidays; **La Mesa Park** (tel. 505/445–2301), 1 mile south of Raton, June–Labor Day, Sat. and Sun.; **Downs at Albuquerque** (tel. 505/262–1188), New Mexico State Fairgrounds, East Central Avenue, Albuquerque, Jan.–June 15, Wed., Fri.–Sun., holiday Mon.; **Ruidoso Downs Racetrack** (tel. 505/378–4431), Ruidoso, early May–Labor Day, Thurs.–Mon., holidays; **San Juan Downs** (tel. 505/326–4551), 7 miles east of Farmington, last weekend in Apr.–Labor Day, Sat., Sun., and holidays; **Sunland Park Racetrack** (tel. 505/589–1131), 45 miles south of Las Cruces (5 miles north of El Paso, Texas), mid-Oct.–mid-May, Wed., Fri.–Sun., holidays.

Quarterhorse racing's Triple Crown events—Kansas Futurity, Rainbow Futurity, and All-American Futurity—take place in mid-June, mid-July, and Labor Day, respectively, at Ruidoso Downs.

Hot-Air Balloons The Albuquerque International Balloon Fiesta, held in early October, draws the largest number of spectators of any sporting event in the state (*see* Festivals and Seasonal Events, above).

Rodeos Rodeos are a big draw from early spring through autumn. Besides the big events in Santa Fe, Albuquerque, and Gallup, every county in the state has rodeo competition during its county fairs. Major all-Indian rodeos take place at Stone Lake on the Jicarilla Reservation, on the Mescalero Apache Reservation, at the Inter-Tribal Ceremonial in Gallup, and at the National Indian Rodeo Finals in Albuquerque.

National and State Parks and Monuments

National Parks **Carlsbad Caverns National Park** (3225 National Parks Hwy., Carlsbad 88220, tel. 505/785–2232 or 505/785–2107 for 24-hr recorded information), in the southeastern part of the state (27 miles southwest of Carlsbad on U.S. 62/180), contains one of the largest and most spectacular cave systems in the world. Of the more than 70 caves in the park, only two, Carlsbad Cavern and New Cave, are open to the public. No camping is permitted in Carlsbad Caverns National Park, but nearby Brantley Lake State Park, the newest state park in New Mexico, and Lincoln National Forest have camping facilities. A number of commercial sites in Carlsbad and at White's City, 7 miles northeast of the caverns, are also available.

National Monuments The National Parks Service also maintains a score of national monuments in New Mexico. They are **Aztec Ruins National Monument** (Box 640, Aztec 87410, tel. 505/334–6174); **Bandelier National Monument** (Box 1, Suite 15, Los Alamos 87544, tel. 505/672–3861); **Capulin Volcano National Monument** (Box 94, Capulin 88414, tel. 505/278–2201); **Chaco Culture National Historic Park** (Star Rte. 4, Box 6500, Bloomfield 87413, tel. 505/988–6716); **El Malpais National Monument and Conservation Area** (Box 939, Grants 87020, tel. 505/285–4641); **El Morro National Monument** (Rte. 2, Box 43, Ramah 87321–9603, tel. 505/783–4226); **Fort Union National Monument** (Watrous 87753, tel. 505/425–8025); **Gila Cliff Dwelling National Monument** (Rte. 11, Box 100, Silver City 88061, tel. 505/536–9461); **Pecos National Historical Park** (Drawer 418, Pecos 87552, tel. 505/757–6032); **Petroglyph National Monument** (contact National Park Service, Southwest Region, Box 728, Santa Fe 87504, tel. 505/988–6430); **Salinas Pueblo Missions National Monument** (Box 496, Mountainair 87036, tel. 505/847–2585); and **White Sands National Monument** (Box 458, Alamogordo 88310, tel. 505/479–6124).

State Monuments For a look at New Mexico's past, you might want to visit one of the five state monuments. **Coronado State Monument** (NM 44, off I–25, tel. 505/867–5351), 18 miles north of Albuquerque, preserves ruins of a prehistoric Indian pueblo; it has self-guided trails, a visitor center and a museum, and is adjacent to a state park. **Jemez State Monument** (NM 4, 1 mi north of Jemez Springs, tel. 505/829–3530) is home to ruins of a 17th-century mission church and pueblo. **Lincoln State Monument** (U.S. 380, 12 mi east of Capitan, tel. 505/653–4500), **Fort Selden** (Radium

Springs exit off I–25, 13 mi north of Las Crucas, tel. 505/526–8911), and **Fort Sumner** (2 mi east of the town Fort Sumner, on Billy the Kid Rd., tel. 505/355–2573) all give insight into the 19th-century territorial period of New Mexico. For more information, contact the **Monument Division, Museum of New Mexico** (Box 2087, Santa Fe 87504, tel. 505/827–6334).

State Parks   Established in the 1930s, New Mexico's state park system is composed of 45 parks located throughout the state, ranging from the high mountain lakes and pine forests of the north to the Chihuahuan Desert lowlands to the south. Pristine and unspoiled, they offer every conceivable outdoor recreational facility. For maps and brochures, contact the **State Parks and Recreational Division** (Energy, Minerals, and Natural Resources Department, 408 Galisteo St., Box 20003, Santa Fe 87503, tel. 505/827–0291).

Indian Reservations

Two general classifications of Native Americans live in New Mexico: the Pueblos, who established an agricultural civilization here many centuries ago, and the descendants of the nomadic tribes who came into the area much later—the Navajos, Mescalero Apaches, and Jicarilla Apaches. The **Jicarilla Apaches** live on a reservation of ¾ million acres in north-central New Mexico, the capital of which is Dulce. The terrain varies from mountains, mesas, and lakes to high grazing land, suited to cattle and horse ranching. The tribe has a well-defined tourist program promoting big-game hunting, fishing, and camping on a 20,000-acre game preserve. On July 4, a rodeo and powwow dancing are held in Dulce, and nearly all the tribe members gather at Stone Lake on September 14 and 15 for the fall festival—two days of dancing, races, and a rodeo. For more information, contact the **Tourism Department, Jicarilla Apache Tribe** (Box 507, Dulce 87528, tel. 505/759–3242).

A reservation of a ½ million acres of timbered mountains and green valleys is home to the **Mescalero Apaches** in southeastern New Mexico. The tribe owns and operates the most elegant luxury resort in the state, Inn of the Mountain Gods, as well as Ski Apache, 16 miles from Ruidoso. Guests at the resort may golf, swim, fish, hike, skeet shoot, and, in season, go on guided big-game hunts. A summer racing season in Ruidoso and the winter ski season at Ski Apache make tourism the tribe's major enterprise, but ranching and lumbering are also important to the economy. An annual celebration, including powwow dancing, a rodeo, arts and crafts, and food booths, is held on July 4 in Mescalero, the reservation's only town. A large campground is also operated by the Mescalero Apaches on one of their fishing lakes. For general information, contact the **Mescalero Apache Tribe** (Box 176, Mescalero 88340, tel. 505/671–4494); for Inn of the Mountain Gods, call 505/257–5141; and for Ski Apache, call 505/336–4357.

The **Navajo** Reservation, home to the largest Native American group in the United States, covers 16 million acres in New Mexico, Arizona, and Utah. More than any other tribe, the Navajos are still nomadic, following flocks from place to place and living in hogans (mud and pole houses). There are a few towns on the reservation, but for the most part it is a vast area of stark pinnacles, colorful rock formations, high desert, and mountains;

the land encompasses several national and tribal parks, some of which include campgrounds. Navajos are master silversmiths and rug weavers, and their work is available at trading posts scattered throughout the reservation. There are no specific feast days, but the tribe frequently holds "sings," sometimes lasting up to nine days, which are part of complex healing rites. Visitors are welcome, but it would be a matter of luck to come across one of these ceremonies. The tribe encourages tourism; for more information, contact the **Navajo Tribal Tourism Office** (Box 663, Window Rock, AZ 86515, tel. 602/871–4941).

Pueblo Villages   Traveling across country, one is immediately impressed with the many recently built forts, Native American villages, and trading posts that dot the landscape everywhere from New Jersey to Cleveland. In some places, "Indians" in jeans and sports jackets sign in for work in the morning, change into tribal regalia, and then spend the rest of the day making pots and baskets and performing dances and other ancient rituals for the entertainment of tourists. Such places may be sincere in their efforts to portray Native American life and culture, but they often come across as inane and theatrical. But not so in the West where reservations are perhaps the only places left where traditional Native American culture and skills are retained with a sense of dignity and pride. Descendants of the highly civilized Anasazi, the Pueblo peoples of Northern New Mexico in particular, continue to preserve their customs amid a changing world. Each pueblo has its own personality, history, and specialties in art and design.

Before venturing off to visit the pueblos, you'd do well to visit the striking **Indian Pueblo Cultural Center** in Albuquerque (2401 12th St. NW, tel. 505/843–7270), which exhibits and sells the best of arts and crafts from all the New Mexico pueblos; coming here will help you decide which of the pueblos to visit. Native American ceremonial dances are held during summer weekends, and photography is allowed (photographing of Native American rituals is not allowed at any of the individual pueblos).

Fall, when the pueblos celebrate the harvest with special ceremonies, dances, and sacred rituals, is the best time to visit. The air is fragrant with curling piñon smoke. Clusters of *ristras* (red chilis) decorate many homes, with the chiles destined to add their distinct flavor to stews and sauces through the winter. Drums throb with insistent cadence. Dancers adorn themselves with some of the most beautiful turquoise and jewelry seen anywhere. The atmosphere is lighthearted, evocative of a country fair: Excited children laugh and scamper, and wives chuckle and gossip, conversing in tongues—Tewa, Keresan, Tiwa—both strange and fascinating to outsiders.

Pueblo Etiquette— Each pueblo has its own regulations for the use of still cameras,
Do's and Don'ts camcorders, and movie cameras, as well as for sketching and painting. Some pueblos, such as San Juan and Santo Domingo, prohibit photography altogether. Others, such as Santa Clara, prohibit photography at certain times, such as during ritual dances. Still others allow photography but require a permit, which usually costs about $5 for a still camera and up to $35 for the privilege of setting up an easel and painting all day. Be sure to ask permission before photographing anyone in the pueblos; it's also customary to give the subject a dollar or two for

agreeing to be photographed. Indian law prevails on the pueblos, and violations of photography regulations could result in confiscation of cameras. Restrictions for the various pueblos are noted in the individual descriptions found in the pueblos sections in Chapters 3, 4, and 5.

Possessing or using drugs and/or alcohol on Indian land is forbidden.

Ritual dances often have serious religious significance and should be respected as such. Silence is mandatory. That means no questions about ceremonies or dances while they're being performed. Don't walk across the dance plaza during a performance, and don't applaud afterward.

Kiva and ceremonial rooms are restricted to pueblo members only.

Cemeteries are sacred. They're off-limits to all visitors and should never be photographed.

Unless pueblo dwellings are clearly marked as shops, don't wander or peek inside. Remember, these are private homes.

Many of the pueblo buildings are hundreds of years old. Don't try to scale adobe walls or climb on top of buildings, or you may all come tumbling down.

Don't litter. Nature is sacred on the pueblos and defacing of land can be a serious offense.

Dining

When it comes to eating out, visitors to New Mexico are in for a treat. A delicious and extraordinary mixture of Pueblo Indian, Spanish Colonial, and Mexican and American frontier cooking, all steeped and bubbling over the centuries like *sopa de pollo* (chicken soup), the regional cuisine is not only good, it's good for you. Mexican restaurants are especially popular and are almost universally inexpensive. Nutrition experts say that the basic staple diet of the Mexican peasant is among the healthiest in the world. Beans provide carbohydrates and protein. Corn, from which tortillas are made, offers protein and calcium. Chiles, one of the most versatile seasonings known, used in everything Mexican and New Mexican, by themselves contain an entire storehouse of vitamins and minerals; they're particularly loaded with vitamin C.

New Mexico also has numerous Chinese restaurants, where freshness is a key to everything served. Many of the dishes are steamed, all brimming with natural vitamins and goodness, with hardly a glob of cholesterol in sight. Many New Mexico restaurants offer buffalo meat (stews, steaks, and burgers), which has numerous fans, especially among people who are allergic to beef or are adhering to a low-cholesterol diet; others like its distinctive taste or simply enjoy eating a throwback to pioneer days. And of course there are a fair share of trendy and contemporary restaurants, particularly in the Santa Fe and Taos areas, as well as a respectable offering of gourmet grill rooms, French, Italian, Japanese, Greek, and other ethnic establishments.

The following list of names and terms may prove helpful for the newcomer to New Mexico who doesn't know what a great taste treat lies in store:

Aguacate. Spanish for avocado, the key ingredient of guacamole. Also may be served halved at breakfast time, with a squeeze of lemon, or quartered or sliced as a garnish.

Albondigas. Meatballs, usually served with vegetables in a broth.

Burrito. A warm flour tortilla wrapped around meat, beans, or vegetables. Burritos are occasionally crisp fried; filled with meat, fish, or chicken; and topped with refried beans, shredded lettuce, and chopped tomatoes.

Chayote. A light green, pear-shape vegetable (it looks like a squash) with edible seeds.

Chile relleno. A large, mild green chile pepper, peeled, stuffed with cheese or a special mixture of spicy ingredients, dipped in batter, and fried.

Chiles. Mexico's infamous hot peppers, which come in an endless variety of sizes and in various degrees of hotness, from the thumb-size jalapeño to the smaller and often hotter serano. They can be canned or fresh, dried or cut up into salsa.

Chimichanga. The same as a burrito above, only deep-fried and topped with a dash of sour cream or salsa.

Chorizo. Well-spiced Spanish sausage, made with red chile.

Enchilada. A rolled corn tortilla, filled with meat, chicken, seafood, chiles, or cheese; covered with salsa; and baked. The ultimate enchilada is made with blue Indian corn tortillas. New Mexicans order them flat, sometimes topped with a fried egg.

Flauta. A tortilla filled with cheese or meat and rolled into a flutelike shape (*flauta* means flute) and lightly fried. When eaten, they're usually dipped into a spicy sauce.

Frijoles refritos. Refried beans, often seasoned with lard, cheese, or a little river of pumpkin-seed oil.

Guacamole. Mashed avocado, mixed with tomatoes, garlic, onions, lemon juice, and hot sauce, used as a dip, a sauce, or a side dish.

Huevos rancheros. New Mexico's answer to eggs Benedict—eggs doused with chile and sometimes melted cheese, served on top of a tortilla. They're good accompanied by chorizos.

Jicama. A large, brown-skinned root, shaped like a turnip. Sweet and crisp, it's either cooked or peeled and eaten raw.

Nopales. Leaves of the prickly-pear cactus, available canned (*nopalitos*) or fresh.

Posole. Resembling popcorn soup, this is a sublime marriage of lime hominy, pork, chile, garlic, and spices.

Quesadilla. A folded tortilla, filled with cheese and warmed or lightly fried so the cheese melts.

Sopaipilla. Puffy deep-fried bread, served with honey.

Taco. A corn or flour tortilla, fried and made into a shell that's then stuffed with spicy meat or chicken, and garnished with shredded lettuce, radishes, chopped tomatoes, onions, olives, and grated cheese.

Tamale. Crushed Indian corn and finely chopped meat, seasoned with red pepper, rolled in a corn shuck, then steamed or baked.

Tortilla. Thin pancake made of corn or wheat flour, used as bread, as an edible "spoon," and as a container for other foods. Locals place butter in the center of a hot tortilla, roll it up, and eat it as a scroll. It is also useful for scooping up the last bit in a bowl of chili.

Verde. Spanish for "green." Salsa chile verde is a green chile sauce.

Lodging

In the early days of the American West, it wasn't uncommon for a cowboy, with one too many tequilas under his belt, to ride his horse right through the front door of a hotel and into the lobby. Hotels were more informal in those days and scarce—so scarce, in fact, that guests frequently not only had to share rooms with total strangers, but had to share beds with them as well. Traces of that informality remain in New Mexico to this day, albeit not to such extremes. You'll never be intimidated by management or staff, by dress codes, or by menus you can't read. Bellboys usually wear clean white shirts and jeans, and the switchboard operator or the desk clerk may call you by your first name.

At the same time, New Mexico is a hot tourist destination that attracts lots of upscale travelers. As a result, prices have been escalating steadily in the past few years and are likely to continue to climb as long as a steady stream of fat cats continues to show up and pay them. Low-season rates, which fluctuate, tend to be 20% lower than during the peak tourist months of July and August. Reservations are also easier to obtain during low season. In addition to hotels, New Mexico offers a broad range of alternative accommodations, from charming bed-and-breakfasts in quaint residential areas to small alpine lodges near the primary ski resorts.

Home Exchange Exchanging homes is a low-cost, relaxing way to enjoy a vacation in another part of the country, especially if you plan a lengthy visit. **International Home Exchange Service** (Box 3975, San Francisco, CA 94119, tel. 415/435–3497) publishes three directories a year. The $45 membership entitles you to one listing and all three directories (there is an additional charge for postage). Photos of your property cost an additional $10, and listing a second home costs $10. **Vacation Exchange Club, Inc.** (Box 820, Haleiwa, HI 96712, tel. 800/638–3841) specializes in both international and domestic home exchanges. The club publishes three directories a year, in February, April, and August, and updated, late listings throughout the year. The annual membership, which includes your listing in one book, a newsletter, and copies of all publications (mailed first class), is $50. **Loan-a-Home** (2 Park La., Apt. 6E, Mount Vernon, NY 10552, tel. 914/664–7640), which publishes two directories (in December and June) and two supplements (in March and September) each year, is popular with professors on sabbatical, businesspeople on temporary assignment, and retired people on extended vacations. There is no annual membership fee or charge for listing your home, but one directory and a supplement costs $35. All four books cost $45.

Credit Cards

The following credit card abbreviations are used: AE, American Express; DC, Diners Club; D, Discover; MC, MasterCard; and V, Visa. It's a good idea to call ahead to check on an establishment's credit-card policies.

2 Portraits of New Mexico

New Mexico

By D. H. Lawrence

Superficially, the world has become small and known. Poor little globe of earth, the tourists trot round you as easily as they trot round the Bois or round Central Park. There is no mystery left, we've been there, we've seen it, we know all about it. We've done the globe, and the globe is done.

This is quite true, superficially. On the superficies, horizontally, we've been everywhere and done everything, we know all about it. Yet the more we know, superficially, the less we penetrate, vertically. It's all very well skimming across the surface of the ocean, and saying you know all about the sea. There still remain the terrifying underdeeps, of which we have utterly no experience.

The same is true of land travel. We skim along, we get there, we see it all, we've done it all. And as a rule, we never once go through the curious film which railroads, ships, motorcars, and hotels over the surface of the whole earth. Peking is just the same as New York, with a few different things to look at; rather more Chinese about, etc. Poor creatures that we are, we crave for experience, yet we are like flies that crawl on the pure and transparent mucous-paper in which the world like a bon-bon is wrapped so carefully that we can never get at it, though we see it there all the time as we move about it, apparently in contact, yet actually as far removed as if it were the moon.

As a matter of fact, our great-grandfathers, who never went anywhere, in actuality had more experience of the world than we have, who have seen everything. When they listened to a lecture with lantern-slides, they really held their breath before the unknown, as they sat in the village school-room. We, bowling along in a rickshaw in Ceylon, say to ourselves: "It's very much what you'd expect." We really know it all.

We are mistaken. The know-it-all state of mind is just the result of being outside the mucous-paper wrapping of civilization. Underneath is everything we don't know and are afraid of knowing.

I realized this with shattering force when I went to New Mexico.

This essay is taken from Phoenix: The Posthumous Papers of D. H. Lawrence. *Lawrence visited New Mexico with his wife, Frieda, in the early 1920s as part of an extended tour of Europe, Mexico, and the American Southwest. The couple lived in a ranch in Taos where Lawrence continued to write.*

New Mexico, one of the United States, part of the U.S.A. New Mexico, the picturesque reservation and playground of the eastern states, very romantic, old Spanish, Red Indian, desert mesas, pueblos, cowboys, penitentes, all that film-stuff. Very nice, the great South-West, put on a sombrero and knot a red kerchief round your neck, to go out in the great free spaces!

That is New Mexico wrapped in the absolutely hygienic and shiny mucous-paper of our trite civilization. That is the New Mexico known to most of the Americans who know it at all. But break through the shiny sterilized wrapping, and actually *touch* the country, and you will never be the same again.

I think New Mexico was the greatest experience from the outside world that I have ever had. It certainly changed me for ever. Curious as it may sound, it was New Mexico that liberated me from the present era of civilization, the great era of material and mechanical development. Months spent in holy Kandy, in Ceylon, the holy of holies of Southern Buddhism, had not touched the great psyche of materialism and idealism which dominated me. And years, even in the exquisite beauty of Sicily, right among the old Greek paganism that still lives there, had not shattered the essential Christianity on which my character was established. Australia was a sort of dream or trance, like being under a spell, the self remaining unchanged, so long as the trance did not last too long. Tahiti, in a mere glimpse, repelled me; and so did California, after a stay of a few weeks. There seemed a strange brutality in the spirit of the western coast, and I felt: O, let me get away!

But the moment I saw the brilliant, proud morning shine high up over the deserts of Santa Fe, something stood still in my soul, and I started to attend. There was a certain magnificence in the high-up day, a certain eagle-like royalty, so different from the equally pure, equally pristine and lovely morning of Australia, which is so soft, so utterly pure in its softness, and betrayed by green parrot flying. But in the lovely morning of Australia one went into a dream. In the magnificent fierce morning of New Mexico one sprang awake, a new part of the soul woke up suddenly, and the old world gave way to a new.

There are all kinds of beauty in the world, thank God, though ugliness is homogeneous. How lovely is Sicily, with Calabria across the sea like an opal, and Etna with her snow in a world above and beyond! How lovely is Tuscany, with little red tulips wild among the corn: or bluebells at dusk in England, or mimosa in clouds of pure yellow among the grey-green dun foliage of Australia, under a soft, blue, unbreathed sky! But for a *greatness* of beauty I have never experienced anything like New Mexico. All those mornings when I went with a hoe along the ditch to the Cañon, at the ranch, and stood, in the fierce, proud silence of the Rockies, on their foothills, to look far over the desert to the blue mountains away in Arizona, blue as chalcedony, with the sage-brush desert sweeping grey-blue in between, dotted with tiny cube-crystals of houses, the vast amphitheatre of lofty, indomitable desert, sweeping round to the ponderous Sangre de Cristo mountains on the east, and coming up flush at the pine-dotted foot-hills of the Rockies! What splendor! Only the tawny eagle could really sail out into the splendor of it all. Leo Stein once wrote to me: It is the most aesthetically-satisfying landscape I know. To me it was much more than that. It had a splendid silent terror, and a vast far-and-wide magnificence which made it way beyond mere aesthetic appreciation. Never is the light more pure and overweening than there, arching with a royalty almost cruel over the hollow, uptilted world. For it is curious that the land which had produced modern political democracy as its highest pitch should give one of the greatest sense of overweening, terrible proudness and mercilessness: but so beautiful, God! so beautiful! Those that have spent morning after morning alone there pitched among the pines above the great proud world of desert will know, almost unbearably how beautiful it is, how clear and unquestioned is the might of the day. Just day itself is tremendous there. It is so easy to understand that the Aztecs gave hearts of men to the sun. For the sun is not merely hot or scorching, not at all. It is of a brilliant and unchallengeable purity and haughty serenity which would make one sacrifice the heart to it. Ah, yes, in New Mexico the heart is sacrificed to the sun and the human being is left stark, heartless, but undauntedly religious.

And that was the second revelation out there. I had looked over all the world for something that would strike *me* as religious. The simple piety of some English people, the semi-pagan mystery of some Catholics in southern Italy, the intensity of some Bavarian peasants, the semi-ecstasy of Buddhists or Brahmins: all this had seemed religious all right, as far as the parties concerned were involved, but it didn't involve me. I looked on at the religiousness from the outside. For it is still harder to feel religion at will than to love at will.

I had seen what I felt was a hint of wild religion in the so-called devil dances of a group of naked villagers from the far-remote jungle in Ceylon, dancing at midnight under the torches, glittering wet with sweat on their dark bodies as if they had been gilded, at the celebration of the Pera-hera, in Kandy, given to the Prince of Wales. And the utter dark absorption of these naked men, as they danced with their knees wide apart suddenly affected me with a *sense* of religion. I *felt* religion for a moment. For religion is an experience, an uncontrollable sensual experience, even more so than love: I use sensual to mean an experience deep down in the senses, inexplicable and inscrutable.

But this experience was fleeting, gone in the curious turmoil of the Pera-hera, and I had no permanent feeling of religion till I came to New Mexico and penetrated into the old human race-experience there. It is curious that it should be in America, of all places, that a European should really experience religion, after touching the old Mediterranean and the East. . . . A vast old religion which once swayed the earth lingers in unbroken practice there in New Mexico, older, perhaps, than anything in the world save Australian aboriginal taboo and totem, and that is not yet religion.

You can feel it, the atmosphere of it, around the pueblos. Not, of course, when the place is crowded with sight-seers and motor-cars. But go to Taos pueblo on some brilliant snowy morning and see the white figure on the roof: or come riding through at dusk on some windy evening, when the black skirts of the silent women blow around the white wide boots, and you will feel the old, old root of human consciousness still reaching down to depths we know nothing of: and of which, only too often, we are jealous. It seems it will not be long before the pueblos are uprooted.

But never shall I forget watching the dancers, the men with the fox-skin swaying down from their buttocks, file out at San Geronimo, and the women with seed rattles following. The long, streaming, glistening black hair of the men. Even in ancient Crete long hair was sacred in a man, as it is still in the Indians. Never shall I forget the utter absorption of the dance, so quiet, so steadily, timelessly rhythmic, and silent, with the ceaseless downtread, always to the earth's centre, the very reverse of the upflow of Dionysiac or Christian ecstasy. Never shall I forget the deep singing of the men at the drum, swelling and sinking, the deepest sound I have heard in all my life, deeper than thunder, deeper than the sound of the Pacific Ocean, deeper than the roar of a deep waterfall: the wonderful deep sound of men calling to the unspeakable depths.

Never shall I forget coming into the little pueblo of San Filipi one sunny morning in spring, unexpectedly, when bloom was on the trees in the perfect little pueblo more old, more utterly peaceful and idyllic than anything in Theocritus, and seeing a little casual dance. Not impressive as a spectacle, only, to me, profoundly moving because of the truly terrifying religious absorption of it.

Never shall I forget the Christmas dances at Taos, twilight, snow, the darkness coming over the great wintry mountains and the lonely pueblo, then suddenly, again, like dark calling to dark, the deep Indian cluster-singing around the drum, wild and awful, suddenly arousing on the last dusk as the procession starts. And then the bon-fires leaping suddenly in pure spurts of high flame, columns of sudden flame forming an alley for the procession. . . . Never shall I forget the Indian races, when the young men, even the boys, run naked, smeared with white earth and stuck with bits of eagle fluff for the swiftness of the heavens, and the old men brush them with eagle feathers, to give them power. And they run in the strange hurling fashion of the primitive world, hurled forward, not making speed deliberately. And the race is not for victory. It is not a contest. There is no competition. It is a great cumulative effort. The tribe this day is adding up its male energy and exerting it to the utmost—for what? To get power, to get strength: to come, by sheer cumulative, hurling effort of the bodies of men, into contact with the great cosmic source of vitality which gives strength, power, energy to the men who can grasp it, energy for the zeal of attainment.

It was a vast old religion, greater than anything we know: more starkly and nakedly religious. There is no God, no conception of a god. All is god. But it is not the pantheism we are accustomed to, which expresses itself as "God is everywhere, God is in everything." In the oldest religion, everything was alive, not supernaturally but naturally alive. There were only deeper and deeper streams of life, vibrations of life more and more vast. So rocks were alive, but a mountain had a deeper, vaster life than a rock, and it was much harder for a man to bring his spirit, or his energy, into contact with the life of the mountain, and so draw strength from the mountain, as from a great standing well of life, than it was to come into contact with the rock. And he had to put forth a great religious effort. For the whole life-effort of man was to get his life into direct contact with the elemental life of the cosmos, mountain-life, cloud-life, thunder-life, air-life, earth-life, sun-life. To come into immediate *felt* contact, and so derive energy, power, and a dark sort of joy. This effort into sheer naked contact, *without an intermediary or mediator*, is the root meaning of religion, and at the sacred races the runners hurled themselves in a terrible cumulative effort, through the air, to come at last into naked contact with the very life of air, which is the life of the clouds, and so of the rain.

It was a vast and pure religion, without idols or images, even mental ones. It is the oldest religion, a cosmic religion the same for all peoples, not broken up into specific gods or saviours or systems. It is the religion which precedes the god-concept, and is therefore greater and deeper than any god-religion.

And it lingers still, for a little while in New Mexico: but long enough to have been a revelation to me. And the Indian, however objectionable he may be on occasion, has still some of the strange beauty and pathos of the religion that brought him forth and is now shedding him away into oblivion. When Trinidad, the Indian boy, and I planted corn at the ranch, my soul paused to see his brown hands softly moving the earth over the maize in pure ritual. He was back in his old religious self, and the ages stood still. Ten minutes later he was making a fool of himself with the horses.

Horses were never part of the Indian's religious life, never would be. He hasn't a tithe of feeling for them that he has for a bear, for example. So horses don't like Indians.

But there it is: the newest democracy ousting the oldest religion! And once the oldest religion is ousted, one feels the democracy and all its paraphernalia will collapse, and the oldest religion, which comes down to us from man's pre-war days, will start again. The skyscraper will scatter on the winds like thistledown, and the genuine America, the America of New Mexico, will start on its course again. This is an interregnum.

New Mexico Crafts

By Suzanne Carmichael

Suzanne Carmichael is the author of The Travelers Guide to American Crafts: East of the Mississippi and West of the Mississippi, and of travel and craft articles for such publications as the New York Times, USA Weekend, and Northwest Magazine.

Purchasing gifts while traveling can be a superb indulgence that provides lasting, vivid mementos of an isolated Indian reservation, a posh urban gallery district, or traditional Hispanic religious observances. On the other hand, it can be a frustrating experience if you don't know where to locate top-notch crafts made by local artisans and sold at reasonable prices. The most reliable way to assure that you return home with high-quality souvenirs is to learn what items are unique to the area you are visiting and then integrate your shopping with your planned itinerary.

New Mexico provides a wealth of craft alternatives: Traditional Pueblo and Navajo Indian, Hispanic, and avant-garde contemporary work vie for the buyer's attention and offer an artistic introduction to the state's multiethnic population. Visits to artisans' studios, old-fashioned Indian trading posts, and annual craft shows can lead you from sophisticated Santa Fe to remote mountain villages.

Native American Crafts

Two general classifications of Indians live in New Mexico: the Pueblos, who established an agricultural civilization many centuries ago, and the descendants of the nomadic tribes who came into New Mexico much later than the Pueblos: the Navajos, Mescalero Apaches, and Jicarilla Apaches.

New Mexico's legacy of Native American crafts includes distinctive Pueblo Indian and Navajo pottery, textiles, and jewelry that can be found everywhere, from airport, motel, and specialty shops to gas stations and roadside stands. The challenge is to find top-notch, authentic work. Some so-called Indian crafts are actually made in Taiwan or Mexico. Others labeled "genuine Indian made" are mass-produced with shoddy materials and inferior workmanship.

To get an idea of how to judge quality, visit the Native American collections at the Indian Pueblo Cultural Center (Albuquerque) or the Wheelwright Museum or the Museum of Indian Arts and Culture (both in Santa Fe). These museums also have gift shops that sell high-quality items at reasonable prices. Long-established galleries and Indian dealers are another option. Most top-notch shops will have a range of prices and knowledgeable salespeople who can answer your questions. If everything in a shop is inexpensive, it's probably attributable to the poor quality of the goods, rather than to a low overhead. It's best to shop elsewhere.

One way to add an adventurous detour to your trip is to buy directly from craftspeople. Inquire at pueblo governors' offices or look for signs outside reservation homes. Although visiting artisans is not a guarantee of quality, it does provide an unforgettable introduction to both crafts and their makers.

Other sources of high-quality wares include Native American festivals, fairs, and powwows (ceremonial gatherings) that exhibit the work of many artisans and showcase native dancing, story-telling, and food. The best annual events in New Mexico are Gallup's Inter-tribal Indian Ceremonial, held the second and third weeks of August; Santa Fe's Indian Market, held the weekend following the third Thursday in August; and the Northern Indian Pueblo Council Craft Show, held in July (dates vary). For more information, contact the Inter-tribal Indian Ceremonial Association (Box 1, Church Rock 87311, tel. 505/863–3896 or 800/233–4528); Indian Market c/o Southwestern Association on Indian Affairs (Box 1964, Santa Fe 87501, tel. 505/983–5220); and ENIPC (Eight Northern Indian Pueblos Council) (Box 969, San Juan Pueblo 87566, tel. 505/852–4265).

Pueblo Indian Crafts Pueblo craftspeople continue traditions begun over 1,000 years ago, when their ancestors first made fired earthenware pottery for storage and cooking, wove cloth and baskets, and used turquoise and shell for personal adornment. Although colors, designs, and materials have altered somewhat, the dominant traditions of the work have remained undisturbed for centuries.

Pueblo pottery has changed from a purely functional craft to a highly prized decorative art. Most potters use traditional methods and local materials, creating vessels from coils of clay smoothed with pieces of wood, gourd, or shells. Pots are then dried, burnished with stones for increased smoothness, and fired outdoors. Designs are added after firing, using yucca-fiber brushes and paint made from colored sand and rock.

Shapes and functions vary, ranging from shallow plates, bulbous pots, and tall storage vessels to double-necked wedding vases. Some pottery is plain, and some is covered with motifs resembling ancient petroglyphs—stylized birds and animals, zigzag bolts of thunder, or legendary spiritual forms. Many pueblos are known for specific designs and color combinations, although individual artisans' work may differ.

Acoma pottery features intricate geometric patterns, a dizzy profusion of black, dark orange, and white motifs spiraling up the sides. In contrast, San Ildefonso and Santa Clara artisans create subtle jet-black pieces, often highly polished, sometimes deeply carved. Other pueblos' distinguishing characteristics include San Juan's polished red pottery, banded at the bottom with incised beige clay; Isleta's red-and-black designs on a white background; Zia's bright orange–and-white pieces with ancient sun symbols; Zuni's dark brown patterns on white; and Picuris's simple, unadorned pottery made from bronze-color, mica-flecked clay. In all cases, look for pieces that are symmetrically shaped with smooth rims and neatly painted designs.

Storyteller figures are another pottery specialty, particularly for Cochiti artisans. This type of ceramic sculpture portrays a stately Indian matron surrounded by a horde of small children, sitting on her lap, curling near her feet, and perching on her shoulders, listening to her recount ancient legends.

Santo Domingo and Zuni jewelry can be a stunning wardrobe accent. Santo Domingos painstakingly grind strings of turquoise or shell into smooth, sinuous ropes of color known as *heishi* ("he-she") necklaces. In contrast, the Zuni create elaborate, inlaid jewelry that resembles miniature mosaics. Individual stones are set inside narrow silver bands in a variety of motifs, from geometric designs to Zuni dance figures—and even Disney characters. There are many variables in the quality of stones and workmanship, so buy pueblo jewelry only from reputable dealers.

For a dollop of personal magic, consider acquiring a "fetish": a small stone animal or bird, sometimes with a miniature arrowhead on its back, intended to endow its owners with good luck, power, or successful hunting. Look particularly for Zuni fetishes, which stand alone like miniature sculptures, decorate pottery, or are strung on necklaces.

Other crafts to watch for are Jemez braided yucca-leaf baskets, Cochiti drums made from hollowed-out logs, San Ildefonso embroidery (geometric designs on cloaks and shawls), and Santa Ana wood crosses inlaid with straw designs. And keep an eye out for contemporary ceramics with unusual colors and designs or ones that sport sculptural accents, from slithering lizards to rows of gaily colored corncobs.

Navajo Indian Crafts Although two-thirds of the 16-million-acre Navajo reservation lie in Arizona, the remaining one-third dominates northwestern New Mexico. Navajo craftspeople in both states are known for the variety and quality of their woven wool rugs, as well as their turquoise and silver jewelry.

Sheepherders for centuries, Navajos learned to weave from Pueblo Indians during the 18th century. The Navajo's early work, brown-and-white striped blankets, was supplanted in the late 19th century by rugs with complex designs and brilliant colors. Contemporary rugs continue traditional patterns, such as boldly jagged "eye-dazzler" designs, "pictorials" featuring animals and other figures, and *yei* rugs that duplicate sandpainting designs.

If you're thinking of purchasing a Navajo rug, make sure that it's made entirely of wool (no linen or cotton threads), that the wool is of even thickness, that the design is neatly woven, and that the colors are uniform throughout. A good source for Navajo rugs is the Crownpoint Rug Weavers' Auctions, held every six to seven weeks at the Crownpoint Elementary School, 57 miles northeast of Gallup. Even if you don't buy anything, it's worth the trip to see the colorful jumble of up to 400 rugs and to hear the shouted bids and auction babble.

Navajo jewelry traces its origin to the mid-19th century. Tribal craftsmen learned metal smithing from Mexican artisans, then developed their own styles and designs. Early pieces were often made from hammered silver coins and decorated with stamp work. Although turquoise beads date back to prehistoric times, Navajos did not combine the stone with silver until the late 1800s. Today, in addition to turquoise, artisans use a variety of semiprecious stones, such as coral and lapis lazuli.

Contemporary Navajo jewelry ranges from simple rings and cast-silver bracelets to massive necklaces and *concha* belts (named for the stamped silver disks strung together on narrow leather bands). Again, because there are so many variables in the quality of stones and workmanship, you should buy only from reputable dealers. Also, be leery of assertions of an item's age or merit simply because it was pawned by its Native American owner and is now for sale; although items in "pawn" displays may be antique and of excellent quality, this is not always the case.

Kachinas In addition to Pueblo and Navajo crafts, shops specializing in Native American tribal arts often sell a variety of "kachina" dolls. True kachinas, however, are made only by the Hopi Indians of Arizona. These colorfully painted wood figures, sporting intricate masks as well as fabric, leather, and feather costumes, are miniature versions of the elaborate regalia worn by dancers in Hopi religious ceremonies. They serve a variety of functions, including the instruction of children in the tribal religion, and range in size from 3 to 18 inches.

Within the past 20 years, Navajo carvers (and some Anglos) began creating kachina-type dolls for sale. Although attractive and often well executed, these are not part of the true kachina tradition. If you are a stickler for authenticity, purchase your kachinas on the Hopi reservation in Arizona or from a reputable dealer who will provide written documentation that the maker is Hopi.

Hispanic Crafts The Hispanic influence in New Mexico began with Coronado's abortive search for gold in 1540. Waves of missionaries and colonizers followed as the Mexican empire extended north. Dependent upon their own skills to provide many of the basic necessities, the settlers used local materials to fashion household goods and religious items. Although their work reflected Spanish and Mexican influences, they gradually developed distinctive styles and techniques, particularly in weaving, religious carvings, and ornamental tinsmithing.

Today these unique crafts are still produced, often by descendants of the original artisans. Traditional Hispanic work can be found throughout the region, especially in shops near the Plaza in Santa Fe and in Albuquerque's Old Town. To see the full array of Hispanic crafts and meet individual artisans, visit Santa Fe's annual Spanish Market, held the last week of July (for more information contact the Spanish Colonial Arts Society, Box 1611, Santa Fe 87501, tel. 505/983–4038).

For a personal introduction to Hispanic weaving, take the "High Road" from Santa Fe to Taos through the Sangre de Cristo mountains (Routes 76 and 3). A number of weaving shops along the narrow, winding highway are open to the public; visitors can watch the work being done at huge looms, then browse in small showrooms. In Chimayo, at Ortega's Weaving Shop (Box 325, Chimayo 87522, tel. 505/351–4215), the family's eighth generation creates "Chimayo/Rio Grande" textiles—rugs, place mats, coats, and purses, all woven from pure wool—dominated by large lozenge-shaped medallions surrounded by colorful stripes.

Other Hispanic weaving styles include the "Tree of Life," in which roadrunners, birds, and fanciful animals perch on outstretched tree limbs; "Saltillos," large diamond-shaped centers surrounded by vividly colored, interlocking diamonds; and "Trampas-Vallero" work, dominated by eight-pointed stars reminiscent of quilt patterns. Many contemporary pieces interpret traditional styles in dazzlingly creative ways.

The creation of *santos*, representations of saints, is one of New Mexico's oldest Hispanic craft traditions. Used in churches or for personal devotions, most santos are relatively rustic, more closely allied to folk art than to the elaborate icons found in European churches. They come in two forms: carved and painted three-dimensional figures called *bultos*, and paintings executed on wood slabs, called *retablos*. One of the more popular saints to appear in either form is San Isidro, the patron saint of Spanish farmers who was so pious his fields were plowed by angels.

Although contemporary *santeros* (saint makers) may use everything from ceramics to sequins in their work, more traditional artisans employ materials and techniques that have remained unchanged since the early 17th century. If authenticity is important, look for santos made of cottonwood and painted with natural pigments derived from native minerals, clay, and vegetables.

Another Hispanic craft, ornamental tinwork, also evolved from the privations of this remote northern frontier of the Mexican empire. Early Franciscan friars brought along Mexican silversmiths to create chalices, crosses, and other religious embellishments. However, silver soon ran short, so tin was substituted, and the more intricate European techniques were necessarily replaced by simpler methods, including stamping and puncturing. Over the centuries, tinwork came to be used for a variety of decorative items, as well as for religious paraphernalia. Among the more interesting pieces made today are mirrors and picture frames surrounded by punched designs and inlaid with flecks of copper, brass, or even embroidery. Look also for candlesticks, lamp shades, and jewelry boxes.

Contemporary Crafts New Mexico's contemporary artisans work in every medium, particularly wood, textiles, and ceramics. Although the focus of their work varies from abstract forms to functional housewares, many reflect New Mexican colors: the splashy hues of mountain sunsets, the subtle pastels of cactus flowers, the flamboyant reds of dried chiles. Other craftspeople incorporate traditional Indian or Hispanic motifs in their work or use them as a starting point for irreverent takeoffs, such as santos made from car parts or ones celebrating liberated women.

Among other items, look for massive, yet graceful Southwestern furniture. Chests, armoires, and other pieces are generally made of unvarnished wood with carved detailing that may recall the staggered lines of pueblo rooftops or may incorporate stylized sunbursts. For a less practical— but more portable—purchase, consider witty wood folk sculptures, perhaps a permanently startled cat, a ferociously grinning lion, or other creatures of indeterminable ancestry.

To find top-notch contemporary crafts, visit Albuquerque's annual New Mexico Arts & Crafts Fair (5500 San Mateo, NE, Suite 111, Albuquerque 87109, tel. 505/884–9043), held for three days at the end of July. Started in 1961, the event showcases over 200 New Mexican artisans who create everything from leather clothing to musical instruments. The rest of the year, visit craft galleries scattered throughout Albuquerque, Santa Fe (especially along Canyon Road), and Taos. A good place to help you decide where to begin your craft foray is *The Wingspread Collector's Guide*, two comprehensive directories (one covers Albuquerque, the other Santa Fe and Taos), which describe galleries and provide detailed maps, glossaries, and articles on collecting New Mexican crafts. They're available from Wingspread Communications (Box 13566-H, Albuquerque 87192, tel. 800/873–4278).

3 Santa Fe and Vicinity

With its crisp, clear air and bright, sunny weather, Santa Fe couldn't be more welcoming. Perched on a 7,000-foot-high plateau at the base of the Sangre de Cristo Mountains, the city is surrounded by the remnants of a 2,000-year-old Pueblo Indian civilization, and filled with evidence of Spanish rule. Add rows of chic art galleries, smart restaurants, and shops selling Southwestern furnishings and cowboy gear, and you have a uniquely appealing destination that is growing increasingly popular every year.

La Villa Real de la Santa Fe de San Francisco de Asis (the Royal City of the Holy Faith of Saint Francis of Assisi) was founded in 1609 by Don Pedro de Peralta, who planted his banner in the name of Spain; St. Augustine, Florida, is the only city in the United States that's older. Santa Fe's Paseo de Peralta—a paved loop that approximates the former walls of the original Spanish colonial outpost—still protects the vital core of the city, if only symbolically. The town plaza, laid out in 1609 and now filled with Native American vendors, has been the site of bullfights, public floggings, gun fights, Indian wars, political rallies, and promenades, as well as public markets.

In 1680, the San Juan Indians drove the Spanish out, burning their churches and missions and turning the Palace of the Governors into a tribal dwelling. But the tide turned again 12 years later, when General Don Diego de Vargas returned with a new army from El Paso and recaptured Santa Fe without firing a shot. To commemorate Don Diego's triumph, the annual La Fiesta de Santa Fe has been held every year since 1712. The country's oldest community celebration traditionally takes place the weekend after Labor Day, with parades, mariachis, pageants, melodramas, arts and crafts shows, and nonstop private parties. Though the best known, La Fiesta de Santa Fe is but one of numerous opportunities for revelry throughout the year—everything from a celebration to start the rodeo season in mid-July to traditional Indian pueblo dances at Christmas.

The road from the south, one of the two main arteries into town, is the once-grand El Camino Real (Royal Highway). As spectacular for its time as the transcontinental Pan American Highway is today, El Camino Real originally stretched from Mexico City to Santa Fe, bringing an army of conquistadores to the northernmost reaches of their New World conquest. Now, however, visitors who drive along the last five-mile stretch into town from the south will find it lined with motels, gas stations, fast-food restaurants, launderettes, and convenience stores.

The Old Santa Fe Trail from the northeast also brought newcomers—first traders to sell goods to the Spanish, then settlers from Missouri and beyond. The covered-wagon days of this famous route ended with the arrival of the railroad—the Atchison, Topeka and Santa Fe, a line made far more famous, perhaps, by the Andrews Sisters' hit recording than by its initial arrival in town in 1880. The Old Santa Fe Trail has survived the ravages of time and progress with far more grace than has El Camino Real, giving first-time visitors a more accurate impression of the town that lies ahead: The route is lined with splendid Southwest-style homes made of adobe and stucco. As one approaches town, the buildings become larger and closer together, but Santa Fe remains mercifully free of skyscrapers; a town ordinance keeps all buildings within a five-story limit.

Melded into the landscape with their earthen colors and rounded, flowing lines—and thus difficult to see from afar— the adobe pueblos of the area's original inhabitants were so styled as a means of protection from enemy Indian tribes and, later, from Spanish explorers. Today the distinct Pueblo-style architecture that has come to characterize Santa Fe and its environs attracts rather than repels visitors—although the predominance of adobe, pure or ersatz, flat-roofed colonial style or climbing pueblo fashion, can be a bit overwhelming. As a result of the tendency to build in this style, the State Capitol, the Santa Fe Hilton, the Camera Shop of Santa Fe, and Furr's Supermarket all look pretty much alike.

Santa Fe is the smallest state capital in the country and the only one without a major airport. The city's population, an estimated 55,000, swells to nearly double that figure during the peak summer season and again in the winter, when skiers arrive, lured by the challenging slopes of the Santa Fe Ski Area and those of nearby Taos Ski Valley. Geared for tourists, Santa Fe can put a serious dent in your travel budget. Hotel rates are on a par with top hotels and resorts in popular spots all over the globe, and prices charged for contemporary artwork in Santa Fe—the third major art center in the country after New York and Los Angeles—can be astonishingly high.

Essential Information

Important Addresses and Numbers

Tourist Information
The **Santa Fe Convention and Visitors Bureau** (201 W. Marcy St., Box 909, 87504, tel. 505/984–6760 or 800/777–2489) has Santa Fe visitors' guides, brochures, maps, and calendar listings. **Santa Fe Chamber of Commerce** (333 Montezuma, Box 1928, 87501, tel. 505/983–7317) is geared more to the traveling businessperson than to the tourist, but is a good source for referrals, as well as for maps, brochures, and general information. The **New Mexico Economic Development and Tourism Department** (Joseph M. Montoya Bldg., 1100 St. Francis Dr., 87503, tel. 505/827–0291) offers a wealth of booklets and printed material on all areas of New Mexico. The **BBS Bulletin Board** (tel. 505/988–5867), a computerized library, carries ski and tourist information for Santa Fe. Except for long-distance calls, the 24-hour service is free to anyone with a modem-equipped computer.

Emergencies
Fire, ambulance, police (tel. 911).

Medical Emergency Room. St. Vincent Hospital (455 Saint Michaels Dr., tel. 505/983–3361; 24-hour hospital hot line, tel. 505/989–5242).

Medical Clinics. Ambulatory Surgical Center of Santa Fe (102 Faithway St., tel. 505/982–6317), **Lovelace** (901 W. Alameda, tel. 505/986–3656; 440 Saint Michaels Dr., tel. 505/986–3566).

Dental Clinics. Medical Dental Center (465 Saint Michaels Dr., tel. 505/982–2578) will see walk-in patients on an emergency basis.

Late-Night Pharmacies
Lee Pharmacies (**Medical Center Pharmacy**, 465 Saint Michaels Dr., tel. 505/983–4359, and **Fraser Pharmacy**, 505 Old Santa Fe

Trail, tel. 505/982–5524) and **Medicap Pharmacy** (2801 Rodeo Rd., tel. 505/471–6177) all offer 24-hour emergency service.

Other Numbers Weather information (tel. 505/988–3437).

Time and temperature (tel. 505/473–2211).

Arriving and Departing

By Plane *See* the Arriving and Departing section in Chapter 1, Essential Information.

By Rail **Amtrak's** (tel. 800/872–7245) *Southwest Chief* serves Santa Fe via the village of Lamy, 17 miles from town, daily on routes from Chicago and Los Angeles. A connecting Amtrak shuttle bus service (tel. 505/982–8829 in Santa Fe, tel. 505/988–4511 in Lamy) is available to and from town.

By Bus **Greyhound/Trailways** (858 Saint Michaels Dr., tel. 505/471–0008) offers comprehensive daily service to and from Santa Fe.

By Car Although located in a secluded mountain setting, Santa Fe is easily accessible; it's a day's drive from several metropolitan areas from points north and south via I–25 or U.S. 84/285.

Getting Around Santa Fe

Downtown Santa Fe is easily maneuvered by foot, with the majority of its museums, galleries, shops, and restaurants located within a comfortable radius of the famous Santa Fe Plaza. But you'll need transportation for the city's outer reaches, including such attractions as the International Folk Art Museum and the Museum of Indian Arts and Culture. Even a tour of the art galleries along Canyon Road can be a hilly 2-mile stretch.

By Car Following is a list of car-rental services in Santa Fe: **Adopt-A-Car** (3570 Cerrillos Rd., tel. 505/473–3189), **Agency** (3157 Cerrillos Rd., tel. 505/473–2983), **Avis** (Garrett's Desert Inn, 311 Old Santa Fe Trail, tel. 505/982–4361), **Budget** (1946 Cerrillos Rd., tel. 505/984–8028), **Hertz** (100 Sandoval, in the Hilton of Santa Fe lobby, tel. 505/982–1844), **Snappy** (3012 Cielo Court, tel. 505/473–2277), and **Thrifty** (1718 Cerrillos Rd., tel. 505/984–1961).

By Taxi Public transportation in town is monopolized by **Capital City Cab Company** (tel. 505/989–8888), the only taxi service in Santa Fe. The taxis aren't metered; you pay a flat fee determined by the distance you're going. There are no official cab stands in town; you must phone to arrange a ride—and if you're lucky, a cab will show up. Rates for various points within the city range from $4 to $7. You can pick up a 40% taxi discount coupon at the Santa Fe Public Library (145 Washington Ave., tel. 505/984–6780).

By Limo If you're feeling flush or the occasion warrants, you can call the **Dream Limousine Service** (tel. 505/884–6464), **Elegante Luxury Transportation Service** (tel. 505/473–1115), or **Limotion VIP Limousine Service** (tel. 505/982–5466). Fares average about $35 per hour, with generally a two-hour minimum.

By Trolley Santa Fe's long-popular Chile Line Trolley was recently discontinued.

Opening and Closing Times

Store and commercial hours may vary from place to place and season to season (remaining open longer in summer than in winter), but the following is a general guide: banks, weekdays 9–3; museums, daily 10–5; stores, Monday–Saturday 10–6; post office, weekdays 8–5.

Guided Tours

General-Interest Tours **Afoot in Santa Fe Walking Tours** (211 Old Santa Fe Trail, 87501, tel. 505/983–3701) offers a get-acquainted, close-up look at the city with the help of resident guides.

Gray Line of Santa Fe (229 N. Guadalupe St., 87501, tel. 505/983–9491) features a variety of daily tours leaving from and returning to the Santa Fe Bus Depot (hotel and motel pickups by advance arrangement). Taos, Bandelier Cliff Dwellings, Los Alamos, and the Santa Clara Indian Pueblo are among the company's destinations. In winter, the availability of tours is subject to road and weather conditions.

Recursos (826 Camino de Monte Rey, Suite A-3, 87501, tel. 505/982–9301) runs historical, cultural, and nature tours.

Santa Fe Detours (La Fonda Hotel lobby, 100 E. San Francisco, 87501, tel. 505/983–6565) includes tours by bus, river, and rail; city walks; trail rides; and ski packages.

Special-Interest Tours **Art Tours of Santa Fe** (301 E. Alameda, 87501, tel. 505/988–3527) specializes in visits to historic sites, museums, galleries, artists' studios, private homes, and collections; tours are accompanied by authorities in art, archaeology, and New Mexican history.

Ghost Tours of Santa Fe (500 Montezuma Ave., Sanbusco Market Center, 87504, tel. 505/983–0111) takes its often-apprehensive group of evening travelers on an eerie, 90-minute journey through the alleyways, hidden graveyards, and haunted buildings of downtown Santa Fe, where, it is believed, witches once roamed and ghosts of broken-hearted women and gamblers still linger.

House and garden tours have always been popular in Santa Fe and are scheduled periodically, depending on the mood and disposition of property owners and guides. The **Santa Fe Architect Society** (tel. 505/983–7421) opens a different home each year to visitors, usually in August, a week after the Sunday of Indian Market Weekend. **Behind Adobe Walls and Garden Tours** (tel. 505/983–6565 or 800/338–6877) generally schedules tours during the last two Tuesdays of July and the first two Tuesdays of August. Contact the Convention and Visitors Bureau (*see* Essential Information, above) for late-breaking house-tour announcements.

Rojo Tours (228 Old Santa Fe Trail, 87501, tel. 505/983–8333) offers a variety of specialized trips—to view wildflowers, Indian ruins and cliff dwellings, galleries and studios, Native American arts and crafts, and private homes—as well as adventure tours, such as ballooning, white-water rafting, hiking, and riding, all with hotel and motel pickups.

Southwest Adventure Group (Sanbusco Market Center, 500 Montezuma, 87501, tel. 505/983–0876 or 800/766–5443), along with adventure tours, also has a number of special-interest offerings, such as guided photo walks, studio tours of artists' galleries and workshops, and craft and cooking-tasting tours.

Studio Entrada (Box 4934, Santa Fe 87502, tel. 505/983–8786) gives informal tours of the studios and ateliers of some of Santa Fe's best-known artists and craftspeople, enabling visitors to buy directly from the artists, often at considerable savings from gallery prices.

Learning Experiences **Santa Fe School of Cooking** (116 San Francisco St., tel. 505/983–4511) offers both night and day classes that allow visitors to capture the flavor of regional New Mexican fare. Classes range from a two-hour basic demonstration exploring the rich flavors and history of northern New Mexican cuisine to more elaborate undertakings, with chefs from Santa Fe's better restaurants sharing their secrets and expertise. The results, good or bad, may be eaten. The beginning class is $25; other rates vary depending on the class. Headed by Susan Curtis and Jennifer Livesay, who suggest reservations be made in advance, the school is located on the upper level of Plaza Mercado, only a block from the main Plaza.

Travel Photography Workshop is a week-long photography blitz headed by Lisl Dennis, a noted photographer whose work appears regularly in *Outdoor Photographer* and other major publications and who has authored a number of books on photographic techniques. Tuition of $1,125 includes workshop sessions, photo field trips to Chimayo, Rancho de Taos, and Taos, critiques, lodging, and some meals. Lisl Dennis and her husband, author Landt Dennis, also offer a number of international photography workshop tours. For inquiries, contact Travel Photography Workshop in Santa Fe (Box 2847, Santa Fe 87504, tel. 505/982–4979, fax 505/983–9489).

Exploring Santa Fe

Humorist Will Rogers said on his first visit to Santa Fe, "Whoever designed this town did so while riding on a jackass, backwards and drunk." While the maze of narrow streets and alleyways may confound motorists, it's a delight for shoppers and pedestrians, who will find attractive shops and restaurants, a flowered courtyard or yet another eye-catching gallery to explore, at just about every turn.

Highlights for First-time Visitors

Beneath the portals of the Palace of the Governors (*see* Tour 1)
Canyon Road art galleries (*see* Tour 2)
Cathedral of St. Francis (*see* Tour 2)
Loretto Chapel (*see* Tour 3)
Museum of International Folk Art (*see* Tour 3)
Santa Fe Plaza (*see* Tour 1)

Tour 1: Santa Fe Plaza

Numbers in the margin correspond to points of interest on the Santa Fe map.

A get-acquainted stroll of the city begins logically enough with
❶ the historic **Plaza** that forms its heart. Originally laid out in

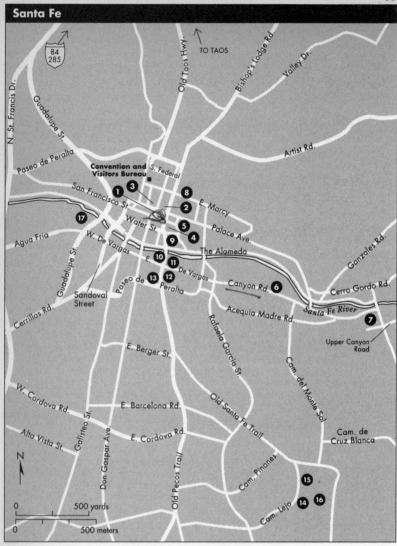

Santa Fe

Barrio de Analco, **10**

Canyon Road, **6**

Cathedral of St. Francis, **5**

Cristo Rey Church, **7**

Fort Marcy, **8**

La Fonda, **4**

Loretto Chapel, **9**

Museum of Fine Arts, **3**

Museum of Indian Arts and Culture, **15**

Museum of International Folk Art, **14**

Oldest House, **11**

Palace of the Governors, **2**

San Miguel Mission, **12**

Santa Fe Plaza, **1**

Santuario de Guadalupe, **17**

State Capitol Building, **13**

Wheelright Museum of the American Indian, **16**

1609–10 as the city's center for religious and military activities by New Mexico governor Don Pedro Peralta, it witnessed the revolt of the Pueblo Indians in 1680 and the peaceful recapture of Santa Fe in 1692. It once held a bullring, was the site of fiestas and fandangos, and was the actual end of the Santa Fe Trail, where freight wagons would unload after completing their arduous journeys. The American flag was raised over it in 1846, as was the standard of the Confederate army, some 20 years later, before Santa Fe was recaptured by Union forces. For a time it was a tree-shaded park, complete with a white picket fence, and later, in the Gay '90s, an expanse of lawn, where uniformed bands played from within the ornate gazebo at its center. Today, lined with shops, art galleries, and restaurants, it is as much the heart of the city as ever.

❷ The pueblo-style **Palace of the Governors,** bordering the northern side of the Plaza on Palace Avenue, is the oldest public building in the United States. Built at the same time that the Plaza was laid out, it has been the key seat of government for four separate flags—Spain, Mexico, the Confederacy, and the U.S. territory that preceded New Mexico's statehood in 1912—serving as the residence for 100 Spanish, Indian, Mexican, and American governors.

Since 1913, the Palace has been the central headquarters of the **Museum of New Mexico,** a state-museum system that includes four museums in Santa Fe—the on-premise **History Museum,** the adjacent **Museum of Fine Arts,** the **Museum of Indian Arts and Culture,** and the **Museum of International Folk Art**—and five state monuments scattered about New Mexico: the prehistoric ruins at **Jemez** and **Coronado,** the historic frontier forts **Sumner** and **Selden,** and the historic community of **Lincoln.** A two-day pass for $6 allows admission to all state museums and monuments. For information, call 505/827–6474.

Permanent exhibits at the **History Museum** in the Palace of the Governors chronicle 450 years of New Mexico history. In addition to displays of furniture, clothing, and housewares, a collection of rare mural-size works, painted on elk and bison hides, depicts key historical events. Themes of changing exhibits may include frontier firearms and the Civil War in New Mexico. In the same building, the Museum of New Mexico Press prints books, cards, and booklets on antique presses and offers bookbinding demonstrations, lectures, and slide shows. With advance permission, students and researchers have access to an extensive historical research library and collections of rare maps and manuscripts, as well as photographs (more than 120,000 prints and negatives). *Box 2087, 87504–2087, north side of the Plaza (Palace St.), tel. 505/827–6474. Admission: $3.50 adults, children under 16 free. Open daily 10–5. Closed Mon. during Jan. and Feb.; Thanksgiving, Christmas, and New Year's Day.*

Under the shaded portals of the Palace of the Governors, **local Indian vendors** display and sell their wares as they've been doing for centuries. With few exceptions, the more than 500 vendors who are registered to sell under the portals are all members of New Mexico pueblos or tribes. All merchandise on sale is required to meet Museum of New Mexico standards: Items are all handmade or handstrung in Indian households; silver jewelry is either sterling (92.5% pure) or coin silver (90%

pure); all metal jewelry bears the maker's mark, which is registered with the museum. Prices tend to reflect the high quality of the merchandise and the mastery of art forms that require years of apprenticeship and learning. Books, regional magazines, owners and sales clerks at reputable shops, and the vendors themselves are all good sources of information about Indian arts and crafts. No bargaining is allowed (except perhaps discreetly when purchasing two or more items), and no photographs should be taken, unless permission is requested and granted.

3 Across from the Palace of the Governors (turn right upon exiting and cross Lincoln Avenue), the **Museum of Fine Arts,** dating from 1917, was Santa Fe's first Pueblo Revival–style structure. More than any other building, it inspired the architectural trend in the region that continues to this day. Inside, the ceilings are made of split cedar *latillas* (branches set in a cross-hatched pattern) and hand-hewn *vigas* (beams); many excellent examples of Spanish Colonial–style furniture are on display. The 8,000-piece permanent collection emphasizes the work of regional artists, including Georgia O'Keeffe and the Taos Masters (Ernest Blumenschein, Bert Geer Philips, Joseph Henry Sharp, and Eanger Irving Couse, among them), as well as of Mexican (such as Diego Rivera), Southwestern, and American Indian artists. Sculpture is displayed in three adjoining courtyards. *107 Palace Ave., tel. 505/827–4455. Admission: $3.50 adults, children under 16 free. Open daily 10–5. Closed Mon. during Jan. and Feb.; Thanksgiving, Christmas, and New Year's Day.*

4 If you cross to the far corner of the Plaza, where Shelby and East San Francisco streets meet, you'll find yourself virtually in the lobby of Santa Fe's landmark hotel, **La Fonda** (*see* Lodging, below). Built in 1864 and refurbished several times in recent years, the hotel is still known fondly as "The Inn at the End of the Trail" because of its past history as a gathering place for cowboys, trappers, pioneers, soldiers, drummers, and frontier politicians. It's still a major social setting for many of the town's activities.

Time Out Stop in at the lunch counter of **Woolworth's** on the Plaza (58 E. San Francisco St., tel. 505/982–1062)—the only Woolworth's in New Mexico, opened in 1931—for some of its famous Frito pie. A small portion of this tasty concoction of Fritos, chili, and cheese costs $2.35 and a large portion, $3.79.

Tour 2: Cathedral of St. Francis, Canyon Road

If the day's not too hot and you're in good physical condition, this tour can be done by foot. Be aware, however, that Canyon Road is a long stretch, all uphill. In most cases, it's a good idea to drive.

5 A block east of the Plaza, the magnificent **Cathedral of St. Francis** is one of the rare departures from the city's steadfast pueblo design: Founded by Jean Baptiste Lamy, Santa Fe's first archbishop, it was built by French architects in 1869 in a French Romanesque style, with Italian stonemasons adding the finishing touches. The inspiration for Willa Cather's novel *Death Comes for the Archbishop*, the circuit-riding young

Lamy, credited with resuscitating the Catholic faith in New Mexico, is buried in the crypt beneath the church's high altar. A small adobe chapel on the northeast side, the remnant of an earlier church built on the site, reveals the Spanish architectural influence so noticeably missing from the cathedral itself. Inside the chapel, *La Conquistadora*, Our Lady of the Conquest, is the oldest representation of the Madonna in the United States. This statue accompanied Don Diego de Vargas on his peaceful reconquest of Santa Fe in 1692, a feat attributed to the statue's spiritual intervention. Every Friday the faithful adorn *La Conquistadora*, now the patron saint of New Mexico, with a new dress. *131 Cathedral Pl., tel. 505/982–5619. Open daily. Mass celebrated daily at 6, 7, and 7:45 AM, 5:15 PM; Sun. at 6, 8, and 10 AM, 12 noon and 7 PM.*

If you bear right from the St. Francis Cathedral to the end of Cathedral Place and turn left on Alameda for another block, **❻** crossing Paseo de Peralta, you'll come to **Canyon Road,** which once served as an Indian trail. During the early part of the century, woodcutters with their loaded burros used *El Camino de Cañón* as a route into town, where they sold bundles of chopped wood door to door. The road's 2-mile stretch from the center of town is now Santa Fe's most fashionable street, lined with many of the city's finest art galleries, shops, and restaurants— described affectionately by locals as "the art and soul of Santa Fe." If you're driving, remember that parking is at a premium on Canyon Road. A shopping complex at the lower end (225 Canyon Rd.) provides parking and rest rooms for customers only. The municipal parking lot at the juncture of Canyon Road and Camino del Monte Sol costs $1 per hour.

Upper Canyon Road is the city's high-rent district, containing some of its most elegant homes. At its terminus is the historic **Randall Davy House** (Upper Canyon Rd., tel. 505/983–4609), once the home and studio of one of the most prolific early Santa Fe artists and since 1975, the regional headquarters of the National Audubon Society. It's open for public tours daily, 9–5.

❼ The **Cristo Rey Church,** at the corner of Upper Canyon Road and Cristo Rey, 1.5 miles from the Plaza, was built in 1939 to commemorate the 400th anniversary of Coronado's exploration of the Southwest. Built the old-fashioned way, with parishioners mixing the more than 200,000 mud-and-straw adobe bricks themselves and hauling them into place, it's the largest adobe structure in the United States and is considered by many to be the finest example of Pueblo-style architecture anywhere. No less impressive is the church's magnificent 225-ton stone *reredos* (altar screen). *1107 Cristo Rey, tel. 505/983–8528. Open daily 8–6.*

Time Out When you need a respite from shopping, drop into **Celebrations** (613 Canyon Rd., tel. 505/989–8904), informal and casual, for a light snack. The place runs a thriving catering service.

If you don't want to spend the day along Canyon Road, another option when you're at St. Francis Cathedral is to head north. Within 600 yards of the Plaza, on a hill northeast of the city, lie **❽** the ruins of **Fort Marcy,** the first American military post in the Southwest (the entrance is near the corner of Paseo Peralta and Otero Street). Something of a white elephant that never justified its massive size (the walls are 9 feet high and 5 feet thick), the adobe fort—named after William L. Marcy, the secretary of war under President Polk—was eventually abandoned. Only a few mounds of earth mark its former existence, but the overview from the hilltop of the city and of nearby mountain ranges (and, on a clear day, of the Sandia Mountains bordering Albuquerque) is spectacular. Also on the Fort Marcy hilltop, the huge white **Cross of the Martyrs,** raised and dedicated during the fiesta, September 1920, commemorates the lives of the 23 Franciscan monks who were killed by Indians in the Pueblo Revolt of 1680.

Tour 3: Along the Old Santa Fe Trail

The first part of this tour can be done on foot, but you'll need a car to go beyond the State Capitol building. Most of the sights noted are along the route of the Old Santa Fe Trail, but the final two, the Institute of American Indian Arts Museum and Santuario de Guadalupe, are at opposite ends of town, both south of the Plaza, but not particularly accessible from the Santa Fe Trail.

Behind the La Fonda hotel and just to the left on the Old Santa Fe Trail is the **Loretto Chapel.** Started in 1873, the French-Romanesque chapel, modeled after the famous Parisian church Sainte-Chapelle, was built concurrently with the Cathedral of St. Francis; the same French architects and Italian stonemasons worked on both projects. The chapel is known for the "Miraculous Staircase" that leads to the choir loft. Legend has it that the chapel was almost finished when it became obvious that there wasn't room enough to complete a staircase to the choir loft. In answer to the prayers of the cathedral's sisters, an old, bearded man arrived on a donkey, built a 20-foot staircase—using only a square, a saw, and a tub of water to season the wood—and then disappeared as quickly as he came. Many of the faithful believe it was St. Joseph himself. Considered an engineering marvel, the staircase contains two complete 360-degree turns, a double helix with no central or visible support; no nails were used in its construction and the wood is like none found in the region. *200 Old Santa Fe Trail, tel. 505/984–7971. Admission: 50¢ adults, children 12 and under free. Open daily 9–5.*

Continuing south along the Old Santa Fe Trail, crossing the bridge over the Santa Fe River, one block farther, you'll come to **Barrio De Analco** (now called East De Vargas Street), believed to be one of the oldest, continuously inhabited streets in the United States. Settled in the early 1600s by Mexican Indian mercenaries and Spanish colonists, it's also the oldest Spanish settlement in Santa Fe, excepting the Plaza area. Interpretive plaques highlight some of the more historic houses, including the Crespin, Alarid, Bandelier, and Boyle homes.

Here too, on the right, you'll find **The Oldest House,** little more than a tacky curiosity. Claimed to be the most ancient dwelling in America, built by Indians more than 800 years ago, it is constructed of "puddled" adobe, which predates the brick type. The building is now operated by a privately leased gift shop and museum, where T-shirts and souvenirs are sold. In the rear, a lifelike Indian dummy sits at a table with its head atilt beside a half-open coffin supposedly containing the remains of a Spanish soldier. A few antique pots and pans, a lamp, and some tools complete the "museum" display. *215 E. De Vargas, tel. 505/ 983-3883. Admission free, donation suggested. Open daily 9-5.*

12 Across the street, heading back toward the Sante Fe Trail, you'll see the **San Miguel Mission.** The oldest church still in use in the United States, the earth-hued adobe structure was built in 1636 by the Tlaxcala Indians (they originally came to New Mexico as servants of the Spanish troops and clergymen). Badly damaged in the 1680 Pueblo Revolt, it was rebuilt in 1710. On display in the chapel is the San José Bell, weighing nearly 800 pounds, believed to have been cast in Spain in 1356 and brought to Santa Fe via Mexico several centuries later. This simple church, filled with priceless statues and paintings, is a must for any visitor to Santa Fe. *401 Old Santa Fe Trail, tel. 505/983-3974. Admission free. Open Mon.–Sat. 11:30-4, Sun. 1-4:30.*

Time Out Next door to the San Miguel Mission, **Upper Crust Pizza** (329 Old Santa Fe Trail, tel. 505/983-4140) is a good place to sit and enjoy a slice out on the patio, watching the passing parade on Old Santa Fe Trail.

13 A block south of the San Miguel Mission, across the Santa Fe Trail, is the **State Capitol building,** built in 1966. Known as "the Roundhouse" (and sometimes "the Bullring"), it is modeled after a Southwestern Indian *zia,* representing the Circle of Life; four short walls symbolizing the four winds, four directions, four seasons, and the four sacred obligations of Native American mythology radiate from the central circular structure. Visitors may view the Governor's Gallery, as well as numerous historical and cultural displays, and enjoy 6 acres of landscaped gardens containing roses, sequoia, plum, and almond trees. *715 Alta Vista, tel. 505/984-9600. Admission free. Guided tours offered. Open 8-5 weekdays.*

14 About a mile farther south along the Old Santa Fe Trail, take the Camino Lejo turnoff. On the right, perched on a hillside overlooking the city, is the **Museum of International Folk Art,** the premier museum of its kind in the world. You'll need a car or taxi to get there; it's two miles from the Plaza and almost all uphill. Charming, handmade creations are everywhere you look—a Madonna painted on tin; papier-mâché pears and apples; a devil made from bread dough; rag dolls; clay pots; and much, much more. Founded by Florence Dibell Bartless, a collector who built the museum and donated it and her collection of over 4,000 pieces of folk art to the state, the museum opened in 1953. In 1978, designer and architect Alexander Girard turned over to the museum his lifelong collection of folk art—over 106,000 items. The Museum of International Folk Art was again enriched in 1989 with the opening of a new $1.1 million Hispanic Heritage Wing, designed to display Hispanic folk art from the Spanish Colonial period (in New Mexico, 1598–1821) to the present. The 5,000-piece exhibit includes religious folk art—particularly *bultos* (carved wooden statues of saints) and *retablos* (holy images painted on wood or tin). Along with the permanent collection, the museum frequently presents visiting exhibits, such as the Masks of Mexico, Village Clothing of Czechoslovakia, and Turkish Traditional Art Today. A gift shop carries textiles, dolls, jewelry, ornaments, and other folk art objects, as well as the excellent color-illustrated book *The Spirit of Folk Art,* to help explain it all. *706 Camino Lejo, tel.*

505/827–8350. Admission: $3.50 adults, children under 16 free. Open daily 10–5. Closed Christmas, New Year's Day, Thanksgiving, and Mon. during Jan. and Feb.

⑮ Next door, the **Museum of Indian Arts and Culture,** the newest (1987) addition to the museums of Santa Fe, focuses on the history and contemporary culture of New Mexico's Pueblo, Navajo, and Apache Indians. Along with its extensive collection of Southwestern Indian arts and crafts, the museum offers art demonstrations; Native American food concessions; and a Learning and Research Center, where visitors can weave on a Navajo loom or beat a Pueblo drum. Workshops and classes for children and adults are offered regularly. *710 Camino Way, tel. 505/827–8941. For hours and prices, see Museum of International Folk Art, above.*

⑯ The privately owned **Wheelwright Museum of the American Indian,** housed in a building shaped like a traditional Navajo hogan behind the Museum of International Folk Art, first opened in 1937. Founded by Mary Cabot Wheelwright, it houses works of all American Indian cultures, exhibited on a single-subject rotating basis—silverwork, jewelry, pottery, basketry, paintings. On the lower level, the Case Original Trading Post is modeled after those that dotted the Southwestern frontier over a hundred years ago. During the early part of July, the museum holds its annual Wheelwright Week, with Indian markets, demonstrations, dances, and ceremonial and story-telling sessions. *704 Camino Lejo, 87505, tel. 505/982–4636. Admission free, $2 donation suggested. Open daily 10–4:45.*

⑰ Another of Santa Fe's historic gems lies at the other side of town. **Santuario de Guadalupe,** at the terminus of El Camino Real, 3½ blocks southwest of the Plaza, is the oldest shrine to Our Lady of Guadalupe, patron saint of Mexico, in the United States. It was built by Franciscan missionaries between 1776 and 1795 and has adobe walls nearly three feet thick. A museum administered by the nonprofit Guadalupe Historic Foundation, the Santuario contains several noteworthy paintings, including a priceless 16th-century work by Venetian painter Leonardo de Ponte Bassano, depicting Jesus driving the money changers from the temple, and a portrait of Our Lady of Guadalupe, one of the largest and finest oil paintings of the Spanish Southwest, by Mexico's renowned Colonial painter José de Alzibar. Other highlights are an authentic 19th-century sacristy; a pictorial-history archives; a library devoted to Archbishop Lamy, furnished with many of his personal possessions; and gardens containing a number of plants from the Holy Land. Many local religious ceremonies, dramatic performances, art and educational events, and concerts are held at the Santuario. Adjacent is Agua Fria Street, filled with colorful shops and restaurants, all part of the Guadalupe Historic District. *100 Guadalupe St., tel. 505/988–2027. Admission free, donation suggested. Open daily (weekdays only during the winter) 9–4.*

Santa Fe for Free

Although Santa Fe can be a very expensive town indeed, much of the joy and exuberance expressed during the city's many fiestas and festivals spills over onto the visiting public, without charge. *See* the Festivals and Seasonal Events section in Chapter 1, Essential Information, to find out what's in town when you're planning to visit. In addition to the festivals noted there, the Spanish Colonial Arts Society (Box 1611, 87501, tel. 505/983–4038) sponsors the **Traditional Spanish Market** each year on the Plaza during the last full weekend in July. **Las Fiestas de Santa Fe,** beginning the Friday morning after Labor Day and lasting three days (tel. 505/988–7575), and the spectacular **Indian Market,** held for two days each August (tel. 505/983–5220) with more than 800 Native American artists participating in juried competition, are both free. So is the ten-day **Santa Fe Festival of the Arts** (tel. 505/988–3924 for information), which twice each year—in the middle of May and October—showcases the finest paintings, lithography, and sculpture of area artists. *See also* The Arts and Nightlife section, below, for a listing of free concerts.

There's no charge for admission to the **Governor's Gallery** in the State Capitol (*see* Tour 3 above). And it's free to enter the **Indian pueblos** outside Santa Fe, with their colorful ceremonial dances and tempting handicraft shops, excluding fees charged for parking and camera permits. A festive culmination of the Christmas season takes place with many *Matachines* and other holiday dances at the surrounding Indian pueblos.

What to See and Do with Children

The **Museum of International Folk Art** (*see* Tour 3, above), with its colorful and fantasy-filled exhibits, is a great place to take children any day, but its **Saturdays Are for Kids** program is especially fun for them. Activities range from adobe making to wood carving to creating Valentines, clay fishes, or Polish snowflakes. Minimasterpieces are displayed in the museum's special **Children's Gallery.** Advance registration is required; prices range from $3 to $4, depending on the age and grade of the child, with discounts for combined sessions, each of which lasts two to four hours. For registration or inquiries, call Judy Lokenvitz, Coordinator of Children's Programs, Museum of International Folk Art, tel. 505/827–8350.

Santa Fe Adventures for Kids (Sambusco Market Center, 500 Montezuma Ave., tel. 505/983–0111) runs a variety of exciting—and well-supervised—programs for children. Kids can float down the Rio Grande with an Indian storyteller, journey back to the days of the Old West on a horse-drawn wagon driven by a stuntman, or learn Native American sand painting and pottery making. During the ski season, supervised full-day downhill ski packages are available to the Chipmunk ski area for children aged 7–12. Groups are generally limited to 20; the minimum age for participation in some programs is 4, for others, 7. Fees range from $20 for a two-hour visit to the Children's Museum, with snacks, to $60 for the Raft Ride on the Rio Grande and Pueblo Visit, to $72 for the ski packages. Parents are welcome to participate as well, and many do.

Santa Fe Children's Museum, next to the New Mexico Repertory Theater, less than a mile from the Plaza, offers stimulating hands-on exhibits in the arts and sciences. A solar greenhouse, waterworks, giant bubbles, oversize geometric forms, and a climbing area with a simulated 18-foot mountain-climbing wall all contribute to the museum's great popularity. Special performances—puppets, storytellers, and the like—and programs—including talks by scientists and artists—are offered on different days. A gift shop is open during museum hours. *1050 Old Pecos Trail, tel. 505/989–8359. Admission: $2 adults, $1 children 18 and under. Open Wed.–Sat. 10–5, Sun. noon–5. Closed Mon. and Tues.*

Off the Beaten Track

The **Cumbres & Toltec Scenic Railroad** (in Chama, a two-hour drive from Santa Fe via I–84) runs the 64 miles each way between Chama and Antonio, Colorado, on the only surviving portion of track alongside the old 1,200-mile mountain route that the Denver and Rio Grande was forced to build when the Santa Fe beat it to Ratan Pass. A veritable rolling museum of antique narrow-gauge engines, equipment, and stock—including snow-fighting attachments that date back to 1889 and are still working—the train provided the setting for key scenes in the film *Butch and Sundance: The Early Years*. It snakes back and forth over the Colorado border, whistle blowing and coal smoke belching; the climb up Cumbres Pass is so steep that a second engine is required to pull it up the grade. During the ride, the brakeman and conductor deliver a lively nonstop commentary about the history of the line and interesting sidelights about passing scenes. Dress warmly; the train is drafty. And take along sunglasses to protect your eyes from soot and cinders. *500 Terrace Ave., Chama, tel. 505/756–2151. Fares: one-way, returning by bus, $45.50 adults, $23 children 2–11. The train leaves at 10:30 daily, Memorial Day weekend–mid-Oct.*

A kind of Williamsburg of the Southwest, **El Rancho de las Golondrinas** (the Ranch of the Swallows), some 15 miles south of Santa Fe, is a reconstruction of a small New Mexican agricultural village. Originally a *paraje*, or stopping place, on El Camino Real, the village has restored buildings from the 17th and 18th centuries. Guided tours highlight Spanish colonial lifestyles in New Mexico from 1660 to 1890; visitors view a molasses mill, threshing grounds, and wheelwright and blacksmith shops, as well as a mountain village and a *morada*, meeting place of the order of Penitentes. Sheep, goats, and other farm animals wander about the sprawling 200-acre complex. During the Spring and Harvest Festivals, on the first weekends of June and October, respectively, the village comes alive with traditional music, Spanish folk dancing, and food and crafts demonstrations. There's a museum gift shop on the premises, but the nearest restaurant is four miles away. *Cienega, 15 mi south of Santa Fe on I–25, tel. 505/471–2261. Admission: $3 adults, $2 senior citizens, $1 children 5–12; during festivals, the rates are $5 for adults, $3 for senior citizens, and $1 for children 5–12. Open Apr. 1–Oct. 31, daily 8–4.*

Founded as a Spanish colonial outpost in 1614, when it was built largely from the rocks of Pueblo Indian ruins, **Galisteo** is now a charming little village popular with artists and with horsemen who keep their animals boarded here (trail rides and rentals are available). There's a small church, open only on Sunday for services, a graveyard, and an old working brewery that welcomes visitors for tours and an occasional sampling. Twenty-three miles south of Santa Fe (take I–25 east to U.S. 285 south, then NM 41 south), Galisteo is mercifully free of fast-food and souvenir shops.

Ojo Caliente Mineral Springs (take I–25 to Espanola, then U.S. 285 to Ojo Caliente, tel. 505/583–2233) was considered a sacred spot by the Native Americans who inhabited this area centuries ago. Today this famous turn-of-the-century resort, with its five bubbling hot springs, one hour north of Santa Fe, offers mineral baths, massages, facials, herbal wraps, a hotel-motel, gift shop, and a restaurant. Canyon Ranch this isn't; don't expect an up-to-date luxury spa. Come if you want to take a trip back in time when it was fashionable to come and "take the waters" (they contain healthful doses of some minerals not usually associated with beneficial effects, such as arsenic).

National Parks and Monuments

Chaco Culture National Historic Park. Set in a canyon 17 miles long and 1 mile wide, with cliff faces rising 330 feet, are the remains of 13 fully developed pueblos and about 400 smaller settlements. Pueblo Bonito, the largest prehistoric Southwest Indian dwelling ever excavated, contains 800 rooms covering more than 3 acres. This dwelling, the magnificent kivas, and other ancient structures, including a 1,200-mile network of paved roads and a solstice marker, all testify that the area was the highest point in the Anasazi culture, which peaked about AD 1150. Located at the park site is a visitors' center, museum, and petroglyph displays. Overnight camping is permitted April through October.

To get here from Santa Fe, heading south–southwest via NM 44, in the direction of Bloomfield, drive to Cuba, NM, and continue on to Anasazi. At Anasazi, head west (right) and drive on the dirt road all the way to Chaco Culture National Historic Park. The trip takes about 3½ to 4 hours. *Star Rte. 4, Box 6500, Bloomfield 87413, tel. 505/988–6716. Admission: $5 per car, $2 per bus passenger. (The Golden Age Passport, issued to U.S. citizens 62 and older, allows free admission to all occupants of the same car, regardless of their age.)*

Pueblos Near Santa Fe

Cochiti Pueblo. The Cochiti Pueblo is located on the west bank of the Rio Grande near recreational facilities at Cochiti Lake (about 45 minutes from Santa Fe, west of I–25) which are administered by the U.S. Army Corps of Engineers. These include picnic tables, boat ramps and rentals, RV hookups, and a beach for swimming. The pueblo is known for its excellent crafts and jewelry, storyteller pottery figures, leather, beadwork, and drums. The latter play a significant role in Cochiti ceremonials on the July 14th Feast Day in honor of San Buenaventura. Most of the people of the pueblo work in Santa Fe or Albuquerque, but enough members of the tribe continue to farm and practice craft-making to maintain the tribal traditions and culture. *Box 309, Cochiti 87041, tel. 505/465–2244. Admission free. Permission to visit from the tribal governor's office is suggested. Open daily 8–5. No cameras, recorders, or sketchbooks are allowed.*

Jemez Pueblo. Located in the red sandstone canyon of the Jemez River, west of Santa Fe (northwest of Bernalillo, off NM 44), the Jemez Pueblo is noted for its polychrome pottery and fine baskets made from yucca fronds. The Jemez reservation, encompassing 88,000 acres, contains two recreational sites,

Holy Ghost Springs and Dragon Fly Pond, on NM 4 near the pueblo. Fishing licenses for both areas can be acquired from the Jemez game warden for $2 to $5 per day, depending on the season. Hunting permits are also available. The village may hold little of interest for the casual visitor. The beautiful San Diego de Jemez Mission at the Jemez State Monument, 20 miles north, is a popular attraction. The great stone mission church was founded in the early 1600s by Fra Geronimo Zarate Salmeron. The pueblo's two major Feast Days are November 12, in honor of Saint James, and August 2, for Our Lady of the Angels. *Box 78, Jemez 87024, tel. 505/834-7359. Admission free. Photography is restricted, except for San Diego Mission.*

Nambe Pueblo. Fifteen miles northeast of Santa Fe (via US 84/285; take a right at NM 4, then look for signs), the Nambe Pueblo is known for its outstanding pottery, especially the famous Nambe cooking pots, made of golden micaceous clay. This ceramic work, along with woven belts, silver jewelry, and beadwork, may be purchased at the pueblo's craft center. Recreational facilities open to the public here include trout fishing, camping, hiking, and picnicking at nearby Nambe Falls and Lake. Contemporary new buildings have replaced the original pueblo and mission church, but the landscape and the stunning views of the Sangre de Cristo Mountains remain unchanged. The pueblo holds ceremonial dances on July 4 (the Nambe Falls Celebration) and on Oct. 4, the Feast Day of Saint Francis of Assisi. *Rte. 1, Box 117-BB, Santa Fe 87501, tel. 505/455-7691 or 505/455-7752. Fishing is allowed for a fee Mar.–Nov., and permits are available for picnicking, camping, and boating. Photo permits may be purchased as well. Fees are $5 for still cameras, $15 for video recorders and movie cameras.*

Pojoaque Pueblo. Drawing visitors from nearby Santa Fe (it's 15 miles north, just off US 84/285), the Pojoaque Pueblo attracts Los Alamos and Espanola residents too. It has more than 25 businesses aimed at the tourist trade, including a visitors' center, tourist information office, tribal-owned supermarket, mobile-home park, and shops offering an extensive selection of northern New Mexican pottery and other traditional arts and crafts for sale. Tribal enterprises, conducted primarily along a commercial strip fronting US 84/285, have made the Pojoaque Pueblo one of the more prosperous in northern New Mexico. However, it has no definable village as such and has virtually ceased to exist as a viable community. Only low mounds scattered in fields and among houses remain of the original settlement. A smallpox epidemic in 1890 nearly wiped out the entire tribe, but its numbers have increased considerably since then, and prospered. The pueblo celebrates its Feast Day on December 12 in honor of Our Lady of Guadalupe. On the first Saturday in August, Pojoaque hosts the Plaza Fiesta, a multicultural celebration that features Native American, Western, and international folk dancing, as well as food and hot-air balloon rides. *Rte. 11, Box 71, Santa Fe 87501, tel. 505/455-2278.*

San Ildefonso Pueblo. This was the home of the most famous of all pueblo potters, Maria Martinez, whose work is now on permanent display in the Millicent Rogers Museum in Taos as well as in other museums throughout the Southwest. She created exquisite designs in red and black pottery from the 1920s to the '80s. The San Ildefonso Pueblo has long been known for its outstanding pottery and boasts a number of highly acclaimed potters as well as other artists and craftspeople, many of whom open their homes to prospective buyers. There are also several trading posts on the pueblo, a visitors' center, and a museum where much of Maria Martinez's work can be seen. Fishing is permitted in a nearby pond. San Ildefonso is one of the more active pueblos in retaining its ceremonial dances and customs. Its Feast Day is celebrated on January 23 when an unforgettable Animal Dance is performed. Buffalo, Deer, and Comanche dances continue throughout the day. *Rte. 5, Box 315-A, Santa Fe 87501, tel. 505/455-2273. Cameras are not permitted at any of the ceremonial dances, but may be used at other times, with a permit. Fees are $5 for still camera; $15 for video recorder, movie camera, or sketching.*

Santa Clara Pueblo. Located just off NM 30, southwest of Espanola, the Santa Clara Pueblo is the home of the beautiful Puye Cliff Dwellings, which rise above it, and of the Santa Clara Canyon with its four ponds, miles of stream fishing, picnicking, and camping facilities. Most of the traditional tribal dwellings have been demolished and replaced by more conventional houses. Santa Clara remains famous nonetheless for its shiny red and black engraved pottery and for its myriad well-known painters and sculptors; visitors who knock on the doors with signs announcing pottery will be invited inside to meet the artists. The population of the pueblo is about 2,000. Self-guided and guided tours are offered to the 740-room Puye Cliff Dwellings, Santa Clara's ancestral home. The Feast Day of St. Clare is celebrated on August 12. *Box 580, Espanola 87004, tel. 505/753-7326. Open daily 8-5. Permits for the use of trails, camping, and picnic areas, as well as for fishing in trout ponds, are available at the sites. Cameras are allowed without special permits, but photography fees may have to be negotiated with individuals photographed.*

Tesuque Pueblo. Built around the year 1250, the Tesuque Pueblo, 10 miles north of Santa Fe along U.S. 84/285, is the home of one of the smallest Tiwa-speaking tribes. Because of its proximity to Santa Fe, it was one of the first pueblos to establish contact with the Spanish and eventually became one of their most vicious foes. It has maintained its identity well and is today one of the oldest and most traditional of the pueblos—listed on the National Register of Historic Places—but unfortunately it's perhaps better known for its bingo parlor than for its arts and crafts. The pueblo has no craft shops or trading posts and most sales are made from private homes. The tribe operates an RV park and general store, among other businesses. Tesuque Farms grows food without the use of pesticides. The pueblo's lands are some of the most beautiful for horseback riding, camping, and fishing, with the majestic Sangre de Cristo Mountains rising in the distance. Wind-eroded sandstone formations, such as nearby Camel Rock, form the "badlands" north of the pueblo. Tesuque celebrates its feast day on November 12 in honor of Santo Domingo with ceremonial dances. It's the one time of the year that the pueblo seems to open its arms and its doors to visitors (bingo players don't have access to most of Tesuque). For directions and information, stop by the administrative office. *Rte. 11, Box 1, Santa Fe 87501, tel. 505/983-2667. Cameras, recorders, and sketch pads not allowed during ceremonial dances (and there's not much to photograph otherwise). Tesuque Pueblo bingo begins at 5 night-*

*ly, with the early-bird special at 6:30 and the main series begin-
ning at 7. For bingo information, call 505/984–8418.*

Shopping

Santa Fe has been a trading post for a long, long time. The
great pueblos of the Hohokam and Anasazi civilizations 2,000
years ago were strategically located between the buffalo-
hunting tribes of the Great Plains and the Indians of Mexico,
who exchanged shells, metals, and parrots for sky-colored turquoise, which was thought to have magical properties. After
the arrival of the Spanish in 1610 and the subsequent development of the West, Santa Fe became the place to exchange silver,
hides, and fur from Mexico for manufactured goods, whiskey,
and greenbacks from the East. And following the building of
the railroad in 1880, all manner of products came and went.

The legacy remains, but today Santa Fe's major commodity is
something known as Santa Fe style, as distinctive as the city's
architecture. The clean lines, strong colors, and Native American patterns that characterize the style have a great deal of
charm. True, because of its popularity, it's become a bit of a cli-
ché; a locally produced poster shows a Santa Fean lying face up
on an Indian rug, surrounded by howling coyote carvings, a
kiva fireplace, a beamed ceiling, a sun-bleached cattle skull, a
string of red chile peppers, and other trendy ornaments. But
the style remains highly infectious just the same—visitors
can't seem to get enough of it and can't wait to take it home.

Santa Fe may strike newcomers as one massive shopping mall,
with stores and shopping nooks sprouting up in the least-likely
places. Nevertheless, a few shopping areas stand out. Canyon
Road is the most famous and most expensive. The downtown
district offers a mix of shops, galleries, restaurants, and craft
nooks within a five-block radius of the Plaza. At the southwest
perimeter of town, the Guadalupe neighborhood is great for
strolling and for relaxing at a sidewalk café as a break from
shopping.

Specialty Stores

Home Furnishings   **Artesanos** (222 Galisteo St., tel. 505/983–5563 or 505/983–
1743), a Mexican marketplace only a block from the Santa Fe
Plaza, has a warehouse-size showroom and an open courtyard
filled with arts and crafts from south of the border—everything from leather chairs to papier-mâché *calaveras* (skeletons
used in Day of the Dead celebrations), tinware, Colonial furniture, Talavera tiles, lighting fixtures, and more. The prices are
reasonable, too.
Foreign Traders (202 Galisteo St., tel. 505/983–6441), a Santa
Fe landmark—founded as the Old Mexico Shop in 1927 and still
run by the same family—offers high-quality handicrafts, antiques, and accessories from Mexico and other parts of the
world. A section of outstanding collectible pieces includes mesquite *escritorio* writing tables, antique wooden tortilla
presses, and burro pack saddles.
Montez Gallery (Sena Plaza Courtyard, 125 E. Palace Ave., tel.
505/982–1828) offers "masterpieces" of New Mexican art, including retablos, bultos, tinwork, furniture, painting, pottery,
weaving, and jewelry, all by Hispanic artists.

Santa Fe Shopping

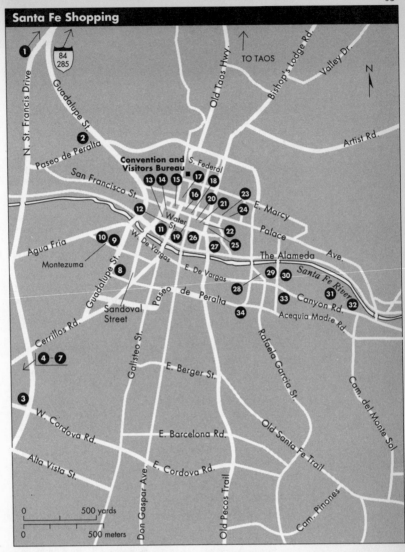

Artesanos, **11**

Bellas Artes, **32**

Canyon Road Fine Arts, **31**

Caxton Books, **14**

Cerillos Road Mercantile and Trading Company, **5**

Coopers Western Wear, **2, 7**

Dewey Galleries, **21**

El Taller on the Plaza, **22**

Elaine Horwitch Galleries, **17**

Fenn Galleries, **34**

Footsteps Across New Mexico, **27**

Foreign Traders, **12**

Galeria Capistrano, **28**

Geranium Slip, **19**

Glenn Green Galleries, **20**

Joshua Baer & Co., **23**

Kachina House and Gallery, **29**

Montez Gallery, **24**

Morning Star Gallery, **30**

Prairie Edge, **26**

Sambusco Outfitters, **10**

Santa Fe Boot Company, **3**

Santa Fe Western Mercantile, **6**

Scheinbaum & Russek, **9**

Spanish Pueblo Doors, **4**

Tom Taylor Boots, **25**

Trade Roots Collection, **15**

Trader Jack's Flea Market, **1**

21st Century Fox Fine Art, **13**

Wadle Galleries, **16**

Wiggins Fine Art, **33**

William R. Talbot Fine Art, **18**

Worldly Possessions, **8**

Spanish Pueblo Doors (2894 Trades West Rd., tel. 505/473–0464), established in 1952, is the buyer's gateway to a wide selection of handcrafted wood doors and gates in Spanish Colonial and custom designs.

Indian Arts and Crafts

Cerrillos Road Mercantile and Trading Company (3741 Cerrillos Rd., tel. 505/471–6329) is one of the leading suppliers of movie props for Hollywood Westerns filmed on location in the area. Peace pipes, tomahawks, Hopi masks, Navajo blankets, muskets, and oil lamps—they're all here at some of the best prices in town. This museumlike shop is 4 miles from the Plaza, but well worth the drive.

Kachina House and Gallery (236 Delgado Rd., tel. 505/982–8415) features an incomparable collection of authentic Hopi kachina dolls, along with a vast selection of Navajo pottery, sculpture, and jewelry.

Prairie Edge (102 E. Water St., El Centro, tel. 505/984–1336) offers classic Lakota art, artifacts, and jewelry, created by contemporary Sioux artists and craftspeople in the style and tradition of the past. Hides, beaded and quilled clothing, shields, weapons, buffalo skulls, and sterling and bead jewelry are all sold here.

Trade Roots Collection (38 Burro Alley, tel. 505/982–8168) is the place to go if you're heavily into Indian ritual objects—outstanding fetishes, fetish jewelry, and Hopi rattles. This handsome showroom, one block west of the Plaza, also has an extensive collection of handwoven rugs, pillows, fabrics, and accessories.

Worldly Possessions (330 Garfield St., tel. 505/983–6090) takes shoppers on a round-the-world treasure hunt, with its bounty of outstanding tribal and folk art, artifacts, textiles, wood carvings, fine art, gifts, and decorative items.

Clothing

Function dictates form in cowboy fashions. A wide-brimmed hat is essential in sun country; not only does it protect the wearer from heat, but it's effective in warding off gnats, flies, and other insects. Cowboy hats made by Resistol, Stetson, Bailey, and other leading firms range in price from $50 to $500, but hats made of exotic materials, such as fur, can go for thousands. Small wonder that when it rains in Santa Fe or Albuquerque, a man is more apt to be concerned with protecting his hat than with letting it protect him.

While tenderfeet may guess that cowboy boots are worn to protect against rattlesnakes, they serve other practical purposes as well. Pointed toes slide easily in and out of the stirrups, and high heels—worn for the same reason by Mongolian tribesmen—help keep feet in the stirrups. Tall tops protect ankles and legs on rides through brush and cactus country and can save the wearer a nasty shin bruise from a skittish horse.

Some Western accessories, now mostly worn to be stylish, were once also functional. A colorful bandanna protected an Old West cowboy from sunburn and windburn and served as a mask in windstorms; when riding drag behind a herd; or, on occasions far rarer than Hollywood would have us believe, when robbing trains. A cowboy's sleeveless vest offered maneuverability during roping and riding chores and provided pocket space that his skintight pants—snug to prevent wrinkles in the saddle area—didn't. Of all the accessories today, however, belt buckles probably are the most important to Western dressers, and it's not unusual for them to spend thousands of dollars for gold ones. Hey, momma, for all those kids who grow up to be cowboys, here's a few places to send them.

Coopers Western Wear (De Vargas Center, tel. 505/982–3388, and Villa Linda Mall, tel. 505/471–8775) features all the top names and top lines—hats, boots, belts, buckles, and complete outfits for the well-dressed cowboy and cowgirl.

Geranium Slip (227 Don Gasper, tel. 505/982–9722) specializes in vintage cowboy boots for those who like their footwear broken in for them, as well as antique clothing and jewelry.

Sambusco Outfitters (550 Montezuma, tel. 505/988–1664), located in the Sambusco Market Center, is where all those tall-in-the-saddle fellas head for jeans, boots, belts, Western shirts, jewelry, and accessories.

Santa Fe Boot Company (950½ Cordova Rd., tel. 505/983–8415) features boots by all major manufacturers, as well as more exotic styles designed by owner Marian Trujillo. The store also sells hats and Western outerwear.

Santa Fe Western Mercantile (6820 Cerrillos Rd., tel. 505/471–3655) offers a seemingly inexhaustible supply of hats, boots, jeans, English and Western saddles, buckles, belts, and feed and health care products for horses and livestock.

Tom Taylor Boots (La Fonda Hotel, tel. 505/984–8181) specializes in fine handmade cowboy boots, belts (ostrich, alligator, and other exotic leathers), and sculptured sterling-silver buckles designed by Jean Taylor.

Books **Caxton Books** (216 W. San Francisco, tel. 505/982–8911), with a new address and expanded space, is perhaps the hottest book nook in New Mexico. It's a meeting place for local writers and the scene of frequent book signings and receptions, with a trio of Spanish folk musicians often playing over the intellectual buzz.

At **Footsteps Across New Mexico** (211 Old Santa Fe Trail, tel. 505/982–9297), the emphasis is on the Land of Enchantment. The shop contains easily the most comprehensive selection of books and guidebooks on Santa Fe and New Mexico, from regional cookbooks to area histories.

Flea Markets

Trader Jack's Flea Market (7 mi north of Santa Fe on U.S. 84/285; tel. 505/455–7874), also known as the Santa Fe Flea Market, has been dubbed the best flea market in America by its habitual legion of bargain hunters. It's open dawn to dusk every Friday, Saturday, and Sunday except during December, January, and February—and sometimes even then if the weather's right. You can buy everything here from a half-wolf puppy or African carvings to vintage cowboy boots, fossils, or a wall clock made out of an old hubcap. Sprawled over 12 acres on land belonging to the Tesuque Pueblo, the flea market is located right next to the Santa Fe Opera. ("There goes the neighborhood," says Trader Jack, when the opera season starts.)

Art Galleries

Santa Fe's brilliant light, limpid skies, and timeless landscape of mountains and mesas have long hypnotized artists. "The world is wide here," said Georgia O'Keeffe, in her usual get-right-to-the-point manner; "it's very hard to feel that it's wide in the East."

Well before the arrival of such artists as Ernest Blumenschein and John Sloan to the state in the early 20th century, an earlier form of art was popular in northern New Mexico. Bultos and retablos, both commonly known as *santos*, or saints, remain a unique, little-heralded art form as indigenous to the Southwest as is an oil painting by Ted DeGrazia. Except for black spirituals, santos are the only non-Indian religious art to originate in America. These devotional images were part of everyday life in Mexico and the American Southwest in the years following the conquistadores and the founding of Christianity in the New World. Today they have captured the attention of serious art collectors and leading museums. Although the santos now being made seem destined more for the tourist trade than for regional churches, no attempt has been made to mass-produce them, and no two are exactly alike. Thus they still retain their unique charm.

Santa Fe is also the epicenter of contemporary Native American art, the breakaway and sometimes satirical styles of Fritz Scholder, R. C. Gorman, Earl Biss, Kevin Red Star, Robert Redbird, Amado Maurilio Pena, and others who are strongly identified with the Santa Fe movement. Before the introduction of blurred images and shocking colors, Native American art was traditionally flat and static, with Bambi-like deer with big, sad eyes and corn dancers in lifeless pueblo rituals. Today, top Native American painters, such as Gorman and Cherokee artist Bert Seabourn, are as celebrated in the galleries of Berlin and Tokyo as they are on Canyon Road.

Santa Fe has 125 art galleries (and no one knows how many painters). The following selection represents a good cross section; the Santa Fe Convention and Visitors Bureau (*see* Essential Information, above) has a fuller listing, and *The Wingspread Collectors Guide to Santa Fe and Taos* (*see* Further Reading in Chapter 1, Essential Information) is a good bet for those who are seriously interested in buying art in Santa Fe.

Bellas Artes (653 Canyon Rd., tel. 505/983–2745), a landmark crafts gallery and sculpture garden, located next to the popular Compound Restaurant, carries a wide selection of contemporary arts and crafts, Pre-Columbian works, ceramics, and textiles.
Canyon Road Fine Arts (621 Canyon Rd., tel. 505/988–9511), one of the city's newest art galleries, specializes in works by early Santa Fe and Taos artists, as well as by selected contemporary impressionist painters.
Dewey Galleries (74 E. San Francisco St., tel. 505/982–8632) is housed in the historic Spiegelberg Building on the south side of the Plaza. In a spacious showroom under the original 20-foot-high pressed tin ceilings, a huge collection of historic Navajo textiles and jewelry, plus paintings and sculpture by contemporary and past artists, are offered.
Dolona Roberts Gallery (293 W. Water St., tel. 505/988–5236) features contemporary Southwestern paintings in all media. A major Santa Fe artist, owner Dolona Roberts is known for her acrylics and pastels of American Indian figures seen from the back, wrapped in brilliantly colored blankets.
El Taller on the Plaza (80 E. San Francisco St., tel. 505/988–9298) was recently formed with the merger of two previous galleries, El Taller Santa Fe and the Plaza Gallery. A full range of

original paintings, drawings, and graphics is available here. Among the artists represented is Amado Pena, a master painter of Mexican and Yaqui ancestry, noted for his bold color schemes and strong graphic use of lines.

Elaine Horwitch Galleries (129 W. Palace Ave., tel. 505/988–8997) sells painting, sculptures, and graphics by internationally known artists as well as by up-and-coming painters from the Southwest. Something of a legend in art circles, Ms. Horwitch died last year. Her legacy includes a gallery in Scottsdale as well.

Fenn Galleries (1075 Paseo de Peralta, tel. 505/982–4631) specializes in works of the celebrated Taos Society of Artists and their successors, in addition to those of early Santa Fe painters, including such luminaries as Maxfield Parrish, Maynard Dixon, and Georgia O'Keeffe. One of the best-known galleries in the Southwest, its list of clients includes former president Gerald Ford, Jacqueline Onassis, Cher, and Cybill Shepherd.

Galeria Capistrano (409 Canyon Rd., tel. 505/984–3024) is owned by Sue DiMaio, who has more than 40 years' experience in collecting and selling Native American art. The gallery, on the first block of Canyon Road, is housed in the historic Delgado Adobe. The warm oak floors and uneven adobe walls soothe the hot, vivid colors on exhibit here.

Glenn Green Galleries (50 E. San Francisco St., tel. 505/988–4168) feature paintings and photographs by internationally known artists. Founded in 1975, the gallery exclusively represents the work of Native American sculptor Allan Houser, one of the most prominent graduates of Santa Fe's Institute of American Indian Arts.

Joshua Baer & Co. (116½ E. Palace Ave., tel. 505/988–8944), a half block from the Plaza, focusses on in 19th-century Navajo wall hangings, serapes, and blankets, as well as prehistoric Mimbres pottery.

Morning Star Gallery (513 Canyon Rd., tel. 505/982–8187) is the largest gallery in the world specializing in antique Native American art and artifacts. Located in a landmark Spanish hacienda and shaded by a huge cottonwood tree, it's a virtual museum of antique basketry, pre-1940 Navajo silver jewelry, Eskimo ivories, Northwest Coast Indian carvings, classic Navajo weavings, and art of the Plains Buffalo culture. (Gallery director Joe Rivera operated trading posts on the Rosebud Sioux Reservation for 12 years.)

Scheinbaum & Russek (328 Guadalupe, Suite M, tel. 505/988–5116) handles contemporary and rare fine-art photographs and limited-edition portfolios. Among photographers represented are Eliot Porter and Mexican master Manuel Alvarez-Bravo.

21st Century Fox Fine Art (217 W. Water St., tel. 505/983–2002), founded by Stephen Fox in 1980, is a huge street-level showroom filled with contemporary Native American paintings and antique pawn jewelry, signed posters and prints, and an excellent collection of photographs of Southwestern and Indian subjects by Yousuf Karsh, Myron Wood, Tracey Pierre, and Edward Curtis. One of Santa Fe's best-known dealers, Fox has coordinated numerous exhibitions of Southwestern and Indian art for universities and museums.

Wadle Galleries (128 W. Palace, tel. 505/983–9219) features works of national and regional painters, bronze and stone sculpture, Pueblo pottery, jewelry, and American folk art. This spacious gallery, with plenty of chairs and seating space, is a good place to unwind and soak up the arty Southwestern ambience.

Wiggins Fine Art (526 Canyon Rd., tel. 505/982–5328) specializes in early- to mid-20th-century American art, with an emphasis on pre–World War II New Mexico. Selected contemporary artists are also represented.

William R. Talbot Fine Art (129 W. San Francisco St., tel. 505/982–1559) features antique maps of the Americas and natural history paintings.

Sports and Outdoor Activities

Participant Sports

Bicycling The streets of Santa Fe are narrow and winding, but the roads and byways are generally level, and the scenery's spectacular. While the city is an ideal size for biking, unfortunately no special bike lanes are available. A suggested route map for bikers can be picked up at the information desk of the Convention and Visitors Bureau (201 W. Marcy St., tel. 505/984–6760). Because of the high density of out-of-state tourist traffic and erratic drivers, bikers are cautioned to keep alert.

Rentals are available at **Downtown Bike Shop** (719 Paseo de Peralta, tel. 505/983–2255), which specializes in mountain bikes such as Fisher and Klein.

Golf **Cochita Lake Golf Course** (5200 Cochita Hwy., Cochita Lake, tel. 505/465–2239) was designed by Robert Trent Jones, Jr., and is set against a stunning backdrop of steep canyons and red-rock mesas. A 45-minute drive southwest of the city, it's rated among the top 25 public golf courses in the country.

Quail Run (3101 Old Pecos Trail, tel. 505/986–2255), opened in 1987, is a beautiful well-balanced course set amid piñon pine and juniper. It has the only kiva-shaped bunkers in the country, designed in the style of local fireplaces. The club is private, so you'll have to find a member to take you.

Santa Fe Country Club (Airport Rd., tel. 505/471–0601), a close-to-town, tree-shaded, semi-private course, was designed over 50 years ago. There's a pro shop, club and electric cart rentals, and private lessons by appointment.

Horseback Riding New Mexico's rugged mountain country has been the scene of many Hollywood Westerns, including, in recent years, *Silverado*. Whether you want to ride the range that Kevin Kline and Gregory Peck rode or just go out and feel tall in the saddle, try the following. Rentals average about $20 an hour.

At **Camel Rock Ranch** (10 minutes north of Santa Fe on U.S. 285, tel. 505/986–0408), 7,000 acres in the high desert of the Tesuque Indian Reservation are available for trail rides, hayrides, overnights, barbecues, mock hangings and gunfights, and barn dancing.

Mountain Mama Packing and Riding Company (Tesuque Pueblo, 10 mi north of Santa Fe off U.S. 84/285, tel. 505/986–1924) has pack trips, trail rides, and Mountain Mama.

Rocking S Ranch (Madrid Hwy., south of Santa Fe, tel. 505/

438–7333) offers Western trail rides for all levels, from beginner to expert, plus bed-and-breakfast.

Santa Fe Stage Line (Galisteo, south of Santa Fe on NM 41, tel. 505/983–6565 or 800/338–6877) offers rentals by the hour, half day, full day, or overnight. It also rents stagecoaches.

Vientos Encantados (Round Barn Stables, Ojo Caliente, one hour north of Santa Fe on U.S. 84/285, no phone) features trail rides and pack trips near the hot mineral springs of northern New Mexico (*see* Off the Beaten Track, above). After a long ride, a hot soak?

Hot-Air Ballooning   All phases of hot-air ballooning are available to the Santa Fe visitor, from hands-on beginning lessons to the traditional champagne-sipping ride. Hot-air ballooning is generally done in the early morning, when there's little wind, so you'll be expected to arrive at the launch site before sunrise. Dress warmly.

Balloons Over Santa Fe (1874 Calle Quedo, Santa Fe 87505, tel. 505/471–2937 or 505/982–8178) offers daily individual or group flights over some of Santa Fe's most gorgeous landscape, weather permitting. Half-hour individual flights cost $90. One-hour brunch flights are $150.

River Rafting   The mention of no other sport conjures up as much excitement as does white-water rafting, and justly so. White-water rafting provides the kind of walloping action-packed thrill that belongs to the rocky, bone-thumping country that gave birth to it. Of course, if you prefer something less invigorating than heart-stopping, hair-raising Class V rapids, there are always more leisurely sightseeing possibilities on a river trip along the Rio Chama or one of the more gentle riverways of northern New Mexico, gliding past colorful mesas, ancient ruins, and fields ripening in the sun. Unless you're a polar bear, the river trips are an option only in the summertime.

Los Rios River Runners (desk in La Fonda Hotel, tel. 505/983–6565 or 800/338–6877) offers a variety of white-water adventures, including the famous Taos Box, a 17-mile run on the rolling rapids of the upper Rio Grande.

New Wave Rafting Company (107 Washington Ave., tel. 505/984–1444) features full, half-day, and overnight river trips, with daily departures from Santa Fe.

Rio Bravo River Tours (1412 Cerrillos Rd., tel. 505/988–1153 or outside New Mexico, 800/451–0708) has professionally guided tours that leave daily from Santa Fe and Taos.

Santa Fe Rafting Company and Outfitters (80 E. San Francisco St., tel. 505/988–4914) features personalized rafting tours. Tell them what you want, they'll do it.

Southwest Wilderness Center (information and reservations through Galisteo News and Ticket Center, tel. 505/983–7262) handles local and international river tours, from the Rio Chama to China.

Running   With the city's 7,000-foot-high altitude, newcomers to Santa Fe may feel as if they're running in the Chilean Andes. Once they adjust, however, they'll find it a great place to slip into their Nikes or Reeboks. The city obliges its runners with a jogging track that runs along the Santa Fe River, parallel to Alameda Street, and one on Washington Avenue near Fort Marcy. There's lots of local organized activity as well, in which visitors may participate. **The Santa Fe Runaround**, a 10-kilometer race held in early June, begins and ends at the Plaza. The **Women's Five-Kilometer Run** is held in early August, and joggers turn out in droves on Labor Day for the most popular run of all, the annual **Old Santa Fe Trail Run**. More a weekly social event than a minimarathon is the **Fun Run** that starts out every Wednesday evening from the Plaza; starting time is 6 PM in summer, 5:30 in winter months. Almost all Santa Fe's running events are organized by the **Santa Fe Striders Running Club** (tel. 505/989–7423).

Skiing The ski season in Santa Fe runs from Thanksgiving through Easter and averages 250 inches of dry-powder snow a year. With blue skies above, blue-silver snow below, and green pines dotting the horizon like exclamation marks, the **Santa Fe Ski Area** has a 1,650-foot vertical rise and more than 40 trails (20% beginner, 40% intermediate, 40% advanced). The resort's six ski lifts include an Easy Street beginner's chairlift and a swift, breath-halting 5,000-foot triple chair to the summit. New Mexico's first quad chairlift, The Santa Fe Super Chief, makes the ride up almost as much fun as the downhill run. Chipmunk is a free run for small fry who measure less than 46 inches in their ski boots, provided they're in the company of a paying adult. Open bowls at the peak and more sheltered runs through the trees make for pleasant skiing even when the high winds blow. A ski-area restaurant, **Evergreen** (High Park Rd., tel. 505/984–8190) offers warming soups and chowders, as well as other hearty dishes.

For ski-area information call the Santa Fe Ski Area (tel. 505/982–4429 or 505/983–9155) or Santa Fe Central Reservations (tel. 505/983–8200, or 800/982–SNOW out of state). The New Mexico Tourism and Travel Division (tel. 505/827–0291) offers a free packet of ski information, and during the season current snow-condition information is available by calling 505/984–0606. For cross-country skiing conditions, contact the **Santa Fe National Forest** office, tel. 505/988–6940.

Tennis Santa Fe has 27 public tennis courts, including four asphalt courts at **Alto Park** (1035½ Alto St.), four concrete courts at **Herb Martinez/La Resolana Park** (Camino Carlos Rey), three asphalt courts at **Ortiz Park** (Camino de las Crusitas), and two asphalt courts at **Old Fort Marcy Commemorative Park** (Prince Ave. and Kearney Ave.). They are all available on a first-come, first-served basis. For the location of additional public facilities, call the City Recreation Department (tel. 505/984–6864). Among the major private tennis facilities, including indoor, outdoor, and lighted courts, are **Club at El Gancho** (Las Vegas Hwy., tel. 505/988–5000), **Sangre De Cristo Racquet Club** (1755 Camino Corrales Rd., tel. 505/983–7978), **Santa Fe Country Club** (Airport Rd., tel. 505/471–3378), and **Shellaberger Tennis Center** (St. Michaels Dr., tel. 505/473–6411). Check for limited membership privileges.

Windsurfing Strong summer breezes and a proximity to numerous lakes have made northern New Mexico a popular destination for windsurfers. **Abiquiu Lake** (40 mi northwest of Santa Fe, via U.S. 84/285; Drawer D, Abiquiu, 87510, tel. 505/685–4371), **Cochiti Lake** (off U.S. 85 between Los Alamos and Santa Fe; Cochiti Lake, PenaBlanca, 87041, tel. 505/242–8302), **Conchas Lake** (three hours east of Santa Fe, via I–25 to Las Vegas and NM 104 to Conchas Lake; Box 976, Conchas Dam, 88416, tel. 505/868–2270), and **Storrie Lake** (an hour east, via I–25 to Las

Vegas; Box 3157, Las Vegas, 87701, tel. 505/424–7278), all with warm water and good winds, have developed a legion of devoted regulars. Most of the windsurfing lakes have no on-site rental facilities, so you'll have to bring your own equipment, which may be rented or purchased from sporting goods and water-sports stores in Santa Fe. **Santa Fe Windsurfing** (905 St. Francis Dr., tel. 505/986–1611) and **Water Sports** (1301 Escalante St., tel. 505/982–8085) both have good selections.

Northern New Mexico is in a constant thunderstorm pattern during the summer, so early morning sessions are recommended for beginning windsurfers or anyone who can't get off the lakes in a hurry. For more information, contact Jeff Backi of **Santa Fe Sailboard Fleet** at tel. 505/471–2176 or write Box 15931, Santa Fe, 87506.

Spectator Sports

Horse Racing Horse racing at the Santa Fe Downs, a beautiful 1-mile track in the foothills of the towering Sangre de Cristo Mountains (on I–25, just 6 minutes west of town) attracts nearly a quarter-million spectators each year. The racing season begins in the middle of June and runs through Labor Day. Races are held each Wednesday, Friday, Saturday, and Sunday and on holidays, with the first race starting at 1:30 PM (except for Friday, at 3 PM). The $100,000 Santa Fe Futurity for two-year-olds is New Mexico's richest thoroughbred purse. There's pari-mutuel betting, of course, a Jockey Club, a Turf Club, ultra-modern grandstands, and plenty of parking, something rare in Santa Fe. For more information, contact **Santa Fe Racing, Inc.** (tel. 505/471–3311).

Dining

A delicious mixture of Pueblo Indian, Spanish Colonial, Mexican, and American-frontier cooking, all steeped and bubbled over the centuries, Santa Fe cuisine is like none other. Recipes that came from Spain via Mexico were adapted for local ingredients—chiles, corn, pork, beans, honey, apples, piñon nuts, jicama, and leaves of the prickly pear cactus—generations ago and have remained much the same ever since. Mexican dishes, such as *carne adovada* (marinated pork), burritos, chile rellenos, *flautas* (rolled corn tortillas filled with shredded beef or chicken), and *chalupas* (literally a "boat" made from a shaped corn tortilla and filled with shrimp, beef, or chicken), are distinct because the flavor is baked in, not poured over. Pinto beans and blue corn or flour tortillas are usually served as side orders.

In northern New Mexico, even Anglo babies cut their teeth on fresh, warm tortillas. And how quickly they develop a taste for *sopapillas*, deep-fried, puff-pastry pillows, drizzled with butter and honey. But it is the chile, whether red or green, that is the heart and soul of northern New Mexican cuisine. Visitors from other parts of the country are always a bit surprised to learn that *ristras*, those strings of bright red chile peppers that seem to hang everywhere, are sold more for eating here than for decoration. More varieties of chiles—upwards of 90—are grown in New Mexico than anywhere else in the world.

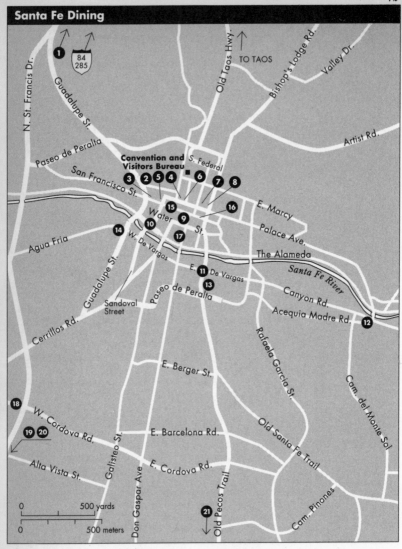

Santa Fe Dining

The Bull Ring, **13**
Cafe Pasqual's, **17**
The Compound, **12**
Coyote Cafe, **9**
423 American
Restaurant, **5**
Legal Tender, **21**
Maria's New Mexico
Kitchen, **18**

El Nido, **1**
The Old House, **15**
Ore House on the
Plaza, **16**
The Palace, **4**
Pink Adobe, **11**
Salsa, **7**
Santacafe, **14**
The Shed, **6**

Shohko-Cafe, **2**
Staab House, **8**
Tecolote Cafe, **19**
La Tertulia, **10**
Tortilla Flats, **20**
Vanessie, **3**

But if you can't stand the heat, you don't have to get out of the Santa Fe kitchen. The city has nearly 200 restaurants to suit all tastes and budgets, from a riot of fast-food outlets on the outskirts of town, particularly along Cerrillos Road, to elegant downtown restaurants near the Plaza, where you can hobnob with film stars and publishers. There are also health food and vegetarian restaurants and a wide selection of ethnic eating places.

Highly recommended restaurants are indicated by a star ★.

Category	Cost*
Expensive	over $25
Moderate	$10–$25
Inexpensive	under $10

*per person, excluding tax (5.8%), service, and drinks

Expensive **The Compound.** With its crisp white linen tablecloths, heavy
★ crystal, gleaming silver, elaborate floral arrangements, white-glove service—and perhaps the only rigidly enforced dress code in Santa Fe—this restaurant shimmers with Old World elegance. The main dining room, draped with colorful fabrics, overlooks an Italian garden where a playful fountain splashes; the other, with Navajo-rug hangings, overlooks a Spanish patio. Described as American Continental, the menu includes breast of chicken in champagne, fresh foie gras, roast loin of lamb, baked salmon, Russian caviar, and raspberries from New Zealand. *653 Canyon Rd., tel. 505/982-4353. Reservations required. Jacket and tie required. AE. Open Tues.–Sat., dinner only.*

The Old House. Pride of the Eldorado Hotel, the Old House specializes in such dishes as cut-to-order New York sirloin, oysters Rockefeller, and a special mixed grill. The masculine setting matches the menu: Dining rooms are Southwestern style, with hardwood floors, beamed ceilings, mohair-covered chairs, and a dominating mural-size painting, *The Rio Grande*, as well as a piano bar and fireplaces. Adjoining the main room is a smaller dining room, decorated with a colorful collection of carved animals from Mexico and New Mexico. *309 W. San Francisco St., tel. 505/988-4455. Reservations required. Jacket and tie advised. AE, DC, MC, V.*

★ **Pink Adobe.** Rosalea Murphey has been the owner of this Santa Fe gold mine for nearly 50 years and still takes a hand in the kitchen; her grandson is one of the managers. Located in a historic three-centuries-old adobe, this is easily the best-known restaurant in town. It's creatively decorated with antique copper pots, wooden shipping chests, painted pine chairs, and early Spanish pottery. Continental, New Orleans Creole, and local New Mexican favorites are served in several cozy dining rooms with fireplaces. No smoking is allowed. *406 Old Santa Fe Trail, tel. 505/983-7712. Reservations required. Dress: informal. AE, DC, MC, V.*

Santacafe. This romantic, low-keyed restaurant, in a thick-walled 200-year-old adobe (the Pedro Gallegos House, two blocks north of the Plaza), is simply decorated with floral bouquets. The menu is inspired by an eclectic array of international cuisines and changes with the season. Chinese dumplings, venison with juniper berry sauce, fresh grilled fish, and a wide variety of breads and desserts are featured. *231 Washington Ave., tel. 505/984–1788. Reservations required. Jacket and tie advised. MC, V. Lunch weekdays, dinner daily.*

Staab House. Beautiful, handcrafted Southwestern furniture, a Victorian bar complete with a brass foot rail, and a large fireplace help set the elegant tone at this well-known restaurant, adjacent to La Posada de Santa Fe. In a delightful conservatory setting, you can dine on seafood and such northern New Mexican favorites as *fajitas del norte* (tortillas filled with chunks of pork, beef, or chicken); in summer you can sit out on the patio beside a bubbling fountain. *330 E. Palace Ave., tel. 505/986–0000. Reservations suggested. Jacket and tie advised. AE, D, DC, MC, V.*

Moderate   **The Bull Ring.** Set in a rambling old Spanish adobe (ca. 1886) next door to the State Capitol, this relaxed, dimly lighted establishment includes steak, pasta, and Spanish red shrimp among its wide selection of New Mexican specialties. In addition to the six crowded dining rooms, there's a popular adjoining lounge, with dancing and entertainment, and a patio, open to diners in the summer. *414 Old Santa Fe Trail, tel. 505/983–3328. Reservations suggested. Dress: casual. MC, V.*

★   **Coyote Cafe.** Formerly a Greyhound bus depot, this is now one of the trendiest spots in town, thanks to its great food and cheerful ambience: bright, flashy colors; modern art; oversize folk art figures; and howling coyote silhouettes everywhere you look. The imaginative menu, which changes daily, offers dishes based on the history and tradition of northern New Mexican cuisine. The signature steak is a 26-ounce ribeye called The Cowboy and served with barbecued black beans and onion rings. Weather permitting, a rooftop cantina is open during the summer months. *132 W. Water St., tel. 505/983–1615. Reservations recommended. Dress: casual at lunch, informal to formal in the evening. MC, V. Closed Tues. during the winter.*

El Nido. This Santa Fe institution has been serving seafood—including excellent broiled salmon and swordfish steak—choice aged beef, prime rib, and New Mexican specialties in cozy, firelit rooms for more than 50 years. (The place was a dance hall and trading post before that.) Located in Tesuque, only five minutes from the Santa Fe Opera, El Nido has long been a favorite of opera fans—and often of the stars themselves. *NM 592 (22) at Bishop's Lodge Rd., 1 mi from Tesuque, tel. 505/988–4340. Reservations advised. Dress: casual but neat. MC, V. Closed Mon.*

423 American Restaurant. Traditional American dishes are served in three small rooms with whitewashed stucco walls, viga ceilings, and swirling overhead fans; for al fresco dining, there's also a charming outdoor patio. One block west of the Hilton and Eldorado hotels, this restaurant is set in a historic adobe home, built in 1850; the floors are made with brick taken from the Old Santa Fe penitentiary. Different fish preparations are featured nightly. The braised lamb shanks, made from a family recipe handed down by the owner's grandmother, are well worth a try. *423 W. San Francisco St., tel. 505/982–1552. Reservations suggested. Dress: informal for lunch, casual but smart for dinner. AE, MC, V.*

La Tertulia. At this lovely restaurant in a converted 19th-century convent, the six small dining rooms are always crowded, but you won't hear your neighbors talking: The walls are three feet thick in places, and there's wall-to-wall carpeting throughout. The restaurant is almost as well known for its splendid Spanish Colonial art collection, including some rare early santos, as for its fine New Mexican cuisine, tangy margaritas, and extraordinary house sangria. *416 Agua Fria, tel. 505/988–2769. Reservations a must. Dress: dressy to informal. AE, MC, V. Closed Mon.*

Legal Tender. It's worth taking a drive 18 miles southeast of town to this saloon and restaurant, opposite the Santa Fe Railroad junction in Lamy. Built as a general store in 1881, it's a Victorian period piece, with its stained-glass lamps, bawdy oil paintings, and turn-of-the-century memorabilia. The menu offers lots of variations on steaks, chops, and chicken, plus a variety of spicy regional dishes. This large place (it seats 250) is popular with locals for Sunday brunch. *In Lamy, just off U.S. 285, tel. 505/982–8425. Reservations not necessary. Dress: informal. AE, MC, V. Closed Mon.*

Ore House on the Plaza. This restaurant is notable for its perfect location, with a dining balcony overlooking the Plaza, and the food's fine, too. Salmon, swordfish, lobster, oysters, ceviche, and steaks are all artfully prepared. Margaritas, the house specialty, come in 64 customized flavors. *50 Lincoln Ave., upstairs on the southwest corner of the Plaza, tel. 505/983–8687. Reservations recommended. Dress: informal. AE, DC, MC, V.*

★ **The Palace.** This lively turn-of-the-century saloon-style restaurant—upholstered banquettes and chairs, crystal chandeliers, and red flocked wallpaper—specializes in northern Italian and French cuisine. Diners choose from a large selection of seafood, steak, veal, and pasta entrées. *142 W. Palace Ave., tel. 505/982–9892. Reservations not required. Dress: informal. AE, D, DC, MC, V.*

Salsa. A handsome brasserie and bar, one block north of the Plaza, Salsa serves up Mediterranean and local cuisine. Specialties include paella; calamari; and tapas, the Spanish finger food designed as an appetizer or as a light meal in itself. The dessert chimichanga, stuffed with spiced cream and goat cheese and served on a pool of raspberry Melba sauce and topped with hot fudge, is worth the calories. *142 Lincoln Ave., tel. 505/989–7171. Reservations suggested. Jacket and tie advised. MC, V.*

Shohko-Cafe. Across the street from the Eldorado hotel, this popular Japanese-Chinese restaurant specializes in tempura combinations, sushi, sashimi, sukiyaki, and teriyaki, along with vegetarian and seafood specials. The 36-foot sushi bar offers 300 artfully prepared varieties. A concession to local tastes is green chile tempura, as well as the handmade Southwestern-style tables and chairs. Dim sum lunches are served on Saturday. *321 Johnson St., at Guadalupe, tel. 505/983–7288. Reservations required. Dress: casual. MC, V.*

Tecolote Cafe. *Huevos rancheros* (eggs served on a tortilla, with hot sauce and refried beans)—New Mexico's unofficial state breakfast—are fabulous at this easygoing place, as are the biscuits, muffins, and coffee (all you can drink). The shirred eggs Tecolote are a luscious combination of baked eggs, sautéed chicken livers, and salsa. *1203 Cerrillos Rd., tel. 505/988–1362. Reservations not required. Dress: informal. AE, DC, MC, V.*

Vanessie. High beamed ceilings and two massive oak tables with highback chairs set a clubby, lodgelike tone for this longtime local favorite. At the same time, a glassed-in kitchen, contemporary paintings, and a tile floor give the place an open, airy feel. You can catch the strains of wistful tunes from the piano bar as you enjoy such specialties as rack of lamb, fish, and filet mignon. *434 W. San Francisco, tel. 505/982–9966. Reservations not required. Dress: formal. MC, V.*

Inexpensive
★ **Cafe Pasqual's.** Only a block southwest of the Plaza, this cheerful, informal place serves regional specialties. Forget the pancakes and order a *chorizo burrito* (Mexican sausages, scrambled eggs, home fries, and scallions wrapped in a flour tortilla and doused with red or green chile sauce) or *huevos motulenos* (eggs, tortilla, chile, fried bananas, cheese, and spicy hot sauce). Though the restaurant is small, it seems larger thanks to high ceilings and huge colorful murals; piñatas, strings of chile peppers, and ceramic pottery add a festive tone. It's open for three meals, with breakfast served all day for sleepyheads. Expect a line outside. *121 Don Gasper, tel. 505/983–9340. No reservations. Dress: informal. MC, V.*

★ **Maria's New Mexico Kitchen.** You haven't been to Santa Fe until you've eaten at this landmark restaurant, in business for over 40 years. In addition to such standard fare as ribs, steaks, and burgers, traditional Mexican specialties and typical local favorites are served daily: homemade tamales, rellenos, blue corn tamales, fajitas, green chile stew. Women in colorful costumes make the tortillas by hand. Margaritas are created from scratch, hand shaken and served with gleaming bits of anticipation shimmering on the glass. The decor is Old Mexico, with piñatas, ceramic pottery, wooden tables, and colorful paper flowers. There's a patio for summer dining and fireplaces lit in winter. *555 W. Cordova Rd., just east of St. Francis, tel. 505/983–7929. Reservations advised. Dress: informal. AE, D, MC, V.*

The Shed. Great homemade pies and tasty New Mexican cuisine make this a luncheon favorite with almost everyone in Santa Fe, judging by the lines. Housed in a rambling, historic adobe hacienda dating to 1692, the restaurant is decorated throughout with festive folk art. Specialties include red chile enchiladas, green chile with potatoes, *posole* (corn chowder), and charbroiled "Shedburgers." *113½ E. Palace Ave., tel. 505/982–9030. Reservations not required. Dress: informal. No credit cards. Lunch only. Closed Sun.*

Tortilla Flats. Between a Taco Bell on one corner and a McDonald's on the other, Tortilla Flats is an oasis of great New Mexican food served in pleasant, informal surroundings. The service is a bit slow, but you'll forget once breakfast arrives—perhaps chorizo Mexicana (spicy red sausage served with a three-egg omelet), a chorizo-and-scrambled-egg burrito, or the traditional huevos rancheros, served with refried beans and good hot coffee that keeps on coming. *3139 Cerrillos Rd., tel. 505/471–8685. Reservations not necessary. Dress: informal. MC, V. Breakfast and lunch only.*

Lodging

Santa Fe is a hot tourist destination that attracts lots of upscale travelers. As a result, prices have been escalating steadily in recent years and are likely to continue to climb as long as a steady stream of fat cats continues to show up and pay them. Low-season hotel rates, which fluctuate considerably from place to place, are generally in effect from the beginning of November until the end of April (excluding the Thanksgiving and Christmas holidays), and then they soar. But the savings are far from spectacular, even at no-frills hotels.

Highly recommended lodgings are indicated by a star ★.

Category	Cost*
Very Expensive	over $150
Expensive	$100–$150
Moderate	$65–$100
Inexpensive	under $65

Prices are for a double room, excluding tax (5.8% in New Mexico).

Hotels

Very Expensive　**Eldorado Hotel.** One of the city's newest and most luxurious hotels—a bit too modern for some—this is located in the heart of ★ downtown, not far from the Plaza. Its rooms are stylishly furnished with carved Southwestern-style desks and chairs, nature prints, and a large upholstered club chair, all in warm, desert colors. Baths are spacious and completely tiled. Many of the rooms have balconies, and all offer views of the Santa Fe mountains. The hotel's Old House restaurant is one of the city's best (*see* Dining, above). *309 W. San Francisco St., 87501, tel. 505/988–4455. 210 rooms and minisuites, 5 suites. Facilities: restaurants, bar, rooftop pool, entertainment, shopping arcade. AE, D, DC, MC, V.*

Inn of the Anasazi. Santa Fe's newest showpiece (opened in 1991), in the heart of the city's historic Plaza district, was clearly designed with the upscale traveler in mind. Each individually designed room has beamed ceilings; a kiva (beehive-style) fireplace; a handcrafted desk, dresser, and tables; and a four-poster bed. Services include a personal attendant who acts as a concierge, twice-daily maid service, and room delivery of exercise bikes upon request. The restaurant serves good regional fare, and a private wine cellar seats up to 12 guests for dinner. Guests can browse in an in-house library, which focuses on the lore and legends of New Mexico and the Southwest. *113 Washington Ave., 87501, tel. 505/988–3030 or 800/688–8100. 60 rooms and suites. Facilities: TV, VCR, film library, stereo, minibar, safe. AE, DC, MC, V.*

Expensive　**Hilton of Santa Fe.** This downtown establishment has a comfortable and spacious lobby—a bit frayed around the edges— with a beamed ceiling, a huge wrought-iron chandelier, and colorful Native American wall hangings. The large, renovated guest rooms, done in muted Southwestern tones of tan, cream, and golden brown, feature locally crafted table lamps, fine modern furniture, and hanging or potted plants. The hotel is built around the Casa de Ortiz, a historic home whose now-enclosed patio houses the hotel's delightful Chamisa Courtyard restaurant, open for breakfast and lunch. The intimate Piñon Grill serves entrées cooked over crackling fires of piñon, mesquite, apple, and hickory. *100 Sandoval St., 87501, tel. 505/*

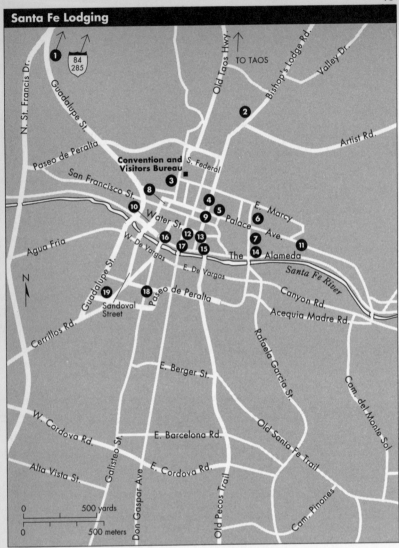

Santa Fe Lodging

Alexander's Inn, **11**

The Bishop's
Lodge, **2**

Eldorado Hotel, **8**

La Fonda, **12**

The Grant Corner
Inn, **3**

Hilton of Santa Fe, **10**

Hotel St. Francis, **13**

Hotel Santa Fe, **19**

Inn at Loretto–Best
Western, **15**

Inn of the Anasazi, **5**

Inn of the Animal
Tracks, **6**

Inn of the
Governors, **17**

Inn on the
Alameda, **14**

La Posada de Santa
Fe, **9**

Preston House, **7**

Pueblo Bonito B & B
Inn, **18**

Rancho Encantado, **1**

Territorial Inn, **4**

Water Street Inn, **16**

988–2811 *or* 800/HILTONS. *155 rooms. Facilities: 2 restaurants, bar, heated outdoor pool. AE, D, DC, MC, V.*

Hotel St. Francis. Listed in the National Register of Historic Places, this tan, three-story building, constructed in 1920, has walkways fronted by turn-of-the-century lampposts. One block southwest of the Plaza, the hotel offers small and simple rooms with high ceilings, casement windows, brass-and-iron beds, marble and cherrywood antiques, and original artwork. Bathrooms feature the original hexagonal tile and porcelain pedestal sinks. Afternoon tea, with scones and finger sandwiches, is served daily in the lobby and, weather permitting, on the veranda. Francisco's restaurant, a local favorite, offers Santa Fe grilled entrées and freshly made pastries. *201 Don Gaspar Ave., 87501, tel. 505/983–5700 or 800/666–5700 outside NM. 81 rooms. Facilities: restaurant, bar, garden patio. AE, MC, V.*

Inn at Loretto–Best Western. Built in the traditional Pueblo style, this hotel has been designed with historical accuracy in mind, with such touches as light fixtures custom made of tinwork or pottery, and Indian mimbres (drawings of legendary birds and animals), petroglyphs, and other ancient designs on the walls. Rooms are decorated in light colors and feature beds with handmade oak headboards and nightstands inlaid with recessed tilework. The inn is adjacent to the famous Loretto Chapel (*see* Tour 3 in Exploring Santa Fe, above). *211 Old Santa Fe Trail, 87501, tel. 505/988–5531 or outside New Mexico, for reservations and information, 800/528–1234. 136 rooms. Facilities: restaurant, lounge, pool, shops, galleries, beauty salon. AE, D, DC, MC, V.*

★ **Inn of the Governors.** Just two blocks from the Plaza, this is one of the nicest hotels in town. A small, intimate lobby makes the traveler feel quickly at home. Standard rooms have a Mexican theme, with bright colors, hand-painted folk art, Southwestern fabrics, and handmade furnishings; deluxe rooms are balconied Southwestern-style minisuites with fireplaces. The dining room specializes in native New Mexican dishes and lighter fare. *234 Don Gaspar (at Alameda), 87501, tel. 505/982–4333 or 800/234–4534 outside New Mexico for reservations and information. Facilities: restaurant, piano bar, patio dining in summer, ground-level and underground parking, swimming pool. AE, D, DC, MC, V.*

Inn on the Alameda. This small, peach-colored hotel on the Santa Fe River offers a personal touch; in addition, it's convenient to both the Plaza and the Canyon Road galleries. Rooms have desert pastel decor, framed posters designed by local artists, and Southwestern furnishings; several have balconies. The hotel has no restaurant, but there are a number of good ones nearby. A complimentary Continental breakfast is served each morning, either in your room or in the lobby. *303 E. Alameda Ave., 87501, tel. 505/984–2121 or 800/289–2122 outside NM. 36 rooms. Facilities: bar, hot tub. AE, DC, MC, V.*

★ **La Fonda.** When Santa Fe was established in 1610, official records show that the town already had an adobe *fonda,* or inn, to accommodate travelers. Two centuries later, the original hotel was still welcoming guests—traders, trappers, mountain men, soldiers, and politicians. The present structure was built on the site of the original inn in 1864 and has been refurbished countless times since. The only lodging directly on the Plaza, it is perhaps also the only hotel in the world that can boast having had both Kit Carson and John F. Kennedy as guests. A spacious tiled lobby is decorated with Spanish Colonial antiques, early Mexican pieces, and classic Native American art. Each room is unique, featuring hand-decorated wooden furniture, wrought-iron light fixtures, beamed ceilings, oak door paneling, and motifs painted by local Pueblo Indian artists; many accommodations have turn-of-the-century pieces, and all the suites have fireplaces. *100 E. San Francisco St., 87501, tel. 505/982–5511 or 800/523–5002 outside NM. 164 rooms, 35 suites. Facilities: enclosed courtyard restaurant, lounge, bar, swimming pool, whirlpool, private dining rooms. AE, D, DC, MC, V.*

La Posada de Santa Fe. This Spanish Colonial inn, only two blocks from the Plaza, is situated on six acres of beautifully landscaped gardens and expansive green lawns shaded by giant elms and cottonwoods. The charming rooms all have fireplaces, beamed ceilings, and Native American rugs. In the center of this hotel complex is the excellent Victorian-style Staab House (*see* Dining, above). *330 E. Palace Ave., 87501, tel. 505/986–0000 or 800/727–5276 outside NM. 116 rooms, 33 suites. Facilities: restaurant, Victorian bar, swimming pool, health-club privileges. AE, D, DC, MC, V.*

Moderate **Hotel Santa Fe.** Opened in 1991, this three-story hotel offers rooms and suites decorated in traditional Southwestern style, with local handmade furniture and Native American paintings, including works by the well-known artist Gerald Nailor. All suites have microwaves and minibars, and smaller rooms have access to a common kitchen. The hotel-lobby bar serves a full breakfast. Controlling interest in the property is owned by the Picuris Pueblo, one of the eight northern New Mexican Native American tribes located in the valley of the Sangre de Cristo Mountains. The hotel gift shop, the only tribal-owned gift shop in Santa Fe, offers prices lower than most nearby retail stores. Hotel guests receive an additional 25% discount. *1501 Paseo de Peralta, 87504, tel. 505/982–1200 or 800/825–9876 outside NM. 40 rooms, 91 suites. Facilities: bar, deli. AE, D, DC, MC, V.*

Bed-and-Breakfasts

Moderate **Alexander's Inn.** This 1903 Victorian house exudes all the charm of an old country inn, with American country-style wooden furnishings, flower arrangements, and lots of open space. A beautiful flowered walkway runs alongside the building. In a lovely east-side residential area, only a few blocks from the Plaza and the Canyon Road shops and galleries, Alexander's Inn serves a generous Continental breakfast, including homemade bread and muffins. *529 E. Palace Ave., 87501, tel. 505/986–1431. 5 rooms, 3 with private baths, 2 with shared bath. MC, V.*

The Grant Corner Inn. Located downtown, but surrounded by a patio and garden, this delightful Colonial-style lodging combines antique Spanish and American country furnishings with potted greens and knickknacks. The rooms feature tile stoves, old-fashioned fixtures, quilts, and Indian blankets. The ample breakfast includes homebaked breads and pastries, jellies, and such unique local treats as blue corn waffles. *122 Grant Ave., 87501, tel. 505/983–6678. 5 rooms with private baths, 6 with shared baths, and 2 with private baths in an adjoining hacienda. MC, V.*

★ **Inn of the Animal Tracks.** Three blocks east of the Plaza, this enchanting 90-year-old restored adobe has beamed ceilings, hardwood floors, handcrafted furniture, and fireplaces. Each guest room is decorated with an animal theme: Whimsical Rabbit, Gentle Deer, Soaring Eagle, Playful Otter, and Loyal Wolf. Be prepared for cuteness: The Whimsical Rabbit room, for instance, is filled with stuffed and terra-cotta rabbits, rabbit books, rabbit drawings and paintings; bunny-rabbit slippers are tucked under the bed. A full breakfast and high tea are served; high tea is also available by reservation for nonguests. *707 Paseo de Peralta, 87504, tel. 505/988–1546. 6 rooms, all with private baths. AE, MC, V.*

Preston House. This 1886 Queen Anne house, the only one of its kind in the city, is tucked away in a quiet garden setting not far from the Plaza. Its pleasant rooms feature period furnishings, Edwardian fireplaces, and stained-glass windows. Fruit bowls and fresh-cut flowers add to the appeal. *106 Faithway St., 87501, tel. 505/982–3465. 15 rooms. AE, MC, V.*

Pueblo Bonito B & B Inn. Minutes from the Plaza, this century-old adobe compound is one of the few bed-and-breakfast inns in Santa Fe that retains the pure Southwest Pueblo design throughout. The handmade and hand-painted furnishings are all in the traditional Old Santa Fe style; work by local Native American and Western artists hangs on the walls, and pottery made by New Mexican craftspeople graces the shelves, bookracks, and mantels. All the rooms have fireplaces. A filling breakfast is served in the main dining room (there's also room service), which has French doors that open onto a patio. *138 W. Manhattan, 87501, tel. 505/984–8001. 12 rooms, 3 suites, all with private baths. Facilities: sun deck. MC, V.*

Territorial Inn. Creature comforts are a high priority in this elegant 100-year-old brick structure, nestled amid restaurants and shops; it's now one of Santa Fe's leading bed-and-breakfasts, only one block from the Plaza. The decor is Victorian throughout; among the well-maintained rooms, No. 9 has a canopied bed and a fireplace. A hot tub is also available, with robes provided. In addition to Continental breakfast, the inn offers afternoon treats, and brandy turndowns in the evening. *215 Washington Ave., 87501, tel. 505/989–7737. 10 rooms, all with private baths. MC, V.*

Water Street Inn. This intimate, restored adobe house blends regional Southwestern furnishings with period antiques. All the rooms have fireplaces and private baths. *427 W. Water St., 87501, tel. 505/984–1193. 6 rooms. MC, V.*

Resorts

Very Expensive **The Bishop's Lodge.** Three miles north of downtown Santa Fe, in the rolling foothills of the Sangre de Cristo Mountains, this resort houses guests in one- and three-story lodges. Geared for families, particularly during the summer, the property offers a variety of outdoor activities, including horseback riding, hiking, skeet shooting, tennis, swimming in an outdoor heated pool and lawn games. Old Southwestern furnishings, such as shipping chests, tables, and desks dating from 1917–20, when the hotel was first built, are found in guest rooms and public spaces, along with tinwork from Mexico and original Native American and Western art. The dining room, one of the finest in the Southwest, offers a bountiful luncheon buffet; Sunday's meal draws large crowds of nonguests from town. Jackets are required for dinner. *Bishop's Lodge Rd., 87504, tel. 505/983–6377. 56 rooms, 18 suites. Facilities: restaurant, bar, heated pool, whirlpool, 18-hole golf privileges, available airport and railroad transfers, supervised children's programs. No credit cards. Closed Jan.–Mar.*

Rancho Encantado. This elegantly casual resort offers horseback riding, indoor and outdoor swimming, hiking, jogging, and seasonal skiing in the rolling, piñon-covered hills above the sprawling Rio Grande Valley. The guest rooms have Southwestern-style furniture, handmade and hand painted by local craftspeople, in addition to fine Spanish and Western antiques from the 1850s and earlier. Some rooms have fireplaces and/or private patios; some are carpeted, while others have tile floors. The acclaimed dining room specializes in rack of lamb and fresh fish. *Located on U.S. 285 near Tesuque, 8 mi north of Santa Fe (Rte. 4, Box 57C), 87504, tel. 505/982–3537. 22 rooms, 10 suites. Facilities: restaurant, 2 pools, heated whirlpool, tennis, golf privileges. AE, DC, MC, V.*

Camping

With its wide open spaces, good roads, and knock-'em-dead scenery, northern New Mexico draws camping enthusiasts and RV road warriors like teenagers to a rock concert. The Santa Fe National Forest is right in the city's backyard and includes the Dome Wilderness (5,200 acres in the volcanically formed Jemez Mountains) and the Pecos Wilderness (223,333 acres of high mountains, forests, and meadows at the southern end of the Rocky Mountain chain). Public sites remain open from May through October. For specifics, call the **Santa Fe National Forest Office** (1220 South St. Francis Dr., Box 1689, 87504, tel. 505/988–6940). Some private campground operators provide literature at the **La Bajada Welcome Center** (La Bajada Hill, 13 mi southwest of Santa Fe on I–25, tel. 505/471–5242). The following are a few of the main campground and recreational vehicle facilities:

Los Campos Recreational Vehicle Park. The only full-service RV park within the city limits, Los Campos even has a swimming pool. Tucked behind a car dealership on one side, it offers open vistas on the other: poplars and Russian olive trees, a dry river bed, and mountains rising in the background. *3574 Cerrillos Rd., 87501, tel. 505/473–1949. Facilities: tent sites ($17.75 plus tax), hookups ($19.75 plus tax for 2 people), showers, bathrooms, LP gas, picnic tables.*

Rancheros de Santa Fe Camping Park. Located on I–25N (at Exit 290 on the Las Vegas Hwy., 10½ mi from the Santa Fe Plaza), this beautiful camping park is on a hill in the midst of a piñon forest. *Las Vegas Hwy., 87505, tel. 505/983–3482. Facilities: RV and tent sites ($13.58 plus $2 per person for more than 2 people), hookups ($16.50), pull-throughs ($17.50), swimming pool, hot showers, grocery, ice, laundry, bathrooms, LP gas available.*

Santa Fe KOA. Set in the southwestern foothills of the Sangre de Cristo Mountains, this large campground is well treed with piñon, cedar, and juniper. *Rte. 3, Box 95-A, 87501, tel. 505/982–1419. Facilities: full hookups ($17.50), tent sites ($11.50, plus $2 per person for more than 2 people), grocery, laundry,* *recreation room (video games, pool, Ping-Pong), bathrooms, showers.*

Tesuque Pueblo RV Campground. This campground, operated by the Tesuque Pueblo Indians, 10 miles north of Santa Fe (St. Francis exit of I–25), is on an open hill with a few cedar trees dotting the landscape; off to the west is the Tesuque River. *Tesuque 87501, tel. 505/455–2661. Facilities: RV and tent sites ($11 plus $2 per person for more than 2 people), 63 full hookups ($14), toilets, showers, drinking water, security gate, laundry.*

The Arts and Nightlife

The Arts

Music   Artistically and visually the city's crowning glory, the famed **Santa Fe Opera** is housed in a strikingly modern structure, a spectacular indoor-outdoor amphitheater carved into the natural curves of a hillside, 7 miles north of the city. Seating 1,773, it overlooks a vast panorama of mountains, mesas, and sky. Blend in some of the most acclaimed singers, directors, conductors, musicians, designers, and composers from Europe and the United States, and you begin to understand the excitement that explodes each July and August amid the tall pines of the Sangre de Cristo Mountains. Founded in 1957 by John Crosby, who remains its general director, the company offers a blend of seasoned classics, neglected masterpieces, and innovative premieres. For schedules and further information, call 505/982–3855, or write the Santa Fe Opera, Box 2408, 87504.

Under the direction of maestro Stewart Robertson, the **Santa Fe Symphony** (tel. 505/983–3530, Box 9692, 87504) performs seven concerts each season (September through May) to sold-out audiences at Sweeney Center. Also from September through May regular concerts are given by the professional chamber **Orchestra of Santa Fe** (tel. 505/988–4640, Box 2091, 87504). Its Mozart Festival in February and its annual holiday presentation of Handel's *Messiah* have become local traditions. In addition, **Santa Fe Summerscene** (tel. 505/989–8062) offers a series of free concerts (rhythm and blues, light opera, jazz, Cajun, salsa, folk, and bluegrass), dance performances (modern, folk), lectures, and story-telling sessions staged on the Santa Fe Plaza each Tuesday and Thursday from mid-June through August at noon and 7 PM.

Theater   On Friday, Saturday, and Sunday nights during July and August, **Shakespeare in the Park** (tel. 505/986–8222, Box 2188, 87504) presents free performances of the Bard's finest at the courtyard of the John Meem Library at St. John's College (Camino de Cruz Blanca, the next left past the cutoff for the International Folk Art Museum on the Old Santa Fe Trail). The music begins at 6 PM, the show at 7. Picnic baskets are welcome, in the tradition of the Old Vic, but, please, no ripe tomatoes. Seating is limited to 350, so it's best to get tickets in advance.

Staging at least four productions each October through May, the beautiful **Greer Garson Theater** (tel. 505/473–6511 or 505/473–6439, College of Santa Fe, Michael's Dr., 87501) is the scene of some of northern New Mexico's most spirited comedies, dramas, and musicals. (The actress for whom it is named is a principal contributor to the college's performing arts program and a resident of Santa Fe.)

Live theatrical performances are also available throughout the year at the **New Mexico Repertory Theater** (tel. 505/983–2382), which presents original, as well as established, dramas and comedies; the **Santa Fe Actors' Theater** (tel. 505/982–8309), dedicated to fostering the growth of the performing arts in Santa Fe and staging the works of playwrights ranging from Euripides to Sam Shepard; the **Santa Fe Community Theater** (tel. 505/988–4262), with its adventurous mix of avant-garde, established drama, and musical comedy; and the **Santa Fe Performing Arts Company** (tel. 505/984–2003 or 505/989–8008), offering a five-week intensive training program for students 8–19, culminating with a major production at the end of the summer session.

Nightlife

The lounges, hotels, and night spots of Santa Fe offer a wide variety of entertainment options, from lively dancing at a frontier saloon to quiet cocktails beside the flickering embers of a piñon fire. You can throw both your wallet and your hip out of joint at any of the following: **The Cargo Club** (519 Cerrillos Rd., tel. 505/989–8790) plays "the hottest dance music in town." **Club West** (213 W. Alameda, tel. 505/982–0099), with its beveled glass windows and U-shaped bar seating patrons on both sides, puts on a different type of musical entertainment each night, from a DJ record spinner to live rock and roll and African rhythms. **Rodeo Nites** (2911 Cerrillos Rd., tel. 505/473–4138) attracts a country-western crowd. **The Bull Ring** (414 Old Santa Fe Trail, tel. 505/983–3328), one of the better restaurants in town (*see* Dining, above), presents a live rock band on weekends. Rock and roll is also the mainstay at **Shooters** (1196 Harrison Rd., tel. 505/438–7777), which offers dance instructions on Wednesday night. **The Red Rooster** (Los Alamos Hwy., tel. 505/455–2724) has a good jukebox.

Check the entertainment listings in Santa Fe's daily newspaper, the *New Mexican,* or the complimentary *Inside Santa Fe,* available at most hotels and shops, for special performances and events.

Excursion 1:
Pecos National Historic Park and Las Vegas

A visit to the ancient New Mexican past and to a contemporary town that lives in the past are highlighted in this pleasant excursion to the region south of Santa Fe.

Pecos National Historic Park

About 25 miles southeast of Santa Fe via I–25, heading in the direction of Las Vegas, Pecos National Historic Park is the site of what was perhaps the greatest Indian pueblo. Located in a fertile valley and strategically situated between the buffalo hunters of the Great Plains and the farmers of the Rio Grande

Valley, Pecos was an early trading center. It was the largest and easternmost pueblo reached by the Spanish conquistadores, who built two missions here in their zeal to convert the Indians to Catholicism, and it became a major landmark on the Santa Fe Trail.

The ruins of the missions and of the excavated and partially stabilized pueblo may be visited on a self-guided tour. Containing more than 1,100 rooms and once the multidwelling home of as many as 2,500 Native Americans, the pueblo was four stories high in places. It was abandoned in 1838, and its 17 surviving occupants moved to the Jemez Pueblo. Today's visitors will find an exhibit and information center at the monument entranceway, where an introductory film is screened. *Pecos National Historic Park, Drawer 418, Pecos 87552, tel. 505/757–6032. Admission: $5 per car, $2 per bus passenger. The Golden Age Passport (issued to U.S. citizens 62 and older) allows free admission to all occupants of the same car, regardless of age.*

Las Vegas

When you leave Pecos, continue on I–25 for about 5 miles until you come to Las Vegas. The antithesis of its Nevada namesake, it was once an oasis for stagecoach passengers on the Santa Fe Trail who were seeking refuge from Indians and outlaws. And it was once, in the late 19th century, one of the state's major centers of commerce. Now the seat of San Miguel County, Las Vegas lies where the Sangre de Cristo Mountains merge with the high plains of New Mexico. At an altitude of 6,470 feet, its climate is delightful—summer days averaging in the low to mid-80s, winter days rarely below freezing. If you like to go traipsing through the past, back to a time when men were slow on words but fast on the draw, you'll enjoy a day or two in this town.

Las Vegas Chamber of Commerce (727 Grand Ave., Box 148, Las Vegas 87701, tel. 505/425–8631) offers brochures and other printed matter about the town and its colorful history. Sheriff Pat Garrett, who killed Billy the Kid, lived here. Teddy Roosevelt held a Rough Riders reunion in the Castaneda Hotel—once a crown jewel in the Fred Harvey chain—which has clearly seen better days. And, fresh from his triumph at San Juan Hill, he announced his candidacy for the vice-presidency in the lobby of the Las Vegas Harvey House. **Theodore Roosevelt's Rough Riders Memorial and City Museum** houses Native American artifacts, documents pertaining to the city's history, and memorabilia from the Spanish-American War. *Chamber of Commerce Bldg., 727 Grand Ave., tel. 505/425–8726. Admission free. Open Mon.–Sat. 9–5; closed Sun. and holidays.*

Las Vegas's 15,000 inhabitants unabashedly live in the past. Today's Las Vegas is built around old churches, old salons, old hotels, old houses, and old shops (many selling memorabilia and antiques of the period). Las Vegas has nine historic districts and some interesting places to stay, including the elegant, historic 1882 Plaza Hotel on the Old Town Plaza (tel. 505/425–3591) and the Inn on the Santa Fe Trail, 2 miles away (tel. 505/425–6791).

Time Out   In Old Town, on the Plaza, **Byron T's Lounge** (Plaza Hotel, 230 Old Town Plaza, tel. 505/425–3591) offers American favorites (steaks, chops, and chicken), as well as Southwestern cuisine, including steaming bowls of chili and hearty soups. Half a block away, **El Realto** (141 Bridge St., tel. 505/454–0037) serves seafood and Mexican specialties in a historic 1890s building furnished with Victorian and early West antiques.

Excursion 2:
Around Los Alamos

With the Jemez Mountains on one side and the Sangre de Cristo range on the other, Los Alamos's mesa-top location provides spectacular scenery and clean mountain air that's pleasantly cool in summer and ideal for outdoor pursuits in winter. There's plenty of fine accommodations, good food, convenient shopping, and several excellent museums. Hundreds of archaeological sites dot the Los Alamos area. Many of the best are located in Bandelier National Park, where cave and cliff dwellings, ancient ceremonial kivas, and other stone structures stretch out for more than a mile as the sheer walls of the Frijoles Canyon rise to a tree-fringed rim, and in Jemez State Monument. Nearby Valle Grande and Soda Dam provide insight into the geology of the region.

Los Alamos, birthplace of the atomic bomb, spreads over fingerlike mesas at an altitude of 7,300 feet. While research continues at the Los Alamos National Laboratory (in areas such as lasers, nuclear energy, superconductivity, and medicine), the community now emphasizes its link to the prehistoric past, promoting the more than 7,000 archaeological sites in the area (*see* Bandelier National Monument, below).

Tourist Information

Los Alamos County Chamber of Commerce (Fuller Lodge, 2132 Central Ave., Box 460 VG, Los Alamos 87544, tel. 505/662–8105) offers a free *Visitors' Guide*, brochures, and other promotional material upon request.

Getting There

Los Alamos is 45 minutes north of Santa Fe (west of U.S. 84/285, on NM 502). **Gray Line of Santa Fe** (tel. 505/983–9491) offers a four-hour tour of Los Alamos and the nearby Bandelier Cliff Dwellings.

Exploring Los Alamos

The community of Los Alamos was founded in absolute secrecy in 1943 as a center of defense research. The disclosure of its existence two years later made international headlines.

Bradbury Science Museum offers visitors a chance to experiment with lasers, use advanced computers, and witness research in solar, geothermal, fission, and fusion energy. You can get a glimpse of World War II's historic Project Y, as well as some of today's advanced science and technology, of the Los Alamos National Laboratory. *Los Alamos National Laborato-*

ry, *Diamond Dr., tel. 505/672–3861. Admission free. Open Tues.–Fri. 9–5, Sat.–Mon. 1–5.*

Housed in a national historic landmark, **Fuller Lodge Art Center** features works of northern New Mexican artists and traveling exhibits of both national and regional importance. The massive log structure, built in 1928, served as the dining and recreation hall for students of the Los Alamos Ranch School before World War II. *Fuller Lodge, 2132 Central Ave., tel. 505/ 662–9331. Admission free. Open daily 9–5.*

Also located on the grounds of the former ranch school, **Los Alamos Historical Museum** displays artifacts of early Native American life, as well as photographs and documents of the community's history, before and after World War II. *Fuller Lodge, 2132 Central Ave., tel. 505/662–4493. Admission free. Open daily 9–5.*

From Los Alamos, take NM 502 (Trinity Dr.) west and then NM 501 (West Jemez Rd.) south until you reach NM 4 at a "T" intersection. Turn left (east) and drive 6 miles to the entrance of **Bandelier National Monument.**

Seven centuries before the Declaration of Independence was signed, egalitarian, compact cities existed in the desert Southwest. Remnants of one of the most impressive of them, the **Anasazi Ruins,** can be seen at Frijoles Canyon in Bandelier National Monument. At the canyon's base, beside a gurgling stream, are the ruins of a three-stories-high pueblo, crumbling walls representing an irregular circle of small stone rooms. Visitors using primitive wooden ladders, rungs lashed into place with leather strips, can squeeze through the doorway and get a feel of living within the cell-like, four-by-four rooms. As the population expanded, additions were made to the original buildings. Natural caves in the soft volcanic tuff nearby were enlarged, and houses were built out from the cliffs.

For hundreds of years, the Anasazi people, early relatives of today's Rio Grande Pueblo Indians, thrived on wild game and crops of corn and beans. Suddenly, for reasons that are still undetermined, the settlements were abandoned. Climatic changes? A great drought? Crop depletion? No one knows for sure what caused the hasty retreat.

Visitors may ponder these and other mysteries while following a paved, self-guided trail through the site. Bandelier National Monument, named after author and ethnologist Adolph Bandelier (his novel, *The Delight Makers,* is set in Frijoles Canyon), contains 37,737 acres of wilderness, waterfalls, and wildlife, traversed by 60 miles of trails. A small museum in the visitors' center focuses on Native American culture and artifacts from AD 1200 to modern pueblo times. Some information about the area's wildlife is also displayed. *Bandelier National Monument, Los Alamos 87544, tel. 505/672–3861. Admission: $5 per car, $2 per bus passenger. The Golden Age Passport (issued to U.S. citizens 62 and older) allows free admission to all occupants of the same car, regardless of age.*

Take a left when you leave the national monument onto NM 4 west and follow the winding, scenic road up through the mountain forest to Jemez Springs; the drive should take about 45 minutes. Between Bandelier and Jemez, you'll pass magnificent **Valle Grande,** the world's largest volcanic caldera, only a fraction of which can be seen from the road. Once a bubbling inferno of steaming lava, it's now a lush green high-mountain valley with herds of grazing cattle. The entire 50-mile Jemez range, formed by cataclysmic upheavals, is now filled with gentle streams, hiking trails, and campgrounds.

Jemez State Monument, on NM 4, one mile north of Jemez Springs, contains another impressive Native American ruin. Approximately 600 years ago, ancestors of the people of Jemez Pueblo built several villages in and around the narrow mountain valley. One of the villages was Guisewa, a name that refers to the numerous hot mineral springs in the area. The Spanish colonists discovered it in 1598 and built a mission that was abandoned in 1630. Jemez is a year-round vacation destination, with hiking, cross-country skiing, and camping in nearby U.S. Forest Service areas. *Tel. 505/829–3530. Admission: $2 adults, $1 children 6–16. Holders of Museums of New Mexico $6 2-day pass admitted free. Open May–Sept. 15, daily 9–6; Sept. 16– Apr., daily 8:30–4:30. Closed for state holidays except July 4, Memorial Day, and Labor Day.*

A mile north of Jemez State Monument, just off NM 4, is a geological wonder known as **Soda Dam.** The so-called dam was created over thousands of years, formed by travertine deposits from mineral precipitation as waters cooled the earth's surface. The site's strange, mushroom-shaped exterior and the natural caves that have formed in and around it create the mystical aura that made it a sacred place to the ancient Native Americans. Numerous artifacts, prayer sticks, and rabbit clubs have been found here, as well as the mummy of a Native American baby wrapped in a blanket. In the warm summer months, the Jemez River at Soda Dam is a popular swimming spot.

Dining and Lodging

Dining **Good Eats Cafe.** Now in its eighth year, this large, friendly restaurant boasts the finest gourmet burgers in town ($5.75), along with chicken-fried steaks, chicken-fried chicken, homemade soups, and heaps of fresh vegetables. Good Eats is a good buy, with generous portions and relatively painless prices. A steak and shrimp dinner tops the menu at $10.50 *1315 Trinity Dr., tel. 505/662–9745. Reservations not required. Dress: casual. MC, V. Closed Sun.*

Lodging **Hilltop House Hotel.** Minutes from the Los Alamos National Laboratory, the three-story Hilltop House is geared toward traveling scientists and businesspeople as well as vacationers. Deluxe rooms have kitchenettes, and mini- and executive suites offer full kitchen facilities. All accommodations are furnished with modern Southwestern-style beds, desks, chairs, and tables. Guests get a complimentary cooked-to-order breakfast on weekdays, and the hotel's Trinity Sights restaurant offers good American and Southwestern cuisine in an elegant, white-tablecloth and flickering candlelight setting. *Trinity Dr. at Central Ave., Box 250, Los Alamos 87544, tel. 505/662–5913. 88 rooms. Facilities: restaurant, lounge, indoor pool, self-service laundromat, car rental agency on premises. AE, DC, MC, V. Moderate.*

Los Alamos Inn. With sweeping canyon views, this sprawling ground-level hotel features modern Southwestern decor. Its dining room, Ashley's Restaurant, does a Sunday brunch that's popular with locals as well as with vacationing visitors. *2201 Trinity Dr., Los Alamos 87544, tel. 505/662–7211. 114 rooms. Facilities: outdoor pool and spa, restaurant, bar. AE, DC, MC, V. Inexpensive–Moderate.*

Excursion 3: The High Road to Taos

If time isn't important, your drive from Santa Fe to Taos can be far more scenic and memorable if you detour a bit, skip the main highway (NM 68), and take the high road, a route by which you can literally travel back in time. The drive through the rolling hillsides studded with orchards and tiny picturesque villages noted for weavers and wood carvers, all set against the rugged alpine mountain backdrop, is stunning. A note of caution, however. As pretty as the high-road country is in winter, when the fields turn deep, soft white and the villages, fences, and naked trees are silhouetted like bold pen-and-ink drawings against the sky, the roads can be icy and treacherous. Check on weather conditions before attempting the drive, or stay with the more conventional Santa Fe–to–Taos route.

Out of Santa Fe past Tesuque on US 84/285, turn northeast at Pojoaque on NM 503 (about 12 mi north of Santa Fe). You'll come first to Nambe Pueblo and the lovely Nambe Falls picnic area. Continue on through the village of Cundiyo to **Chimayo,** sometimes called "the Lourdes of the Southwest." Nestled into the rugged hillsides where gnarled piñons seem to grow from bare bedrock, Chimayo is a town famous for its weaving, regional food, and the **Santuario de Chimayo** (once you reach the village, you can't miss it; signs everywhere point the way). The Santuario is a small, frontier adobe church built on the site where, believers say, a mysterious light came from the ground on Good Friday night in 1810. Some men from the village investigated the phenomenon, trying to find its source. Pushing away the earth, they found a large wooden crucifix. Today the chapel sits above a sacred *pozito* (a small well), the mud from which is believed to have miraculous healing properties, as the dozens of abandoned crutches and braces left at the altar— along with many notes, letters, and photos left behind in thanksgiving and prayer—dramatically testify. The Santuario draws a steady stream of worshipers all year long, but during Holy Week as many as 50,000 people visit. The shrine is a National Historic Landmark, but unlike similar holy places, it remains free of hysteria, and the commercialism is limited to a small adobe shop nearby selling brochures, books, and religious articles. *Tel. 505/351–4889. Admission free. Open daily.*

Chimayo is also known for its colorful weaving. At the junction of NM 520 and NM 76, **Ortega's Weaving Shop** offers high-quality Rio Grande work by a family whose Spanish ancestors brought the craft to New Mexico in the 1600s. Adjacent to the weaving shop is the **Galeria Ortega,** featuring traditional New Mexican Hispanic and contemporary Native American arts and crafts. The mailing address for both shops is Box 325, Chimayo 87522, tel. 505/351–4215.

About 4 miles east–northeast of Chimaya, just off NM 76 (look for the clearly marked signs), is the town of **Cordova.** Hardly more than a mountain village with a small central plaza, Cordova is the center of the regional wood-carving industry. Craftspeople whose ancestors carved santos and other religious and ornamental figures for church altars and private chapels still fashion them here from local wood. There's not much to see in the village, which consists of a schoolhouse, post office, and a few stores, except for the **Saint Anthony of Padua Chapel,** which is filled with beautiful handcrafted statues and retablos.

Cordova supports no less than 35 full-time and part-time carvers. The most famous of them is George Lopez, whose house is just south of the plaza. If you visit, you'll see an Ansel Adams portrait of Jose Dolores Lopez, George's father, considered a creative genius of wood carving; it was taken by the photographer in 1928. Most of the santeros in Cordova have signs outside their homes indicating that the statues are for sale. The pieces are expensive, ranging from several hundred dollars for small ones to several thousand for larger figures. Collectors snap them up at any price.

Continuing north on NM 76, about 1½ miles from Cordova, you'll come to **Trucas,** where Robert Redford shot the movie *The Milagro Beanfield War* (based on a novel written by Taos author John Nichols). This breathtakingly beautiful village is perched on the rim of a deep canyon with the towering Trucas Peaks, mountains high enough to be almost perpetually capped with snow, dominating the horizon. The tallest of the Trucas Peaks is 13,102 feet, the second-highest mountain in New Mexico. Trucas (Spanish for "trout") has a colorful array of shops and galleries, the best known of which is **Cordova's Weaving Shop** (Box 425, Trucas 87579, tel. 505/689–2437). Proprietor Harry Cordova, whose son played a part in the Redford movie, is quick to point out that his shop's back door was also in the film, as the front door of the town's newspaper office.

Next is the village of Trampas, founded in 1751. Turn right on winding NM 75, then left on NM 518 to Talpa and on to Rancho de Taos, site of the famous San Francisco de Asis church. Turn right on NM 68 to Taos.

Dining and Lodging

Dining **Rancho de Chimayo** is where aficionados of northern New Mexican cooking go to find the very best of it. Set in a century-old adobe hacienda tucked into the mountains, with white-washed walls and hand-stripped vigas, cozy dining rooms, and lush, terraced patios, the Rancho de Chimayo is still owned and operated by the family who originally occupied the house. They use locally grown products and recipes that are generations old. (On sale at the cash register and in bookstores everywhere is the new *Rancho de Chimayo Cookbook*, which celebrates native New Mexican fare.) There's a roaring fireplace in the winter and summer dining al fresco. *NM 520, tel. 505/984–2100. Reservations advised. Jacket and tie advised. AE, DC, MC, V. Closed Mon. during the winter. Inexpensive.*

Lodging **Hacienda de Chimayo.** Across the street from the Rancho de Chimayo restaurant and owned by the same people is the Hacienda de Chimayo, more of a country inn than a bed-and-breakfast (though a Continental breakfast is served). Its rooms are all decorated with turn-of-the-century antiques, and each has a private bath and a fireplace. The lovely mountain setting and the charming furnishings make this a delightful place to stay. *NM 520, tel. 505/351–2222. 6 rooms, 1 suite. AE, DC, MC, V. Moderate.*

4 Taos

Introduction

Mysterious, spiritual, and ageless, Taos is an enchanted town of soft lines and delineations that once viewed will remain etched in the mind forever. Romantic courtyards, stately elms and cottonwood trees, narrow streets, and the profusion of adobe all add to its timeless appeal.

Just as layers of history can be read on the rock walls of the 650-foot-deep Rio Grande Gorge, carved into the otherwise table-flat landscape just west of Taos, so, too, are layers of history revealed in the town itself. The tawny-colored one- and two-story adobe buildings that line the two-centuries-old Plaza reveal the influence of Native American and Spanish settlers. Overhanging balconies supported by slender beams were added later by American pioneers who came west after the Mexican War of 1846. Many of the roads extending from the Plaza are still unpaved today; when it rains, they're not unlike the rutted streets of yesteryear. Taos is actually three towns in one.

The Taos Pueblo, 2 miles north of the commercial center of Taos, is the home of the Taos-Tiwa Indians, whose apartment-house-style pueblo dwelling is one of the oldest continually inhabited communities in the United States. Life here predates Marco Polo's 13th-century travels in China and the arrival of the Spanish in America in 1540. The northernmost of the 19 Pueblo Indian settlements scattered throughout the Rio Grande Valley, Taos Pueblo is now the home of some 200 of the more than 2,000 members of the reservation (most of whom live in fully modern homes elsewhere on the pueblo's 102,000 acres). It retains much of its rich cultural heritage, as exemplified by the soft, flowing lines of the dramatic architecture and in the seasonal dances performed on the open plaza. The Taos Pueblo has no electricity, no telephones (except at the visitors' center), and no plumbing; water is carried by bucket from the crystal-clear stream that rushes through the pueblo's center. A sign reading "Please, No Wading" warns thoughtless tourists away from this sacred river, the pueblo's only source of drinking water. Unlike many Native American tribes that were forced to relocate to government-designated reservations, the Taos Pueblo Indians have resided at the base of the 12,282-foot-high Taos Mountain for centuries, remaining a link between prehistoric inhabitants who originally lived in the Taos Valley and their descendants who reside there now.

Ranchos de Taos, located four miles south of town, presents a separate and distinct face. This adobe-housed farming and ranching community, settled by the Spanish centuries ago, has one of the most beautiful churches in the Southwest. The San Francisco de Asis Church, with its massive, buttressed adobe walls and graceful towers, is a revered sanctuary to local parishioners, as well as a prime example of Early Mission architecture. Its graveyard, or *campo santo*, is one of the most photographed in the country, its beauty surpassed only by the church's wealth of religious artifacts and paintings. The church is the focal point of St. Francis Plaza, where a number of picturesque shops and galleries are located.

And so here at the point where the sky meets the mountains, the three different faces of Taos merge—the town itself, the Taos Pueblo, and the Ranchos de Taos—with a combined population of fewer than 4,000, in that magnificent 6,950-foot-high plateau setting. In many ways Taos is still very much a frontier town. In the dry summer months, dust covers everything, affording the place a comfortably worn, weathered look.

Essential Information

Important Addresses and Numbers

Tourist Information Brochures, maps, a calendar of events, and general information are available from the **Taos County Chamber of Commerce** (229 Paseo del Pueblo Sur, Post Office Drawer 1, Taos 87571, tel. 505/758–3873 or 800/732–8267 outside NM). Its Visitor's Information Center, located two blocks south of the Plaza on Paseo del Pueblo Sur, is open 9 AM–6 PM daily during the summer months, 9 AM–5 PM daily during the rest of the year.

Emergencies **Fire, medical,** or **police** (tel. 911). **Taos police** (tel. 505/758–2216), **state police** (tel. 505/758–8878).

Ambulance (tel. 505/758–1911).

Hospital emergency room: Holy Cross Hospital (Paseo del Pueblo Sur, tel. 505/758–8883).

Late-Night Pharmacies **Taos Pharmacy** (S. Santa Fe Rd., tel. 505/758–3342); **Revco Discount Drug Center** (1102 Paseo del Pueblo Sur, tel. 505/758–9891); **Rick's Pharmacy** (Pioneer Rd., Red River, tel. 505/754–2489); **Springer's Drug** (8254 Springer, tel. 505/483–2356).

Arriving and Departing by Plane

Airport The **Taos Municipal Airport** (U.S. 64, tel. 505/758–4995), 12 miles west of the city, is a low-traffic, low-density facility with a 5,800-foot runway. It services only private air charters. The closest major airport is in Albuquerque, 2½ hours south of Taos.

Charter Airlines For air-charter information, call 505/758–4995.

Between the Airport and Downtown *By Limousine* **Taos Limo** (Box 1351, Taos 87571, tel. 505/758–3524) offers long- and short-stretch limousine service between Taos and Albuquerque airports and into town, as well as to the ski areas and anywhere else within the "Enchanted Circle" region of northern New Mexico, with fares calculated at $35 per hour (two-hour minimum).

By Bus **Pride of Taos** (tel. 505/758–8340) offers daily shuttle service to the Albuquerque Airport ($25 one-day, $45 round-trip).

By Taxi **Faust's Tours** (Box Q, N. Hwy. 3, in nearby El Prado, tel. 505/758–3410 or 505/758–7359) offers radio-dispatched taxis between the Taos airport and town. The cost is around $5.

Arriving and Departing by Car, Train, and Bus

By Car The main route from Santa Fe to Taos is NM 68. From points north, take NM 522; from points east or west, take NM 64. Roads can be treacherously icy during the winter months; call New Mexico Road Conditions (tel. 800/432–4269) before heading out. The altitude in Taos will affect your car's performance, causing it to "gasp" because it's getting too much gas and not enough air.

By Bus **Texas, New Mexico, Oklahoma Coaches** (a subsidiary of Greyhound/Trailways) runs buses once a day from Albuquerque to the Taos Bus Station (corner of Paseo del Pueblo Sur and Paseo del Canyon, tel. 505/758–1144).

By Train **Amtrak** (tel. 800/872–7245) provides service into Lamy Station (County Rd. 41, Lamy 87500) half an hour outside Santa Fe, the closest train station to Taos. **Faust's Tours** (Box Q, N. Hwy. 3, in nearby El Prado, tel. 505/758–3410 or 505/758–7359) offers radio-dispatched taxis to the train station.

Getting Around Taos

Taos, like Santa Fe, radiates around its famous central Plaza and is easily maneuvered by foot. And, like Santa Fe, it has a La Fonda Hotel directly on the Plaza, although the two hotels have no official affiliation. Since the Plaza is the city's prime location, many of the top restaurants, stores, boutiques, and galleries are all on or within its immediate vicinity. The main street through town is Paseo del Pueblo Norte, which turns into Paseo del Pueblo Sur. All the major hotels have ample parking space, and parking areas can be easily found just beyond the Plaza (though space may be tight during the peak summer months). To reach many of the sights of interest outside town, transportation will be necessary.

Car Rentals **Hertz Rent-A-Car** is located on Santa Fe Road (tel. 505/758–1668); **Jeep Trailways Rentals** is at Alpine Lodge, Red River (tel. 505/754–6443); and **Rich Ford Rent-A-Car** is located at the Taos Municipal Airport (tel. 505/758–9501).

By Bus **The Pride of Taos** (tel. 505/758–8340) provides pickups and drop-offs to various points within town. The cost is $5 for the first passenger, $2 for each additional passenger.

By Taxi Taxi service is sparse. However, **Faust's Tours** (Box Q, N. Hwy. 3, in nearby El Prado, tel. 505/758–3410 or 505/758–7359) has a fleet of radio-dispatched cabs.

Opening and Closing Times

Banks, weekdays 9–5; museums, daily 9:30–5:30; stores, daily 9 or 10–5 or 6; post office, weekdays 9–5.

Guided Tours

Orientation **Alpine Air Tourist** (Jackson Hotel Rd., Angel Fire 87710, tel. 505/377–3072) offers bird's-eye-view tours of the Enchanted Circle region. **Pride of Taos Tours** (Box 1192, Taos 87571, tel. 505/758–8340) provides narrated 45-minute trolleylike bus tours of Taos highlights, including the San Francisco de Asis Mission Church that Georgia O'Keeffe painted, the Martinez Hacienda that portrays Spanish colonial life in the 17th and 18th centuries, and Kit Carson's House and Museum near the Plaza. Cost: $5. The departure point for tours, shuttles, and pickups is next to the Chamber of Commerce office on Paseo del Pueblo Sur.

Special-Interest Tours **Native Sons Adventures** (813A Paseo del Sur, tel. 505/758–9342) organizes biking, backpacking, rafting, and snowmobiling expeditions. **Roadrunner Tours** (Box 274, Angel Fire, tel. 505/377–6416) is run by Nancy and Bill Burch, who offer horseback,

jeep, snowmobile, and ski rentals. **Taos Indian Horse Ranch**
(Taos Pueblo, tel. 505/758–3212 or 800/659–3210) features old-
fashioned horse-drawn sleigh rides through the Taos Pueblo
backcountry, winter weather permitting, complete with brass
bells, an Indian storyteller, marshmallows, and green chili
roasts. Escorted horseback tours and hayrides are run through
Indian-held lands during the remainder of the year. (By reservation only. No liquor permitted.)

Walking Tours   **Taos Historic Walking Tours** (Box 2466, Taos 87571, tel. 505/
758–3861) covers all the historically famous homes and sites in a
one-hour tour of the city.

Exploring Taos

Orientation

Taos is a year-round destination. Its fabulous ski slopes beckon
in the wintertime, and summer brings a flood of tourists, both
longtime regulars and newcomers who have heard or read
about the enchanting little town in northern New Mexico and
want to see it for themselves. Situated on a rolling mesa at the
base of the rugged Sangre de Cristo Mountains, where lofty
peaks rise to well over 10,000 feet, Taos has more than enough
attractions to stand on its own and is worth more than a day trip
out of Santa Fe. This adobe-walled town, with its intrinsically
rustic charm, is a world-famous art and literary center, bringing both artists and collectors to the many museums and galleries surrounding the historical Plaza. Another of its primary
draws is that it is a tricultural community, with strong Native
American, Spanish, and Anglo influences. A visit to the Taos
Pueblo north of town is a good introduction to the centuries-old
culture of the Pueblo Indians. Restored haciendas and the famous San Francisco de Asis Church to the south of the Plaza
reflect Taos's strong Spanish heritage. There are also numerous sights of interest outside Taos proper, including the
Enchanted Circle, the Rio Grande Gorge, and the haunts of
well-known Taos personalities, such as D. H. Lawrence and
Georgia O'Keeffe.

Highlights for First-time Visitors

Blumenschein Home (*see* Tour 1)
D. H. Lawrence Shrine (*see* Tour 4)
Historical Plaza Area (*see* Tour 1)
Kit Carson Museum (*see* Tour 1)
Martinez Hacienda (*see* Tour 3)
Millicent Rogers Museum (*see* Tour 4)
Ranchos de Taos and the San Francisco de Asis Church
(*see* Tour 3)
Taos Pueblo (*see* Tour 2)

Tour 1: The Plaza Tour

*Numbers in the margin correspond to points of interest on the
Taos map.*

❶ **The Taos Plaza** bears only a hint of the grace, dignity, and
stateliness of the Plaza in Santa Fe, although its history is
drawn with the same pen. The first Europeans to appear in the

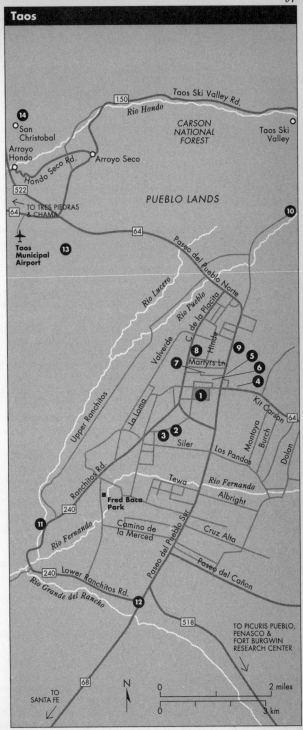

Taos

Taos Valley were led by Captain Alvarado, who was exploring
the area for the 1540 Coronado Expedition. Don Juan de Onate,
the official colonizer of the province of Nuevo Mexico, arrived in
Taos in July 1598. An established mission, trading arrangements with the Taos Pueblo Indians, and abundant water and
timber attracted early Spanish settlers. Because of the many
fires that plagued the city, none of the buildings on the Plaza
predates the 19th century. At the center of the Plaza, the U.S.
flag flies night and day, as authorized by a special act of Con-
gress in recognition of Kit Carson's heroic stand, when he and
his men stood guard over the flag to protect it from Confederate sympathizers during the Civil War. A covered gazebo, donated by heiress and longtime Taos resident Mabel Dodge
Luhan, contains Tio Vivo, an antique carousel that delights
children when it's put into operation during summer fiestas
(three days per year in late July during the Fiestas de Santiago
Y Santa Ana). Tickets are 50¢ per ride.

A walking tour of historic Taos begins logically enough on the
Plaza, with its many smart shops and galleries. Upstairs in the
Burke Armstrong Gallery (121 N. Plaza, tel. 505/758–9016), you
can see the renowned Taos Murals, 10 frescoes painted by early
Taos artists, including several founding members of the Taos
Society of Artists. The gallery building was the original Taos
Old County Courthouse. Inside is the jail cell used in the movie
Easy Rider. On the south side of the Plaza, don't miss the extraordinary **La Fonda de Taos Hotel,** with all its eccentric
charm. For an admission fee of $1, you can enter the manager's
office and view the erotic paintings done by author D. H. Lawrence. The paintings were banned in London, as were many of
the author's books. Hardly scandalous by today's standards,
the paintings are certainly worth a visit for anyone with more
than a passing interest in Lawrence and his work.

Next, take a detour off the southeast corner of the Plaza to
Ledoux Street, where a number of historic adobe buildings can
❷ be explored. Two blocks from the Plaza is the **Blumenschein
Home,** a fully restored, original adobe masterpiece. Ernest L.
Blumenschein was the cofounder of the Taos Society of Artists,
an art colony that flourished from 1912 to 1920. His paintings
and those of his talented wife, Mary Green Blumenschein, and
their daughter, Helen, are on display inside, along with works
of other Taos artists. Blending the sophistication of European
charm with the beauty of classic adobe, the house is furnished
with handmade Taos furniture, as well as European antiques
and artifacts gathered by the artist and his family from all over
the world. The house creates a colorful picture of the life of the
early Taos Society of Artists. *13 Ledoux St., tel. 505/758–0505.
Admission: $3 adults, $2.50 children and senior citizens. Open
daily 9–5. Note: A family ticket is available for $6, admitting
parents and three children under 16. Also, a special combination can be purchased for $7 adults, $5 for children and senior
citizens, that permits admission to the Blumenschein Home,
as well as to the Kit Carson Home and the Martinez Hacienda,
all part of Kit Carson Historic Museums of Taos, a private,
nonprofit organization.*

❸ Farther along Ledoux Street is the **Harwood Foundation Library and Museum,** the former home of Burt C. Harwood, a
member of the original Taos art colony. On display are more
than 100 paintings by early and modern Taos artists, plus rare

santos (saints) carvings done by early Spanish wood carvers—almost all from the private collection of Taos art patron Mabel Dodge Luhan. This is where the Museum of Taos Art exhibits and researches the art, artists, and history of Taos County. It's also the site of the Taos Public Library, which house an excellent collection of volumes on the Southwest, Western and Native American art, and volumes by and about D. H. Lawrence. *238 Ledoux St., tel. 505/758–3063 (library), 505/758–9826 (museum). Admission free. Library open Mon., Thurs., Fri. 10–8, Tues.–Wed. 10–5, Sat. 10–4; museum open weekdays noon–5, Sat. 10–4.*

Time Out Stop off at nearby Guadalupe Plaza to visit the unique shops and galleries and perhaps stop for an espresso or tea at **La Luz Blanca Gallery/Cafe** (118B Calle La Dona Luz, tel. 505/758–7460). If you just want to rest your feet, head for the peaceful garden behind the Harwood Museum.

If you head east from the Plaza across the intersection of Paseo del Norte and Paseo del Pueblo Sur, you'll find more fine shops, some of the best in town. Here, too, is the **Kit Carson Museum,** once home of the famous mountain man and scout who left an indelible mark on the history of Taos. Carson purchased the 12-room adobe home in 1843 as a wedding gift for his young bride, Josefa Jaramillo, the beautiful daughter of a powerful and politically influential Mexican family. Josefa was 14 when Carson, dashing in dun-colored buckskins with long fringes and colorful beadwork, began courting her; he was 32 and already twice married. The couple lived in the house for more than 25 years. Three of the rooms are furnished as they were when the Carson family lived here, offering a glimpse of Taos's rich and colorful history. The rest of the museum is devoted to gun and mountain-man exhibits, as well as to Native American, Spanish, and early Taos antiques, artifacts, and manuscripts. In the patio outside, the Carson House Shop has four rooms filled with gifts and collectibles, Native American art, folk art, jewelry, kachinas, and handcrafted furniture. *Kit Carson Rd., tel. 505/758–0505. Admission: $3 adults, $2.50 children and senior citizens, family and combination tickets are available (see Blumenschein Home, above). Open early Oct.–mid-June, daily 9–5; mid-June–Sept., daily 8–6.*

Back at the intersection of Paseo del Norte and Paseo del Pueblo Sur, turn right and walk to the **Taos Inn,** a historical landmark and the site of the original town well, now a fountain in the hotel lobby. Next door to the Taos Inn is the **Stables Art Center,** the visual arts gallery of the Taos Art Association. The association purchased the handsome adobe building, formerly a private home, in 1952. It was in the stables in back of the house that the association first began exhibiting the work of members and of invited nonmember artists from all over northern New Mexico—thus the gallery's name. The main building was once the home of Arthur Manby, a recluse who gained considerable notoriety by securing himself behind barred doors and snarling guard dogs for most of his 30 years in Taos. The Stables presents changing exhibits almost monthly; all the artwork is for sale. There's also a gift shop, and the Clay and Fiber Gallery (*see* Shopping, below) is next door. *133 Paseo del Pueblo Norte, Taos 87571, tel. 505/758–2036. Admission free. Open Mon.–Sat. 9–5, Sun. noon–5.*

Leaving the Stables, cross Paseo del Pueblo Norte and you'll be on Bent Street, one of the town's major shopping venues, lined **6** with attractive galleries and boutiques. The **John Dunn House** (124A Bent St., no tel.) was the onetime homestead of a notorious Taos gambler and entrepreneur, who founded the town's first transportation company. It contains a number of interesting shops, including G. Robinson Old Prints and Maps and Moby Dickens, a popular and eclectic bookstore and prime gathering spot for the local literati (*see* Shopping, below). Also **7** on this small street is the **Governor Bent Museum.** In 1846, when New Mexico became a United States territory during the Mexican War, Charles Bent, an early trader, trapper, and mountain man, was appointed governor. A year later he was killed in his house by an angry mob protesting New Mexico's annexation by the United States. The well-kept adobe building where Bent lived is filled with his family's possessions, furniture, and Western Americana. Governor Bent was married to Maria Ignacia, older sister of Kit Carson's wife, Josefa Jaramillo. *117 Bent St., tel. 505/758–2376. Admission: $1 adults, 50¢ children. Open daily 10–5.*

Two blocks north of Bent Street on the corner of Armory Street and Placitas Road is the Taos Volunteer Fire Department, **8** home of the **Firehouse Collection.** More than 100 paintings by Taos artists, including some of the town's most famous—Joseph Sharp, Ernest Blumenschein, Bert Phillips, and others—are on display. The paintings are exhibited in the Fire Department's meeting hall, adjoining the station house, where five fire engines are maintained at the ready. An antique fire engine is housed here as well. *323 Placitas Rd., Box 4591, Taos 87571, tel. 505/758–3386. Admission free. Open weekdays 9–4.*

If you head east from the Firehouse back to Paseo del Pueblo Norte, and turn left, you'll come to the wooded, 20-acre **Kit Carson Park,** two blocks farther on. Kit Carson's grave is located here, marked with a *cerquita*, a spiked wrought-iron rectangular fence, traditionally used to outline and protect gravesites. Mabel Dodge Luhan, the art patron and longtime guiding light of the Taos social scene, is also buried in the same small graveyard.

9 A short walk north is the **Fechin Institute,** housed in a traditional Southwestern adobe house with a Russian-style interior. Filled with extraordinary hand-carved doors, windows, and gates, the home was built in 1928 by artist Nicolai Fechin, a Russian émigré who arrived in Taos one year earlier. Fechin designed the extraordinary house, with its exotic handcarved architectural motifs and Russian furnishings, to showcase his daringly colorful portraits and landscapes. Listed in the National Register of Historic Places, the Fechin Institute hosts annual exhibits and special workshops devoted to the artist's unique approach to learning, teaching, and creativity. *227 Paseo del Pueblo Norte, tel. 505/758–1710. Admission: $3 donation suggested. Open May–Oct., Wed.–Sun. 1:30–5:30, or by appointment.*

Tour 2: The Taos Pueblo

Three miles north of town, driving on Paseo del Pueblo Norte, **10** you'll come to Taos's number one tourist attraction, the **Taos Pueblo.** For nearly 1,000 years, the Taos-Tiwa Indians have lived at or near the present pueblo site. The northernmost of New Mexico's 19 Indian pueblos, it is the largest existing multistory pueblo structure in the United States. Continuously inhabited for centuries, it holds within its mud-and-straw adobe walls—frequently several feet thick—a way of life little changed by the passage of time. Two separate buildings rise in earthy magnificence, containing many individual homes built side by side and in layers, with common walls but no connecting doorways. (Because there were neither doors nor windows, access to the dwellings was gained only from the top, via ladders that were retrieved after entering.) Small buildings and corrals are scattered about. The two main buildings, Hlauuma (north house) and Hlaukwima (south house), separated by a creek, are believed to be of a similar age, most likely constructed between AD 1000 and 1450.

The pueblo today appears much as it did when the first Spanish explorers arrived in New Mexico in 1540: Seeing the golden shades of its smooth adobe walls, the conquistadores thought they had discovered one of the fabled Seven Cities of Gold. The outside surfaces are continuously maintained by replastering with thin layers of mud, and the interior walls frequently are coated with thin washes of white earth to keep them clean and bright. The roofs of each of the five stories are supported by large timbers—*vigas*—hauled down from the mountain forests. Rotted vigas are replaced as needed. Smaller pieces of wood—pine or aspen *latillas*—are placed side by side between the vigas; the entire roof is then packed with dirt.

Tribal ritual allows no electricity or running water within the pueblo, where approximately 200 Taos Indians live full time. Some 2,000 others live in conventional homes on the pueblo's land, which extends over 95,000 acres, television antennas poking out from above the roofs. Inside the pueblo, the traditional Native American way of life has endured even after 400 years of Spanish and Anglo presence. The crystal-clear waters of the Rio Pueblo de Taos, originating high above in the mountains at the sacred Blue Lake, still serve as the primary source of drinking water and irrigation. Bread is still baked in outdoor domed ovens, a system unchanged for centuries. Artisans of the Taos Pueblo produce handcrafted wares by using techniques that have been passed down through the generations; the mica-flecked pottery and silver jewelry made in the pueblo are sold at many of the individually owned curio shops within the compound. Great hunters, the Taos Indians are also renowned for their work with animal skins, creating excellent moccasins, boots, and drums.

The pueblo dwellers are about 90% Catholic, but practice their religion alongside ancient Indian religious rites that remain an important part of life in the Taos Pueblo. This combination derives from a concession often made by the Spanish missionaries, who were anxious to convert the "pagan savages." A costumed Indian deer dancer in full regalia often comes thumping down the church aisle during or immediately after the celebration of the Catholic mass. The striking adobe Church of San Geronimo (Saint Jerome, the patron saint of the Taos Pueblo) on the pueblo grounds was completed in 1850 to replace a church that was destroyed by the U.S. Army in 1847 during the Mexican War. With its graceful flowing lines, arched portal, and twin bell towers, the church is a popular subject of photographers and artists (but, please, no photographs inside).

While many religious activities are restricted to tribal members, the public is invited to witness certain ceremonial dances. These include the following: January 1, Turtle Dance; January 6, Buffalo or Deer Dance; May 3, Feast of Santa Cruz–Foot Race and Corn Dance; June 13, Feast of San Antonio–Corn Dance; June 24, Feast of San Juan–Corn Dance; July (2nd weekend), Taos Pueblo Powwow; July 25 and 26, Feast of Santa Ana and Santiago–Corn Dance; September 29–30, Feast of San Geronimo–Sunset Dance; Christmas Eve, Procession; Christmas Day, Deer Dance or Matachines. While there is no charge for general admission to the Taos Pueblo, certain rules must be observed. These include respecting the "restricted area" signs that protect the privacy of pueblo residents and sites of native religious practices; not entering private homes or opening any doors not clearly labeled as curio shops; not photographing tribal members without asking permission; not entering the cemetery grounds; and not wading in the Rio Pueblo de Taos, the community's sole source of drinking water. *Taos Pueblo, Box 1846, Taos 87571, tel. 505/758–9593. Tourist fees: $5 per vehicle (for parking), $10 for tour buses (plus $1 per passenger, 50¢ for students); $5 for a still-camera permit, $10 for a movie-camera permit, artist's sketching fee $15, and artist's painting fee $35. Open daily 8–5:30, except during funerals or religious ceremonies not open to the public.*

Time Out   When you're ready for a quick snack, look for the "Fry Bread" signs on individual dwellings. You can enter the kitchen and enjoy fresh fry bread—bread dough that is flattened and deep fried until it's puffy and golden brown and then topped with honey or powdered sugar—and a cup of coffee while watching the Indian women cook.

Tour 3: The Spanish Colonial Heritage

In Taos, one quickly steps into the town's rich Spanish past with a visit to the outstanding Hacienda Martinez Museum and the cherished, oft-photographed and -painted Ranchos de Taos.

Two miles south of Taos Plaza, on Ranchitos Road (NM 240), is ⑪ **La Hacienda de Don Antonio Severino Martinez,** one of the only fully restored Spanish Colonial adobe haciendas open to the public in New Mexico. The fortlike building, on the banks of the Rio Pueblo, served as the Martinez family's home and a community refuge against Comanche and Apache raids. With massive adobe walls and no exterior windows, the hacienda has 21 rooms surrounding two courtyards. Magnificently restored period rooms illustrate the lifestyle of the Spanish Colonial era, when the only supplies to Taos came by ox-cart on the Camino Real over the "Journey of Death." Built in progressive additions between 1804 and 1827 by Severino Martinez, the house gives testimony to the pure, rich Spanish heritage that survived the rugged colonial conditions and remains to this day. Padre Antonio José Martinez, Severino's son, became a famous leader of his people and founder of *El Crepusculo* (The Dawn), possibly the first newspaper published west of the Mississippi.

Along with the room diplays, the fortresslike house is also used for changing exhibits on Spanish culture and history and photography shows. In addition, there's a working blacksmith's shop, and other living history. In late September the hacienda hosts the annual Old Taos Trade Fair, which reenacts the fall trading fairs of the 1820s, when Plains Indians and trappers came to trade with Spanish and Pueblo Indians in Taos. The two-day event includes traditional crafts demonstrations, native foods, entertainment, traditional-style caravans, and music. *Ranchitos Rd. (NM 240), tel. 505/758–0505. Admission: $3 adults, $2.50 children and senior citizens. Family and combination tickets are available (see Blumenschein Home, above). Open daily 9–5.*

Four miles east of the Martinez Hacienda on Ranchitos Road **⓬** (NM 240) is **Ranchos de Taos** (on NM 68), an adobe-house Spanish Colonial ranching and farming community. An early home of Taos Indians, it was settled by Spaniards in 1716. The centerpiece of Ranchos de Taos is the monumental adobe masterpiece, the **San Francisco de Asis Church,** first built in the 18th century as a spiritual and physical refuge from raiding Apaches, Utes, and Comanches. In a state of deterioration, the church was rebuilt by community volunteers in 1979, using traditional adobe bricks. It's a spectacular example of adobe Mission architecture, and the shapes and shadows of the walls and supporting bulwarks have inspired generations of painters and photographers, including Georgia O'Keeffe, Paul Strand, and Ansel Adams. If you've got a camera handy and want to try it yourself, late afternoon offers the best exposure of the heavily buttressed rear of the church, while morning is best for the front. Bells in the church's twin belfries call faithful Taoseños to services on Sunday and holidays, when worshipers fill the church to overflowing.

In the parish hall nearby, a 15-minute slide presentation explains the history and restoration of the church, and the famous mystery painting, *Shadow of the Cross*, may be seen throughout the day. In the evening the shadow of a cross, which isn't there during the daylight hours, appears over Christ's shoulder. Scientific studies made on the canvas and the paint pigments cannot explain the phenomenon. *Ranchos de Taos, tel. 505/758–2754. Admission free. Open Mon.–Sat. 9–4, on Sun. and holy days during church services: Sun. Mass 7 AM (in Spanish), 9 AM, and 11:30 AM.*

Many of the old adobe homes around Ranchos Plaza now house shops, restaurants, and galleries, including the **Hacienda de San Francisco Galeria** (4 St. Francis Plaza, tel. 505/758–0477), with its collection of fine Spanish Colonial antiques and sculptured bronzes by such masters as Mexico's Francisco Zuniga.

Time Out   **Pilgrim's Rest** (tel. 505/758–9045), a coffee-and-pastry shop on the historic church plaza, is a good place to cool your heels. For a more substantial meal, try **Andy's La Fiesta Restaurant** (*see* Dining, below).

Tour 4: Artistic and Literary Taos

If you have time to visit only one museum in Taos, make it the **⓭** **Millicent Rogers Museum,** 4 miles north of the Plaza, just off

NM 522 (turn left at the blinking light and follow the signs to the museum). Founded in 1953, it contains more than 5,000 pieces of Native American and Hispanic art, the core of Standard Oil heiress Millicent Rogers's private lifetime collection. The granddaughter of Henry Huddleson Rogers, one of John D. Rockefeller's partners in the Standard Oil Company and founder of Anaconda Copper and U.S. Steel, she visited New Mexico in 1947 and, like many others, fell in love with the country and its people. A woman of keen intellect and artistic talent, she became intently interested in the area's culture and art. She gathered baskets, blankets, rugs, jewelry, kachina dolls, santos, carvings, and paintings, a collection that remains unsurpassed of its kind to this day. A recent acquisition of major importance is the pottery and ceramics of Maria Martinez and members of the famous San Ildefonso family of potters. The museum's Hispanic collection, including recently acquired rare pieces of religious and secular artifacts, is equally impressive. Missing, of course, is the presence of Millicent Rogers herself, a striking beauty with a flair for fashion and a love of costumes. A debutante in the heyday of the Jazz Age, she was tall, with a perfectly proportioned figure, a born "clothes horse" with long, painted nails, wide-set eyes, and alabaster skin. Married three times, she numbered among her suitors Clark Gable, Serge Obolensky, Ian Fleming, and James Forrestal. Many of her costumes and jewelry designs are included in the museum's holdings. The Millicent Rogers Museum features permanent and changing exhibits, guided tours on request, and a gift shop, as well as educational activities such as field trips, lectures, films, workshops, and demonstrations. *Box A, Taos 87571, tel. 505/758–2462, fax 505/758–5751. Admission: $3 adults, $2 senior citizens, $1 children (6–16), $6 family groups. Open daily 9–5, except major holidays.*

Leaving the Millicent Rogers Museum, follow NM 522 north for **14** 10 miles, and you'll reach the **D. H. Lawrence Ranch** and the **D. H. Lawrence Shrine.** The noted British author lived in Taos only briefly, about 22 months over a three-year period between 1922 and 1925. He and his wife, Frieda, arrived in Taos at the behest of Mabel Dodge Luhan, who collected famous writers and artists the way some people collect butterflies. Dodge provided them with a place to live, Kiowa Ranch, on 160 acres in the mountains north of Taos. Rustic and remote, it's now known as the D. H. Lawrence Ranch, although Lawrence never actually owned it. Nearby is the smaller cabin where Dorothy Brett, the tagalong companion of the Lawrences, stayed while traveling with the couple. The houses, now owned by the University of New Mexico, are not open to the public. The D. H. Lawrence Shrine, nearby at the end of a step walk on wooded Lobo Mountain, can be visited, however. A small white shedlike structure, it is simple and unimposing. The writer fell ill while visiting France and died in a sanitarium there in 1930. Five years later, his wife, subsequently married in Italy to Angelo Ravagli, had Lawrence's body disinterred, cremated, and brought back to Taos. Frieda Lawrence is buried, as was her wish, in front of the shrine. *Hwy. 522, Box 190, San Cristobal 87564, tel. 505/776–2245. Admission free. The D. H. Lawrence Shrine is open daily.*

Tour 5: The Enchanted Circle

Numbers in the margin correspond to points of interest on the Taos Environs: The Enchanted Circle map.

No visit to northern New Mexico is complete without experiencing the 90-mile day trip through the Enchanted Circle, a breathtaking panorama of deep canyons, passes, alpine valleys, and towering mountains of the verdant Carson National Forest. It's a journey that in many ways will take you into another century. This tour can easily be combined with Tour 4, above. Both the D. H. Lawrence Ranch and the Millicent Rogers Museum are on the loop.

Traveling east from Taos along U.S. 64, you'll soon be winding your way through Taos Canyon, climbing toward 9,000-foot-high Palo Flechado Pass (Pass of the Arrow). On the opposite side of the pass are stunning vistas—Moreno Valley, and the towns of Angel Fire and Eagle Nest. Now known primarily as a

① ski resort, **Angel Fire** was for hundreds of years little more than a long, empty valley, the fall meeting grounds of the Ute Indians. The name derives from the glow that covers the mountain in the late autumn and early winter. It began to develop as a resort in the early 1970s and is fast becoming one of the most comprehensive resort areas in New Mexico. Here you'll find the stunning Vietnam Veterans Memorial, a 50-foot-high gull wing–shaped monument built in 1971 by D. Victor Whetphall, whose son David was killed in that war. The memorial's textured surface captures the constantly changing sunlight of the New Mexican mountains, vividly changing its colors throughout the daylight hours as the sun moves across the sky. It's on the north side of U.S. 64, 8½ miles southwest of Eagle Nest.

② At **Eagle Nest,** a tiny village surrounded by thousands of acres of national forest, you'll get on to U.S. 38 and head over Bobcat

③ Pass (just under 10,000 feet elevation) to **Red River,** another major ski resort, with 33 trails and a bustling little downtown community filled with shops and sportswear boutiques. Red River came into being as a miner's boom town in the last century, taking its name from the river whose mineral content gave it a rich, rosy color. When the gold petered out, Red River died, only to be rediscovered in the 1920s by tourists who were escaping the dust bowl. Situated at 8,750 feet above sea level at the base of Wheeler Peak (New Mexico's tallest mountain), Red River is the highest, if not the loftiest, town in the state. Much of the Old West flavor remains in Red River, with Main Street shoot-outs, a genuine melodrama, and plenty of square dancing and two-stepping. In fact, because of its many country dances and festivals, Red River is affectionately called "The New Mexico Home of the Texas Two-Step."

④ From Red River, the Enchanted Circle heads west to **Questa** (which means "hill" in Spanish), a town settled in the 1840s with considerable difficulty because of Indian raids. In 1870, it was officially established—as were many western towns—with the opening of its first post office; to date, Questa has had only six postmasters. Don't miss St. Anthony's Church, built of adobe with 5-foot-thick walls and viga ceilings. The Red River Trout Hatchery (*see* Taos for Free, below) is also worth a visit. Known as the "Heart of the Sangre de Cristo Mountains," Questa is a small, quiet village, nestled between Taos and the Red River amid some of the most beautiful mountain country in

Taos Environs: The Enchanted Circle

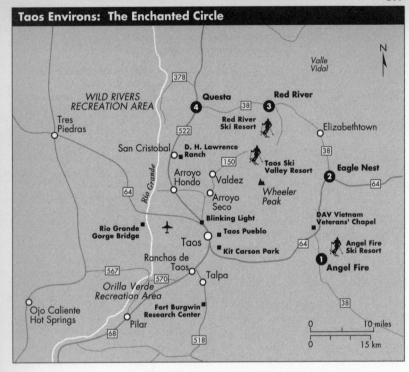

New Mexico. Turning left at downtown Questa's main intersection, you're on your way back to Taos on NM 522, passing through the picturesque communities of San Cristobal and Arroyo Hondo. It's on this last stretch that you can stop and visit the D. H. Lawrence Ranch or the Millicent Rogers Museum, both off NM 522.

Time Out In Red River, stop by the **Sundance** (High St., tel. 505/754–2971) for Mexican food or **Texas Red's Steakhouse** (Main St., tel. 505/754–2964) for steaks, chops, burgers, or chicken. If you want to stay overnight, try the **Red River Lodge** (Box 818, Red River 87558, tel. 505/754–2988), which has 20 moderately priced rooms, hot tubs in the winter, and picnic tables in the summer.

Taos for Free

Taos is a major art center, so it's not surprising that many of the town's major free attractions involve, and evolve from, an appreciation of art. Visitors are welcome to browse through more than 80 art galleries (indeed, in some cases, they may even be pulled in off the street to do so) and to enjoy a number of major museum exhibits free of charge. These exhibits include the Harwood Foundation, the Firehouse Collection, and the Stables Art Center (*see* Tour 1, above). The Taos Inn (tel. 505/758–2233) sponsors a free Meet the Artist Series in spring (mid-May–mid-June) and again in fall (mid-Oct.–mid-Dec.) every Tuesday and Thursday evening at 8 PM. This is a unique opportunity to have one-on-one contact with nationally known artists who are residing in Taos. Another major free attraction is the magnificent San Francisco de Asis Mission Church in Ranchos de Taos (*see* Tour 3, above).

In Questa, about 20 miles north of Taos (at the end of NM 515), the **Red River Trout Hatchery** offers a fascinating look at how the king of freshwater fish is hatched, reared, stocked, and controlled. There's a visitors' center with displays and exhibits, a show pond, and a machine that dispenses fish food, so you can feed the trout yourself. Self-guided tours last anywhere from 20 to 90 minutes, depending on how enraptured one becomes. Guided tours are available for groups, upon request. Parking space and a picnic area are on the grounds. *Box 410, Questa 87556, tel. 505/586–0222. Open daily 9–5.*

Fort Burgwin Research Center, 10 miles southeast of Taos on NM 518, is a restored fort that once housed the First Dragoons of the United States Cavalry (1852–60). Their function was to protect the citizens of Taos and the travelers coming and going from Santa Fe, the territorial capital, from renegade Indians. Museum displays include Native American and Spanish-American artifacts and ecological and archaeological exhibits. Operated by Southern Methodist University of Dallas, Texas, the center also conducts extension courses for its university students, particularly in theater, music, and the arts. Summer concerts, plays, and lectures are presented to the public free of charge. Call for a schedule (tel. 505/758–8322). *Box 300, Ranchos de Taos 87557, tel. 505/758–0322. Admission free. Open daily 9–5.*

What to See and Do with Children

Anyone who has children and goes to Taos without them is bound to regret it. Almost everywhere they turn, parents will find something they wish their children were there to see. The **Taos Pueblo** (*see* Tour 2, above) offers insights into a way of life that has remained virtually unchanged over the centuries. The **Kit Carson Home and Museum** and **Kit Carson Memorial Park** (*see* Tour 1, above), where Carson's grave is located, are bound to be spellbinders. In Kit Carson Park there's a playground for youngsters, picnic tables and grills, an ice-skating rink in winter, and bicycle and walking paths. **Fred Baca Park,** 2 miles west, also has tennis courts, a playground, a baseball field, and a basketball hoops. The Red River Trout Hatchery in Questa (*see* Taos for Free, above) will fascinate the younger set. And if your child is one that has to be bribed, bound, and chained before being dragged screaming and kicking into an art gallery, you may find the Firehouse Collection (*see* Tour 1, above) a painless introduction. After all, there are all those beautiful fire engines to ogle.

Off the Beaten Track

Of **Ghost Ranch/Abiquiu**, artist Georgia O'Keeffe wrote, "When I first saw the Abiquiu house it was a ruin with an adobe wall around the garden broken in a couple of places by fallen trees. As I climbed and walked about in the ruin I found a patio with a very pretty well house and a bucket to draw up water. It was a good-sized patio with a long wall with a door on one side.

That wall with a door in it was something I had to have. It took me 10 years to get it—three more years to fix the house up so I could live in it—and after that the wall with the door was painted many times." After a long history of regular visits to New Mexico and the Southwest, artist Georgia O'Keeffe moved permanently to Abiquiu, New Mexico, in 1949. The rocky desert vistas between Ghost Ranch, where O'Keeffe purchased her first home in New Mexico, and Abiquiu, 20 miles to the south, where she had her second home, are all that remain open to public scrutiny; both homes are in private hands.

Before her death in 1986 at the age of 98, O'Keeffe added special provisions in her will ensuring that the houses would never be turned into public monuments, in order to protect the land she loved so much from an onslaught of tourists. Thus a pilgrimage to O'Keeffe country, a good 60 miles east of Taos (NM 68 south of Espanola, U.S. 84 to Albiquiu; look for a dirt road off 84 marked with a cattle skull highway sign), is purely what the visitor makes of it. Ghost Ranch was originally called El Rancho de los Brujos, the Ranch of the Witches. A Spanish rancher was murdered in the sprawling adobe homestead, and the villagers believed that the voices of the female spirits who roamed there could be heard howling through the nearby canyons. Anglos shortened the name to Ghost Ranch. Possessed or not, the area remains hauntingly beautiful.

Rio Grande Gorge Bridge (west of Taos on U.S. 64) is the second highest expansion bridge in the country. Viewing the dramatic gorge, with the Rio Grande River 650 feet below, is a breathtaking experience. Hold on to your camera and eyeglasses when looking down.

Pueblos Near Taos

Picuris Pueblo. Located off NM 68, between Espanola and Taos, surrounded by the timberland of the Carson National Forest, the Picuris Pueblo operates a museum where samples of mica-flecked pottery and other crafts can be seen and purchased. The Picuris Indians once lived in large six- and seven-story dwellings similar to those still standing at the Taos Pueblo, but they were abandoned in the wake of 18th-century pueblo uprisings. Relatively isolated and a bit run down, Picuris now seems the most economically depressed of all the New Mexico pueblos. A multi-purpose building on the grounds contains the Hidden Valley Restaurant (American and Native American food) and a convenience store, the Picuris Market. Guided tours are conducted to recently excavated areas of the pueblo. Fishing, picnicking, and camping are permitted at nearby trout-stocked Pu-Na and Tu-Tah Lakes. (Fishing and overnight camping permits can be obtained at the Picuris Market.) The 270-member, Tiwa-speaking Picuris tribe governs itself as a separate tribal nation and has no treaties with any foreign country, including the United States. The pueblo's patron saint, San Lorenzo, is honored on August 10. *Box 127, Penasco 87553, tel. 505/587–2957. Admission to the pueblo is free, but a $1 fee is charged for guided tours to the ruins. Camera permits, available at the visitors' center, are required. Fees are $5 for still cameras, $10 for video or movie cameras. Open daily 8–7; the Hidden Valley restaurant is open 11:30–7.*

San Juan Pueblo. Site of the first regional Spanish settlement in 1598 (the first capital of *Nueva Espana*, New Spain), the San Juan Pueblo is situated on the confluence of the Chama River and the Rio Grande, 5 miles north of Espanola on NM 68. Headquarters of the Eight Northern Indian Pueblo Council, it has a beautiful arts center called Oke-Oweenge Arts and Crafts Cooperative where beadwork, jewelry, baskets, textiles, and the pueblo's special thick-walled red and black pottery can be purchased. One of the more picturesque of the pueblos along the Rio Grande, it has two handsome kivas and a French Romanesque–style church, built in the 19th century by Italian stonemasons who modeled it after the St. Francis Cathedral in Santa Fe. The pueblo also conducts public bingo games, and its Tewa Restaurant, near the center of the old village, is the only restaurant serving Native American specialties within the Eight Northern Pueblos. The pueblo has fishing ponds open in the spring and summer, with permits available on the sites. Its Feast Day is June 24. At Christmas, the San Juan dancers perform the Matachines Dance, a colorful adaptation of a Spanish morality play based on the conquest of Mexico. *Box 1099, San Juan 87566, tel. 505/852–4400. Admission free. Open daily. No video cameras, tape recording, or sketching allowed. Still cameras are allowed by permit ($5 per camera) which can be bought weekdays from 8 to 4:30 at the San Juan Pueblo tribal office (behind the post office).*

Shopping

When it comes to shopping, Taos is basically an extension of Santa Fe, with many of the same shops and galleries (as well as some restaurants) represented in both cities. If Taos has any edge over the capital in this regard, it's in the craftsmanship of its Spanish carvers and carpenters, whose techniques have been handed down from father to son for nearly 300 years. Complementing such skills is the work of talented young artists, who have been drawn to the town's legendary reputation as an art center and as a place of spiritual fulfillment. This energy can be seen everywhere in Taos, in the decor of buildings, in the presentation of food in restaurants and dining rooms, in the attitude and enthusiasm of the people, and in the wares that fill the galleries and showcases.

Shopping Districts

The main concentration of shops in Taos is directly on or just off the historic central Plaza. That area includes the John Dunn Boardwalk and Bent Street, running parallel to the Plaza on the north, and Kit Carson Road, extending east off the northeast corner. With plenty of municipal parking just beyond Bent Street, these shopping districts, concentrated as they are, are easy to maneuver by foot. Except for its broad open space in the center, there isn't a spare niche anywhere along the Plaza that isn't a shop or restaurant of some kind or another, from Charley's North and West, two large gift shops on the northwest corner, to the Clothes Horse on the southeast corner. It's pockets of unrelieved commercialism such as these, as appealing as they may be to some, that have critics complaining that Taos is going the way of tourist centers everywhere and is quickly losing its distinctive charm. Cheap souvenir stores and fast-food outlets are popping up everywhere, and the downtown traffic bottleneck is at times beyond comprehension.

Bent Street, happily, seems less overdone. Named in honor of New Mexico's first governor, Bent Street was long home to mountain men, traders, and artists of the Old West. The street now houses some of the finest galleries and shops in town. Kit Carson Road, named in honor of the legendary scout, also hosts top art galleries, as well as El Rincon, the oldest trading post in Taos. In addition, the Ranchos de Taos area, 4 miles south of the Plaza, contains a number of fine shops, including some of the town's priciest.

Galleries

Bert Geer Phillips and Ernest Blumenschein, traveling from Denver on a planned painting trip into Mexico in 1898, stopped in Taos to have a broken wagon wheel repaired—a chance occurrence that led to the development of Taos as a major art center. Enthralled with the dramatic Taos landscape, earth-hued adobe buildings, thin, piercing light, and clean mountain air, they decided to stay. Word of their discovery soon spread to fellow artists. In 1912, the Taos Society of Artists was formed. At its nucleus were Blumenschein, Phillips, Joseph Henry Sharp, and Eanger Irving Coue, all graduates of the celebrated Parisian art school Academie Julian. Members of the society painted in Taos, but shipped their work to art markets on the East Coast and in Europe.

Most of the early Taos artists spent their winters in New York or Chicago teaching, painting, or illustrating to earn enough money to free them for their summers in New Mexico, where they worked under difficult conditions at best, often without running water or electricity. Most were fascinated with Native Americans, their customs, modes of dress, and ceremonies, feeling—rather romantically—a spiritual kinship with them. The society was disbanded in the late 1920s, but Taos continued to attract artists. Several galleries opened, and in 1952 local painters joined to form the Taos Artists' Association, forerunner to today's highly active Taos Art Association. At present, more than 80 galleries and shops display original art, sculpture, and crafts.

BA Gallery (133 E. Kit Carson Rd., tel. 505/758–2239) is the oldest gallery space in Taos. Owner Burke Armstrong handles Old Masters and Southwestern expressionists, especially work in the tradition of Taos narrative art.

Burke Armstrong Gallery (121 N. Plaza, tel. 505/758–9016) offers traditional art in a historic setting, a two-story building that was the original courthouse of Taos. It was the first building on the Plaza to burn down and subsequently the first to be rebuilt, making it the oldest standing structure. On permanent display upstairs are the famous Taos Murals, painted by a number of the founding artists of Taos. Burke, who refurbished the building 20 years ago at his own expense, offers old and modern masters, Indian pottery, and Indian jewelry in three handsome gallery rooms.

Clay and Fiber Gallery (135 Paseo Pueblo Norte, tel. 505/758–8093), located behind the Stables, emphasizes ceramics and cloth work such as handpainted silks and traditional and contemporary weavings.

El Taller Taos Gallery (119A Kit Carson Rd., tel. 505/758–4887) is the exclusive Taos representative of original works by Amado Pena. It also handles sculpture, jewelry, weavings, glass, and clay, as does its sister gallery in Santa Fe.

Gallery Elena (119 Bent St., tel. 505/758–9094) has watercolors by Keith Crown and bronze sculpture by Velroy Vigil, and the work of other artists of regional and national importance. Although relatively new, the gallery's growing reputation continues to attract sophisticated art buyers.

Gallery Rodeo of Beverly Hills (118 Camino de la Placita, tel. 505/758–3622 or 800/776–5767 outside NM), a half block southwest of the Plaza, handles Old Masters, Impressionists, and contemporary internationally renowned artists.

E. S. Lawrence (132 E. Kit Carson Rd., tel. 505/758–8229) shows both traditional and contemporary paintings, as well as Santa Fe–style furnishings.

Mission Gallery (138 E. Kit Carson Rd., tel. 505/758–2861), now in its 30th year, features early Taos artists, early modernists, and important contemporary artists. The gallery is located in the former home of early Taos painter Joseph H. Sharp.

Navajo Gallery (210 Ledoux, tel. 505/758–3250) offers the varied works of Navajo artist R. C. Gorman, widely considered the best Native American artist and probably the best known of all the modern Southwestern artists. Dubbed "the Picasso of Indian Art" by the *New York Times*, Gorman opened the Navajo Gallery in 1968, becoming the first Native American artist to operate his own gallery. A branch of the Navajo Gallery was opened in Albuquerque's historic Old Town district in 1989.

R. B. Ravens (St. Francis Plaza, Ranchos de Taos, tel. 505/758–7322) presents paintings by the founding artists of Taos, weavings, ceramics, and sketches by famous Indian painter Elbridge Ayer Burbank. It also features Navajo textiles, both blankets and rugs, pottery, regalia, and pawn jewelry.

Shriver Gallery (401 Paseo Pueblo Norte, tel. 505/758–4994) handles traditional bronze sculpture and paintings, including oils, watercolors, and pastels, as well as drawings and etchings.

Stewart's Fine Art (108 E. Kit Carson Rd., tel. 505/758–0049), the largest gallery in Taos, specializes in Southwestern realism, from the 17th century to today. Work by Dorothy Brett, longtime companion to Frieda and D. H. Lawrence, can be found here.

Taos Traditions Gallery (221 Paseo Pueblo Norte, tel. 505/758–0016), located next to the Fechin Institute, mainly showcases the work of contemporary artists, including oils, pastels, and watercolors.

The Taos Gallery (403 Pueblo de Norte, tel. 505/758–2475) features Western and Southwestern impressionism and an exclusive collection of bronzes, and the **Taos Gallery 2** (124 Bent St., tel. 505/758–7438) focuses on Southwestern impressionism.

Western Heritage Art (1042 South Plaza, tel. 505/758–4376), established in 1985, handles paintings, alabaster and bronze sculpture, Navajo rugs, and Native American artifacts and pottery. Bill Rabbit and Robert Redbird are among the artists represented here.

Specialty Stores

Home Furnishings **Casa Cristal Pottery** (on Highway 3 in El Prado, tel. 505/758–1530), 2½ miles north of the Taos Plaza, has it all: stoneware, serapes, clay pots, Indian iron-wood carvings, ceramic sunbursts, straw and tin ornaments, *ristras* (strings of chile peppers), fountains, sweaters, ponchos, clay fireplaces, Mexican blankets, clay churches, birdbaths, baskets, tile, piñatas, and blue glassware from Guadalajara. Also featured are antique reproductions of park benches, street lamps, mailboxes, bakers' racks, and other wrought-iron products. Casa Cristal has outlets in Colorado Springs, Colorado, and Velarde, New Mexico.

Dwellings Revisited (107 Bent St., tel. 505/758–3377) offers time-worn authentic, primitive pine furniture, architecturals, and other antique treasures from New Mexico.

At **Hacienda de San Francisco** (4 St. Francis Plaza, Ranchos de Taos, tel. 505/758–0477), you'll find an exceptional collection of Spanish Colonial antiques.

High Mesa Furniture (729 Paseo del Pueblo Sur, tel. 505/758–4253) has a complete line of handcrafted viga and Territorial-style furniture, along with a large selection of Southwestern interiors.

Lo Fino (201 S. Santa Fe Rd., tel. 505/758–0298), in a contemporary adobe, provides one of the largest selections of handcrafted furniture in New Mexico, with the work of 10 top Southwestern furniture and lighting designers featured in one large showroom. Handcarved beds, tables, chairs, cupboards, chests, lamps, and doors are all on display, along with Native American alabaster sculptures, basketry, and pottery.

Native Furniture of Taos (134 Bent St., tel. 505/758–8010), located in the Dunn House Building, offers quintessential Taos furnishings. Much in demand, the distinctive, versatile line of young designer Greg Flores includes small stools, sofas, occasional tables and chairs, benches, *trasteros* (cupboards), and dining sets. Each piece is signed and dated.

Taos Blue (101A Bent St., tel. 505/758–3561) specializes in Taos-style interior furnishings and just about everything else one might need to beautify his or her space. Behind the blue door on the corner of Bent Street and Paseo del Pueblo Norte is a treasure trove of one-of-a-kind accessories. On display are Pawnee/Sioux magical masks, decorated with feathers, horsehair, and scarves; "storyteller figures" from the Taos Pueblo; ceramic dogs baying at the moon; and Native American shields and rattles, sculptures, leather hassocks, and painted buckskin pillows.

Native American Arts and Crafts **Broken Arrow** (222 N. Plaza, tel. 505/758–4304) specializes in collector-quality Native American arts and crafts, including sand paintings, rugs, prints, jewelry, pottery, artifacts, and Hopi kachinas.

Buffalo Dancer (103 E. Plaza, tel. 505/758–8718) buys, sells, and trades Southwest Indian arts and crafts, including pottery, concho belts, kachinas, hides, and silver-coin jewelry.

Don Fernando Curio and Gift Shop (W. Plaza, tel. 505/758–

3791) is the oldest Native American arts shop on the Taos Plaza. It opened in 1938, hoping to catch some business from the newly opened La Fonda Hotel across the Plaza. Guests from La Fonda still wander in to pick out a turquoise bracelet, a kachina mud man, a woven straw basket, or some colorful beads.

El Rincon (114 E. Kit Carson, tel. 505/758–9188), housed in a traditional adobe from the turn of the century, was and still is a trading post, the oldest in Taos. Native American items of all kinds are bought and sold here: drums, feathered headdresses, Navajo rugs, beads, bowls, baskets, shields, beaded moccasins, jewelry, arrows, and spearheads. A free museum of Native American and early Spanish American artifacts is located off the main room of the shop. One of its most prized acquisitions is a pair of Kit Carson's buckskin pants. In back of the shop is the El Rincon Bed and Breakfast, reminiscent of the era when Native Americans often traveled for days on horseback to visit the reservation trading post and were invited to spend the night.

R. B. Ravens (St. Francis Plaza, Ranchos de Taos, tel. 505/758–7322) features the best in Navajo blankets and rugs, historical pots, regalia, pawn jewelry, and fine paintings, many from the founding artists' group of Taos painters.

Tony Reyna's Indian Shops (Kachina Lodge, Paseo del Pueblo Norte, tel. 505/758–2142; on Taos Pueblo Rd., tel. 505/758–3835) are Pueblo Indian owned and operated and offer authentic Native American jewelry, paintings, and kachina dolls.

Clothing **Mariposa Boutique** (John Dunn House, 120 Bent St., tel. 505/758–9028) features original contemporary Southwestern clothing and accessories by leading Taos designers. Handcrafted jewelry is also featured.

Martha of Taos (121 Paseo del Pueblo Norte, tel. 505/758–3102), next to the Taos Inn, specializes in Southwestern-style dresses, broomstick skirts, Navajo blouses, and velvet Navajo dresses with silver.

Overland Sheepskin Company (NM 522, tel. 505/758–8822) has a huge selection of high-quality sheepskin coats, hats, mittens, and slippers, many using Taos beadwork, Navajo rug insets, and buffalo hides for exotic new styles. There are branches in Santa Fe, San Francisco, and the Napa Valley area of California.

The Outfitter (127 Paseo del Pueblo Sur, tel. 505/758–2966) is a one-of-a-kind shop offering made-to-order custom-leather moccasins, cowboy and Mountain Man gear, and women's clothing, along with Native American trade beads, walking sticks, skulls, antiques, and collectibles. The shop is located west of the Taos Plaza, across from the Guadalupe Church; look for the 1776 Freedom Flag out front.

Books **The Brodsky Bookshop** (218 Paseo del Pueblo Norte, tel. 505/758–9468) has a fine selection of contemporary books and Southwestern classics. If you don't see what you want, Brodsky's will order it on the spot.

Fernandez de Taos Book Store (N. Plaza, tel. 505/758–4391), located right on the Plaza, has books, art magazines, and major out-of-town newspapers, such as the *New York Times* and the *Washington Post*.

G. Robinson Old Prints and Maps (124 Bent St., tel. 505/758–2278), located in the John Dunn House, has a wide selection of original antique maps and prints (16th–19th century), Edward Curtis Indian photographs, and rare books.

Moby Dickens (No. 6, John Dunn House, 124 Bent St., tel. 505/758–3050) is roomy and well-lighted, with lots of windows that let in the bright Taos sun. A bookstore for all ages, it has a good selection of contemporary best-sellers, as well as an outstanding selection of books on the Southwest.

Taos Book Shop (122D Kit Carson Rd., tel. 505/758–3733), a half block west of the Taos Plaza in a lovely walled adobe building, is the oldest bookshop in New Mexico. It was founded in 1947 by Genevieve Janssen and Claire Morrill, whose recollections of their years in Taos, *A Taos Mosaic* (University of New Mexico Press), remains by far the best local history of the Taos area. Frequent book signings and receptions for authors are held in the shop, which specializes in out-of-print and Southwestern selections. Complimentary coffee is served. The shop has a second location in the Taos Ski Valley (tel. 505/776–2506), open only during the season.

Ten Directions Books (228C Paseo del Pueblo Norte, tel. 505/758–2725) buys and sells new and used books. It welcomes book searches, locating out-of-print and hard-to-find volumes.

Sports and Fitness

Whether you're going to be pumping iron or jogging along Paseo del Pueblo Norte, the altitude in Taos (over 7,000 feet) takes a toll. Even your car will be gasping, getting too much gas and not enough air. Your body works almost the same way at high altitudes, with decreased oxygen content and decreased humidity. You may experience symptoms of nausea, insomnia, shortness of breath, diarrhea, sleeplessness, and tension. Eat lightly during the first few days and try to avoid alcohol, which aggravates "high altitude syndrome." Keep physical exertion to a minimum. And, voilà!, after a few days, you should be your old self again and ready to hit the road running.

Participant Sports

Bicycling **Bicicletas** (next to the Greyhound Station on S. Santa Fe Rd., tel. 505/758–3522) and **Taos Mountain Outfitters** (114 S. Plaza, tel. 505/758–9292) both have bicycles to rent. The Taos-area roads are steep and hilly and none has marked bicycle lanes. Be cautious; drivers, many from out of state, may be as unfamiliar with a passing bicycle as they are with a passing deer. Serious bikers may want to participate in the annual autumn **Enchanted Circle Wheeler Peak Bicycle Rally and Aspencade,** held on the second weekend in September: Hundreds of cyclists challenge the 100-mile route through Red River, Taos, Angel Fire, Eagle Nest, and Questa, past a brilliant blaze of fall color.

Golf If golf's your game, take your clubs to Angel Fire's 18-hole PGA mountain course, one of the highest in the nation. Contact the **Angel Fire Pro Shop** (Drawer B, Angel Fire 87710, tel. 505/377–3055 or 800/633–7463) for tee times and greens fees. The new **Taos Country Club** (south of Taos at NM 240, tel. 505/758–7300), an 18-hole championship course with separate practice facility, is scheduled to open July 1, 1992. Greens fees for the March–November season are tentatively set at $25.

Health Clubs The **Taos Spa and Court Club** (111 Dona Ana Dr., tel. 505/758–1980) has indoor and outdoor pools, a sauna, a Jacuzzi, tennis and racquetball courts, and aerobics classes. All are open to nonmembers for fees ranging from $8 to $10. Hotel health facilities are generally reserved only for the use of guests.

Jogging The Taos mountain roads are challenging to a jogger, to say the least. You might try the running track that rings the football field at Taos High School (134 Cervantes, tel. 505/758–5230). It isn't open to the public, but no one seems to object if nonstudents, within reasonable numbers, jog there. The paths through Kit Carson Park are also suitable.

River Rafting White-water rafting through the Taos Box section of the Rio Grande Wild and Scenic River is a growing sport in the region. **Native Sons Adventures** (tel. 800/753–7559) and **Rio Grande Rapid Transit** (tel. 800/222–RAFT) offer full- and half-day rafting trips. Contact the **Bureau of Land Management** (tel. 505/758–8851) for a list of other registered river guides or for information on running the river on your own.

Skiing In winter, within a 90-mile radius, Taos offers five ski resorts
Resorts with beginning, intermediate, and advanced slopes, as well as snowmobile and cross-country skiing trails. These resorts include the **Angel Fire Resort** (Drawer B, Angel Fire 87710, tel. 505/377–6401 or 800/633–7463 outside NM), open from December 15 through the first week in April; the **Red River Ski Area** (Box 900, Red River 87558, tel. 505/754–2382), open from Thanksgiving to Easter; the **Sipapu Lodge and Ski Area** (Rte. Box 29, Vadito 87579, tel. 505/587–2240), open from mid-December to the end of March; and the **Taos Ski Valley** (Box 90, Taos Ski Valley 87525, tel. 505/776–2291), open from November 22 through the first week in April.

Cross-country At the **Enchanted Forest Cross-Country Ski Area** (Box 521, Red River 87558, tel. 505/754–2374) the season runs from December 1 to April 7. The **Carson National Forest Service** (Box 558, Taos 87571, tel. 505/758–6200) can provide a good self-guide map of cross-country trails throughout the park.

Swimming The **Don Fernando Municipal Swimming Pool** (124 Civic Plaza Dr., tel. 505/758–9171) is open for recreational swimming from 1 AM to 4 PM daily. The charge is 75¢.

Tennis Kit Carson Park and Fred Baca Park both have free public tennis courts, available on a first-come, first-served basis. For information, call the Taos Department of Parks and Recreation (tel. 505/758–4160). The **Quail Ridge Inn and Tennis Ranch** (Taos Ski Valley Rd., tel. 505/776–2211) has eight Laykold tennis courts (two indoors), which are free to guests. Nonguests can play on the two indoor courts for $35 an hour.

Spectator Sports

Spectator sports include the annual **Rodeo de Taos,** held at the Taos County Fairgrounds in mid-June, and the **Taos Mountain Balloon Rally,** held in a field south of downtown during the last week in October.

Dining

For a city with a population of fewer than 5,000, Taos has an extraordinary number of fine restaurants. As in Santa Fe, many of the restaurants rely heavily on northern New Mexico–style cooking, offering flavorful dishes that are rooted deep in the Spanish culture, with recipes that, for the most part, have been handed down for generations. (*See* Dining in Essential Information, Chapter 1, for an explanation of Mexican food terms.) The clientele at all these establishments is a cross section of locals and seasonal tourists, skiers in the winter and art- and nature lovers in the summer.

Highly recommended restaurants are indicated by a star ★.

Category	Cost*
Very Expensive	over $20
Expensive	$15–$20
Moderate	$10–$15
Inexpensive	under $10

*per person, excluding sales tax (5.8%), service, and drinks

Expensive
★ **Apple Tree.** Located in a historic adobe Territorial house on Bent Street, only a block from the Plaza, the Apple Tree is a popular luncheon and early-dinner spot for locals as well as visitors. A series of intimate dining rooms, divided by open archways, the Apple Tree is cozy and casual. This restaurant has pastel shaded walls and wooden tables flanked with straw chairs. Kiva (beehive) fireplaces burn brightly in winter, and there's patio dining in summer; the large tree in the courtyard gives the restaurant its name. Among the excellent dinner entrées are mango chicken, enchiladas, shrimp quesadillas, filet mignon with shiitake mushrooms, and lamb steak (made from organically raised local lambs). Two hot homemade soups are prepared daily, and Sunday brunch, served from 10 to 3, is a Taos tradition. *123 Bent St., tel. 505/758–1900. Reservations advised. Dress: casual. AE, DC, MC, V.*

★ **Brett House.** Four miles north of Taos, Brett House is the former home and literary salon of Lady Dorothy Brett, friend and frequent traveling companion of Frieda and D. H. Lawrence. Opened in 1983 as a restaurant, it is now one of the finest places to dine in Taos. Chef-owner Chuck Lamendola offers a wide selection of Southwestern and international dishes, including veal scallopini; rack of lamb; roast duckling in ginger sauce; medallions of veal; fresh fish; and, on Wednesday, ethnic specialties (often Greek or French). Service is impeccable and the views of the Sangre de Cristo Mountains are superb. Set in a traditional old Taos adobe, painted white, are four small rooms with half fireplaces, wood floors, and viga ceilings. A few paintings by local artists hang in the bar area, and several articles about Lady Brett are framed on the wall, along with photos of her and a sketch of her by internationally acclaimed Taos artist R. C. Gorman, done just before she died in 1977. *Rte. 522 and Hwy. 150, tel. 505/776–8545. Reservations recommended. Jacket and tie advised. AE, MC, V.*

Don Fernando's. The dining room at the Holiday Inn, 1 mile south of the Taos Plaza, is modern in concept, with Taos flour-

Amigo's Natural Grocery and Juice Bar, **15**

Andy's La Fiesta Restaurant, **18**

Apple Tree, **7**

Bent Street Deli and Cafe, **9**

Brett House, **1**

Carl's French Quarter, **3**

Casa de Valdez, **17**

Chile Connection, **2**

La Cigale Cafe de Paris, **14**

La Cocina de Taos, **10**

Doc Martin's, **8**

Don Fernando's, **16**

Michael's Kitchen, Coffee Shop, and Bakery, **6**

Ogelvie's Bar and Grill, **12**

El Patio de Taos, **11**

Rhoda's Restaurant, **5**

Roberto's, **13**

The Stakeout Bar and Grill, **19**

Villa Fontana, **4**

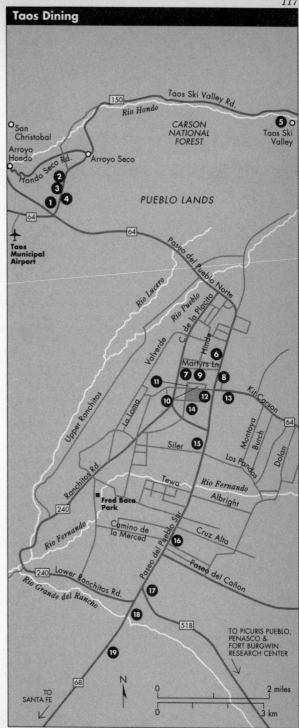

Taos Dining

ishes—kiva fireplaces, Indian art, and handcrafted tables and lamps. Out of its busy kitchen comes a wide selection of authentic Southwestern dishes, including enchiladas Puerto Vallerta (stuffed with crab and baby shrimp), shrimp Veracruz (marinated and grilled), and *carne asada* (broiled steak fillet). The adjoining lounge, Fernando's Hideaway (*see* Nightlife, below), features live entertainment, with intimate seating around a large adobe fireplace. *1005 Paseo del Pueblo Sur, tel. 505/758–4444. Reservations suggested. Jacket and tie advised. AE, D, DC, MC, V.*

Doc Martin's. Long a popular gathering place for locals, the Taos Inn's restaurant is known for fresh fish dishes and traditional American cuisine—steaks, chops, and chicken—prepared with a New Mexican flair. Doc Martin's takes its name from the building's original owner, a local physician who performed operations and delivered babies in the rooms that now make up the dining areas. The decor is the epitome of Southwestern: viga and latilla ceilings (beams and small strips of wood arranged to create a herringbone effect); *nichos* (wall niches) containing pottery and carved wooden santos; fireplaces; balconies with intricately carved railings draped with Indian saddle blankets; and handcrafted wooden tables and chairs. Breakfast and lunch menus are predominantly New Mexican; at dinner the emphasis is on contemporary American fare. The wine list is exceptional. Favorites here include the shrimp burrito smothered in vegetarian chili verde for lunch and pepper-crusted loin of lamb with rosemary mint demiglace for dinner. *Taos Inn, 125 Paseo del Pueblo Norte, tel. 505/758–1977. Reservations suggested. Dress: casual. AE, DC, MC, V.*

Carl's French Quarter. The decor of Carl's French Quarter, where New Orleans cuisine tops the menu, is reminiscent more of Santa Fe than of Bourbon Street: a large stone fireplace, wooden tables and chairs, and a few unimpressive Western paintings on the walls. Owner-chef Carl Fritz features nightly pasta specials, as well as aged Angus beef, quail, and duck. Also recommended are the grilled swordfish with spicy oriental glaze and fettuccine with lobster cream sauce, topped with shrimp and snow crab. *Quail Ridge Inn, Ski Valley Rd., 5 mi north of the Taos Plaza, tel. 505/776–8319. Reservations recommended. Jacket and tie advised. D, DC, MC, V.*

Casa de Valdez. A large A-frame building with wood-paneled walls and beamed ceilings, Casa de Valdez has a rustic, mountain-lodge feeling. The tables and chairs are handmade, as are the colorful drapes on the windows. Owner-chef Peter Valdez specializes in hickory-smoked barbecues, charcoal-grilled steaks, and regional New Mexican cuisine. *Paseo del Pueblo Sur, 2½ mi south of the Taos Plaza, 505/758–8777. Reservations suggested. Dress: casual. AE, MC, V.*

El Patio de Taos. A Taos favorite for over 40 years, El Patio is set in a traditional adobe touted as the oldest structure in Taos (actually, only one of the standing patio walls can truthfully claim that distinction). The main dining room has a skylight above and flagstone floors below, and a fountain covered by a small green sea of potted plants. A second, smaller dining room, which seats 30, has viga ceilings and Western and Native American paintings on the walls. Recently renovated, the restaurant offers classic New Mexican, French, and northern Italian cuisine. Chef Yvon's house specialties include enchiladas con patos (duck), fettuccine Alfredo, New York steak, and blue corn enchiladas. The Caesar salad is probably the best in town.

El Patio has drawn many visiting celebrities over the years. *Teresins La., northwest corner of Taos Plaza, tel. 505/758–2121. Reservations suggested. Jacket and tie advised. AE, D, DC, MC, V.*

Ogelvie's Bar and Grill. Occupying the second floor of an old two-story adobe building on the east side of the Taos Plaza, Ogelvie's is the perfect spot for people-watching from on high, especially from the outdoor patio in summer. Inside, the restaurant's two adjoining dining rooms and full-service lounge are decorated in what has been described as "early Taos thrift-shop": assorted paintings, balloons, vintage black-and-white photos, musical instruments, antique lamps, you name it. Draped tapestries hang from the ceilings, and blue tablecloths cover the handcrafted tables and chairs. The chef and kitchen staff seem far more in control than the decorators, offering prime Angus beef, seafood, and traditional Southwestern and regional specialties that keep people waiting in line to get in. *103 E. Plaza, tel. 505/758–8866. Reservations suggested. Dress: casual. AE, MC, V.*

The Stakeout Grill and Bar. Tucked into the foothills of the Sangre de Cristo Mountains, 8 miles south of Taos, at a place called Outlaw Hill, this old adobe homestead offers views that stretch for hundreds of miles and sunsets that dazzle. Clearly marked by a huge cowboy hat out front, the restaurant's decor is rustic, with wood-paneled walls, viga ceilings, hardwood floors, wooden tables and chairs, and muted-glass wall lamps. Changing exhibits of locally produced Western art and handcrafted silver—all of which is for sale—are displayed throughout. But the main attraction is the food—New York strip steaks, filet mignon, roast prime rib, shrimp scampi, swordfish steak, baked brie, escargots, French onion soup, Caesar salad. *Stakeout Dr. (NM 68), tel. 505/758–2042. Reservations suggested. Dress: casual. MC, V.*

★ **Villa Fontana.** A two-story adobe with a Continental ambience, the newly opened Villa Fontana is the former Casa Cordova, refurbished and remodeled, all aglow with newness and candlelight. Its two intimate dining rooms, with gleaming hardwood floors and well-appointed tables, starched linens and sparkling crystal, set a classic tone found in many of Europe's finest restaurants. Master chef Carlo Gislimberti and his wife Siobhan offer authentic northern Italian cuisine, including the house specialty of locally picked wild mushrooms and a variety of seasonal game, such as venison, duck, and pheasant. *Taos Ski Valley Rd., ⁹⁄₁₀ of a mi north of the blinking light, tel. 505/758–5800. Reservations recommended. Jacket and tie advised. D, DC, MC, V.*

Moderate **Andy's La Fiesta Restaurant.** Spectacularly sited in one of the 250-year-old adobe buildings that made up the fort built by Spanish settlers in Ranchos de Taos, Andy's serves northern New Mexican cuisine, utilizing longtime family recipes. The enchiladas are a favorite here; *carne adovada* (pork marinated in chile Caribe) is another house specialty. Steaks and seafood round out the menu. In keeping with the unique architecture, the decor of the dining room and adjoining lounge is early Spanish; there are viga ceilings and wall niches containing antique santos and retablos. Even the cash register is over 150 years old. Soft lighting, greenery, and beige tablecloths create a soft, intimate atmosphere. *St. Francis Plaza, Ranchos de*

Taos, tel. 505/758–9733. Reservations suggested. Jacket and tie advised. MC, V. Closed Sun. and Mon.

Chile Connection. Six minutes north of the Taos Plaza on Ski Valley Road, Chile Connection is housed in a sprawling ranch-style adobe building with a large patio offering spectacular mountain views. The patio is open for dining in summer and on mild sunny winter days; otherwise, meals are served in three separate dining rooms, each with a kiva fireplace, handcrafted tables and chairs, Western art, and decorations from south of the border. Specialties of the house include blue corn tortillas, homemade salsa, buffalo burgers and steaks, and fajitas. The blaring large-screen TV in the bar is annoying, but the great margaritas served there almost dull its effect. There's also a gift shop offering packaged spices and chile souvenirs. *Ski Valley Rd., tel. 505/776–8787. Reservations suggested. Dress: casual. AE, D, DC, MC, V.*

★ **La Cocina de Taos.** The giant lettering in front of this typical New Mexican adobe building on the north side of the Taos Plaza identifies yet another popular restaurant offering regional specialties—chile rellenos, *pollo mole poblano* (chicken with a spicy chocolate sauce), fajitas, and carne adovada—as well as American standards. The two main dining rooms are separated by stained-glass murals (one depicting St. Francis Church in Ranchos de Taos, and the other the Taos Pueblo). The handmade tile-topped tables, left bare for lunch, are covered with wine-colored tablecloths at night. A private dining room in back near the bar features caricatures of local celebrities done by local artist Scratch Rhodes, some dating back to 1952 when the restaurant opened. *North Plaza, tel. 505/758–2412. Reservations suggested. Jacket and tie advised. AE, MC, V.*

Rhoda's Restaurant. Nestled at the base of famed Al's Run in the Taos Ski Valley, Rhoda's is a haven for hungry skiers who can dine while watching fellow enthusiasts lift off to the snowy summits. Set in a wood frame building with lots of windows, it also offers dining outdoors on the sundeck. This sunny, pleasant restaurant has handcrafted pine tables and chairs, peach-colored tablecloths and napkins, and fresh floral bouquets on the tables. Chef Richard Reyes's daily specials include pasta selections, seafood and poultry, and traditional New Mexican specialties, plus such unusual regional dishes as elk and buffalo brochette. Especially good is *pollo Monterey*, chicken breast with cheese and chili. Full bar service is available. *Resort Center, Taos Ski Valley, tel. 505/776–2005. Reservations suggested. Dress: casual. AE, MC, V. Closed Apr. 8–Thanksgiving.*

Inexpensive **Amigos Natural Grocery and Juice Bar.** In front of a building that looks like ancient adobe—it's actually composed of railroad ties with adobe plastering—is the grocery store, with its wide assortment of health foods, organic eggs, honey, and fresh local fruit and produce. In back is the natural-food café and juice bar, where blenders purr away, turning carrots, apples, berries, and giant stalks of celery into nectar. Home-baked breads and rolls go well with the juices and fresh daily selections of vegetarian entrées. The bare-bones café section seats 40 on tables and benches. There's also outside seating, weather permitting. *325 Paseo del Pueblo Sur, tel. 505/758–8493. No reservations. Dress: casual. No credit cards. Open daily 11–5.*

Bent Street Deli and Cafe. It's simple and unpretentious, but the place to go if you're dying for a Reuben sandwich. An extensive selection of deli-style food is offered, along with croissants, cappuccino, soups, salads, sandwiches, and desserts. Beer and wine are available, and there's patio dining in the summer. *120 Bent St., tel. 505/758–5787. No reservations. Dress: casual. No credit cards.*

★ **La Cigale Cafe de Paris.** This plastered adobe building, one block south of the Plaza, is a turn-of-the-century French bistro resurrected in Taos. La Cigale features traditional bistro cooking from the four corners of France at what almost appear to be turn-of-the-century prices. Breakfast begins with fresh-baked, buttery croissants (the pastry chef is just off the boat) and European coffees. Lunch features homemade soups, salads, baguette sandwiches, *plats du jour*, and fresh pastries. Dinner specialties include steaks with classic sauces, fish, and fondue. The decor is also French bistro, with bare wood tables, a marble floor, and lots of light. Colorful travel posters adorn the walls alongside large photos by French masters taken during the early part of the century. Live jazz is performed in the evenings and during Sunday brunch when eggs Benedict with béarnaise sauce, crêpes, and more of those good butter croissants are offered. *Pueblo Alege Mall, tel. 505/751–0500. No reservations. Dress: informal. AE, MC, V. Open daily in summer; closed Tues. in winter.*

★ **Michael's Kitchen, Coffee Shop, and Bakery.** It seems almost required by law that all Western communities have one top spot for breakfast; in Taos, this is it. Housed in a traditional old adobe, four blocks north of the Plaza, Michael's has been turning out huevos rancheros, tortilla *renadas* (diced ham and scrambled eggs wrapped in a tortilla), and other good things to get the day going for over 15 years. The restaurant's unique decor reflects its past as a curio shop—an antique washing machine, a wood-burning stove, vintage picture frames and mirrors, a turn-of-the-century coat rack, 10-gallon hats, Indian pottery, and a pitcher and commode. The ceilings are beamed, the floors are polished hardwood, and the tables and chairs are all hand-crafted. Chef-owner Michael Ninneman also serves lunch and dinner, but it's breakfast that brings the faithful back for more. *304 Paseo de Pueblo Norte, tel. 505/758–4178. Reservations not required. Dress: casual. MC, V. Open 7 AM–8 PM.*

Roberto's. Housed in a 150-year-old adobe, across from the Kit Carson Museum, this New Mexican restaurant affords an ambience of rustic elegance and grace. Owners Bobby and Patsy Garcia reveal a deep-rooted love for their native heritage, using prized recipes handed down through the Garcia family for generations to create authentic native dishes from scratch. Three intimate dining rooms are decorated in Southwestern style throughout, with art and cherished family antiques, including handcrafted lamps and furniture. The margaritas and chile rellenos are particularly good. *E. Kit Carson Rd., tel. 505/758–2434. Reservations suggested for dinner. Dress: casual. MC, V. Closed Tues.*

Lodging

Taos is a tourist town and offers a broad range of accommodations from which to choose. There are hotels and motels to suit every need and budget, from big-name chains with all the extra amenities to smaller roadside establishments offering basic accommodations. There's no drastic variation in hotel rates from season to season, but you'll find more rooms available in the spring and fall.

Most of the art and social events take place during the summer months; lodging rates are about 20% higher during the peak summer period (July and August) and reservations are highly recommended during this time.

With the development of the Taos Ski Valley and several other nearby ski resorts in the mid-1950s, Taos, long a virtual ghost town in winter, blossomed into one of the premier ski destinations in the country. Depending on snow conditions, the season generally runs from about the third week in November through the first week in April. Skiers now have many deluxe resorts to choose from for comfortable and convenient accommodations.

In order to accommodate the large influx of visitors into their small town, many Taos residents decided to open up their homes. Bed-and-breakfast Taos-style means traditional adobe houses and haciendas, some 200 years old, and special Southwestern-flavor breakfasts—blue corn pancakes and huevos rancheros. Innkeepers often act as concierges, directing guests to specialty shops, arranging river rafting or hot-air balloon excursions, or suggesting the perfect place to dine.

Highly recommended lodgings are indicated by a star ★ .

Category	Cost*
Very Expensive	over $140
Expensive	$95–$140
Moderate	$50–$95
Inexpensive	under $50

All prices are for a standard double room, excluding 3% room tax, 6.4% city sales tax or 5.75% county sales tax, and service charges.

Hotels/Motels
Expensive
★

Taos Inn. Only steps from the Taos Plaza, this sprawling hotel is a prized local landmark, exemplifying Southwestern rustic charm with its adobe walls, wood-burning fireplaces, hand-stripped viga ceilings, American Indian carpets, and wrought-iron fixtures. It's listed in the National Register of Historic Places; parts of the structure date back to the 1600s. The guest rooms, all individually furnished in warm Southwestern style, are filled with antiques; hand-loomed Zapotec Indian bedspreads; custom-made Taos-style furniture built by local artists; and fireplaces created by Carmen Velarde, the local Michelangelo of fireplace design. In summer there's dining al fresco on the patio. The Western paintings on the walls of the dining rooms, as well as in the dramatic, two-story lobby, are all for sale. The comfortable, inviting lobby is built around the old town well, from which a fountain now bubbles forth; nearby

Taos Lodging

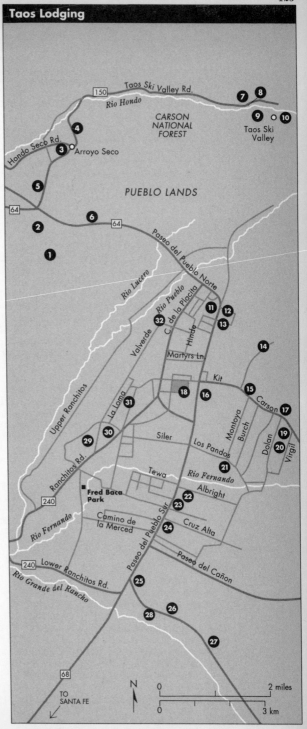

is a sunken fireplace, rimmed with *bancos* (cushioned adobe seating areas). Most of the town's shops and restaurants are within walking distance of the hotel, which is adjacent to the Stables Art Center and the Taos Community Auditorium. *125 Paseo del Pueblo Norte, Taos 87571, tel. 505/758–2233 or 800/ TAOS–INN. 39 rooms. Facilities: restaurant, bar, lounge, library, wine shop. AE, DC, MC, V.*

Moderate **Don Fernando de Taos Holiday Inn.** One mile south of the Taos Plaza, this is one of the newest hotels in Taos, but it has a venerable past. The original Don Fernando, built in the 1920s by a German entrepreneur, was considered one of the most charming hotels in the Southwest. At the time, Taos was populated by a colorful assortment of Indians, trappers, miners, and desperadoes. Hotel guests were met at the train depot in Lamy by guides from the Fred Harvey Company and then endured an arduous 12-hour journey by Model-T Ford to the hotel. The old Don burned to the ground in 1933, and the new one rose in its place in 1989. It's built in a distinct Pueblo-style design, with rooms grouped around central courtyards and connected by meandering walkways. Accommodations are tastefully appointed with handcarved New Mexican furnishings, accented with specially designed fabrics in rich Southwestern colors. Many of the rooms have kiva fireplaces. Suites named after D. H. Lawrence, Lady Brett, and others of the charmed literary circle miss a bet by not including a memento or two—not even a photograph—of their celebrated namesakes. Because of its amenities, including the lounge, this is probably the best choice for single travelers. *1005 Paseo del Pueblo Sur, Drawer V, Taos 87571, tel. 505/758–4444 or 800/HOLIDAY, fax 505/758–0055. 126 rooms. Facilities: restaurant, lounge, bar, pool, Jacuzzi. AE, MC, V.*

El Monte Lodge. Nestled among cottonwoods in a quiet residential area four blocks east of the Taos Plaza, the El Monte Lodge has been in business for over 50 years. It consists of several one-story white-painted adobe buildings, similar to guesthouse cottages in the privacy of their arrangement among the trees. Local color is afforded by beamed viga ceilings, corner fireplaces, bright Native American rugs, and tinwork mirrors and frames. All rooms have refrigerators; some have kiva fireplaces and kitchenettes. A laundry on the premises is available for the guests' use, as are picnic tables outside. Owners George and Pat Schumacher know all the ins and outs of Taos life and are happy to help guests plan their vacation schedules. *317 Kit Carson Rd., Box 22, Taos 87571, tel. 505/758–3171 or 800/828– TAOS. 9 rooms, 4 2-bedroom suites. Facilities: cable TV and refrigerators in rooms, laundry facilities, picnic tables. AE, DC, MC, V.*

El Pueblo Lodge. This low-to-the-ground Pueblo-style adobe, only blocks north of the Taos Plaza, is as practical as it is charming. In-room refrigerators, kitchenettes, and the use of a complimentary guest laundry room make it an ideal home away from home for traveling families. There's even cable TV. The lodge is located on the Ski Valley side of Taos, pointing skiers in the right direction. Room appointments include pale desert colors and traditional Southwestern furnishings—handmade furniture, lamps, and mirrors and Native American and Western art throughout. Many of the rooms have fireplaces. Free Continental breakfast is served in the lobby. *418 Paseo del*

Pueblo Norte, Box 92, Taos 87571, tel. 505/758–8700 or 800/ 433–9612. 46 rooms. Facilities: heated pool and hot tub. MC, V.

Hotel La Fonda de Taos. Built in 1937, on the south side of the Plaza, La Fonda (no affiliation with La Fonda in Santa Fe) catered to European and American celebrities in its heyday. Entering its lobby today is much like entering a European museum. Dark and worn (your eyes will need a moment to adjust after the bright New Mexican sunlight), the lobby is a showcase of framed newspaper and magazine stories, photos, posters, paintings, and Native American artifacts, all illuminated by low-wattage lamps with heat-singed shades; two bullfight costumes are mounted near the reception desk. Most are mementos of trips taken by James Karavas, who built the hotel and traveled the world, hobnobbing with the rich and famous. In the office of Karavas's son, Saki, who now owns and operates the hotel, is one of Taos's most celebrated treasures, the "erotic" paintings of D. H. Lawrence, purchased from Lawrence's widow after the artist's death. By today's standards, the naked couples embracing or romping about in the fields are pretty mild stuff, but visitors to Taos still are willing to wait in line and pay the $1 that's charged to view them. The condition of the hotel lobby telegraphs the condition of the guest rooms, which are small and cluttered with Southwestern furnishings that have reached a certain age and dignity over which one no longer speculates. *Taos Plaza, Box 1447, Taos 87571, tel. 505/758– 2211 or 800/833–2211. 24 rooms with bath. Facilities: TV in second-floor lounge only. MC, V.*

★ **Kachina Lodge de Taos, Best Western.** Just down the road from the historic Taos Indian Pueblo and only minutes from the Taos Plaza, the large, comfortable Kachina Lodge is built in a two-story adobe Pueblo-style. A kachina theme runs throughout the hotel, with rare and historic kachina dolls, carved from the root of cottonwood trees, decorating many of the hotel's public areas and others—newer, and somewhat more commercial— offered for sale in the hotel shops and lobby area. Chairs and couches, upholstered in fabrics inspired by Southwest Indian designs and colors, rim the large lobby fireplace. Hopi and Pueblo Indian art hangs on the walls. In the hotel's Kiva Coffee Shop (there's also a Hopi Dining Room and Zuni Cocktail Lounge), a huge handcarved totem pole behind the counter dominates the room. The recently refurbished guest rooms continue the Southwest Indian theme, with handmade, hand-painted furnishings, colorful fabric bedspreads, and decorative lamps. Every night from Memorial Day through Labor Day a troupe from the nearby Taos Pueblo performs ritual dances outside by firelight. During the day, the hotel's seven acres of wooded landscape invite picnics and quiet walks. *N. Pueblo Rd., Box NN, Taos 87571, tel. 505/758–2275 or 800/522–4462, fax 505/758–9207. 122 rooms. Facilities: restaurant, bar, coffee shop, heated pool, hot tub, shopping arcade. AE, D, DC, MC, V.*

Ramada Inn. One mile south of the Taos Plaza, the two-story adobe-style Ramada Inn recently underwent a transformation of sorts, putting more of a Taos stamp on the familiar Ramada mold. The remodeled dining room now features desert colors, Western art, and Native American pottery. The lobby has a fireplace where none burned before. Even the guest-room furnishings have been modified to reflect a Southwestern flavor. The hotel's Cafe Fennell has always specialized in Southwestern and American favorites, but now even the cuisine seems spicier. You can enjoy hors d'oeuvres and a cozy fireplace in the Hearthside Lounge, where guitarist Rufus Perry plays during the week and on weekends during the peak summer months. *Santa Fe Hwy. and Frontier Rd., Box 6257, Taos 87571, tel. 505/758–2900 or 800/272–6232, fax 505/758–1662. 124 rooms. Facilities: indoor heated pool, whirlpool spa with sun deck, dining room, lounge, conference rooms. AE, D, DC, V.*

★ **Sagebrush Inn.** With its graceful portals, enchanting patios, and charming adobe architecture, the two- and three-story Sagebrush Inn is one of the prettiest hotels in town. Built in adobe Pueblo-Mission style in 1929, the inn is furnished with authentic Navajo rugs, rare pottery, Southwestern and Spanish antiques, fine carved pieces, and paintings from many of the old Southwestern masters. Georgia O'Keeffe once lived and painted in one of the third-story rooms. The two large dining rooms (specializing in prime rib and New Mexican cuisine) are decorated in the Southwestern mode, as are rooms and suites, which feature wall niches containing antique religious figures, Native American wall hangings, and Native American–design rugs and bed coverings. Many have kiva fireplaces; some have balconies looking out onto the magnificent Sangre de Cristo mountains. The Sagebrush Village, a recent addition to the Sagebrush Inn, offers alternative family lodging, condominium style. *1508 Paseo del Pueblo Sur, 3 mi south of the Plaza, Box 557, Taos 87571, tel. 505/758–2254 or 800/428–3626, fax 505/758–9009. 83 rooms. Facilities: 2 restaurants, lounge, nightly entertainment, pool, 2 hot tubs, 2 tennis courts. AE, D, DC, MC, V.*

Inexpensive **The Koshari Inn.** Nestled under centuries-old silver aspens in
★ the foothills of Taos Canyon, the Koshari Inn is a former motel that has been painstakingly converting to a traditional Southwestern inn, in the Taos mold. New furnishings include the handmade wooden chairs, desks, end tables, and headboards painted in the pale colors so popular in northern New Mexico. Framed posters by favorite regional artists, including Georgia O'Keeffe and R. C. Gorman, hang on the walls, and the Native American motif is everywhere. Beyond the inn, which is part adobe, part cement block, is the Rio Fernando, more a trickling stream than a mighty river. The inn offers its guests free use of 10-speed all-terrain bicycles for touring the countryside or for trips into town, 2 miles to the west. There's also a small swimming pool on the property for the guests' use. Rooms are spacious, and each has a motel-style private entrance. There's no restaurant, but coffee is served in the lobby. *910 E. Kit Carson Rd., Box 6612, Taos 87571, tel. 505/758–7199. 12 units. Facilities: pool. MC, V.*

Resorts and **Hotel Edelweiss.** This quiet, elegant resort hotel, directly on
Ski Lodges the ski slopes, offers a touch of European alpine flavor, com-
Expensive plete with floral arrangements on the dining tables and fresh-baked breads and rolls at the hotel's La Croissanterie restaurant. The large lobby is dominated by a gigantic fireplace, where après-ski coffee and pastries are served; it's the place to meet and socialize. Owners Ilse and Bernard Mayer make their own hearty soups, sandwiches, and desserts. Rooms are more practical than posh, offering just the basics. *Taos Ski Valley 87525, tel. 505/776–2301. 20 rooms. Facilities: Jacuzzi, sauna, massages. Closed mid-April–Memorial Day. MC, V.*

★ **Quail Ridge Inn and Tennis Ranch.** The 20th century comes to sleepy Taos with this all-things-to-all-people family resort and conference center. One- and two-story modern would-be adobe bungalows offer a variety of room choices—plain rooms, studios with kitchen, one- and two-bedroom suites, and rooms with balconies or patios, all decorated in Southwestern contemporary, with viga ceilings and kiva fireplaces. Carl's French Quarter has excellent food (*see* Dining, above). Five miles north of Taos Plaza, the Quail Ridge offers a touch of modern elegance set against the magnificent natural backdrop of northern New Mexico. What it lacks in rustic charm it makes up for in a host of recreational amenities, from organized trail rides to hot-tub soaks. A free Continental breakfast is included in the room rate. *Ski Valley Rd. (NM 150), Box 707, Taos 87571, tel. 505/ 776–2211 or 800/624–4448, fax 505/776–2949. 110 rooms and suites. Facilities: restaurant, lounge, 4 racquetball courts, 8 Laykold tennis courts (2 inside), heated pool, hot tub, fitness center, squash, volleyball. Complete ski, tennis, rafting, mountain-bike, or fly-fishing packages are available for groups or individuals. D, DC, MC, V.*

Thunderbird Lodge and Chalets. Only 150 yards from the main lifts, on the sunny side of the valley, this large, two-story wood-frame inn is the ultimate ski-lodge resort, owned and managed by live-in residents Elizabeth and Tom Brownell. Its dining room is one of the most popular in the valley, with all breads, soups, salads, entrées, pastries, and ice cream made on the premises. A large conference room also serves as a game room, with TV, board games, and a library. Guest rooms are small and functional, typical of ski-resort accommodations. Supervised children's activities include early dinners, movies, and games. *Box 87, Taos Ski Valley 87525, tel. 505/776–2280 or 505/ 776–2238. 32 rooms. Facilities: whirlpool, sauna, massage, bar, restaurant. MC, V.*

Moderate **Amizette Inn & Restaurant.** A small, wood-frame mountain inn on the banks of the Rio Hondo, 1½ miles from the ski lifts, the Amizette offers all the amenities (as well as the decor) of a traditional Alpine chalet—hot tub, redwood sauna, sun deck, trout stream and hiking trails, and comfortable rooms with queen-size beds, private baths, and color TV. The decor, as you might expect, is Alpine. *Taos Ski Valley Rd., Box 756, Taos Ski Valley 87525, tel. 505/776–2451. 12 rooms. Facilities: hot tub, sauna. AE, MC, V.*

★ **Austing Haus.** Billed as the largest and tallest timber-frame building in the United States, Austing Haus, 1½ miles from the ski lifts, opened in 1984. Over 70,000 board feet of heavy timbers, with more than 3,000 interlocking joints—held together by wooden pegs—were used in its construction. The beams are exposed inside and out, providing structural stability and a pleasantly aesthetic design. All the furniture is handmade as well: Owner Paul Austing, an award-winning chef, is as handy with a mallet and saw as he is with his sauces and soufflés. The full front exterior of the building is paneled glass, offering stunning views of the valley from inside and a glimpse of the cozy interior from outside. The hotel's aptly named Glass Dining Room has an Indian loom with a partially completed blanket mounted on the wall; a fireplace; stained-glass paneling; and large picture windows. House specialties are veal Oscar and steak au poivre. Guest rooms are sparse and functional, not unlike those of ski lodges all over the world. *Taos Ski Valley Rd. (Hwy. 150), Box 8, Taos 87525, tel. 505/776–2649 or 505/776– 2629. 26 rooms with bath. Facilities: restaurant, hot tub, satel-*

*lite TV. Converts to bed-and-breakfast inn during the summer.
MC, V.*

Inexpensive **Abominable Snow-Mansion Skiers' Hostel and Summer Center.**
This large old adobe building, midway between Taos and the
Ski Valley (15 minutes either way), is designed for the budget
minded who don't mind bedding down in bunks, dormitory
style. You can't miss the garish lettering out front, painted directly on the adobe facade. Inside, the front part of the two-
story building is a large general room where everything happens; there are video games, a piano, a fireplace, chairs,
couches, and books. Meals are served here buffet style during
the ski season. There's no food offered during the summer, but
kitchen facilities are available to guests. In back and upstairs
are six dormitory rooms with bunk beds, mostly five beds to a
room; each room has its own bath. During the summer, two of
the rooms are offered as private accommodations. There are
two cabin units out back and an area set aside for tent camping
(conventional and tepee). It's all clean, comfortable, and fun,
and a great way to meet people. *Taos Ski Valley Rd. (Hwy.
150), in Arroyo Seco, Box 3271, Taos 87571, tel. 505/776–8298,
fax 505/776–8746. 96 beds. No liquor permitted during the
summer months. MC, V.*

Bed-and-Breakfasts **Casa de las Chimeneas.** Within walking distance of the Taos
Expensive Plaza (two blocks southeast), Casa de las Chimeneas, meaning
"the House of Chimneys," is so-named because of the many kiva
fireplaces warming each corner of this L-shaped adobe. Each of
the guest rooms has its own private entrance and fireplace and
each is individually furnished with handcarved, hand-painted
traditional New Mexican chests, tables, chairs, and headboards. A special two-room suite includes a large sitting room
with a sofabed. All rooms overlook the inn's formal gardens and
fountains. Large common areas contain cozy nooks for reading
or relaxing. Innkeeper Susan Vernon and her artist husband
Ron Rencher share the stage with two resident cats. Full complimentary breakfasts—served in the guest rooms, on the terrace, or in the dining room—feature huevos rancheros, blue-
corn pancakes with fresh berries and maple syrup, and the
like. Nobody goes away hungry. Hors d'oeuvres are served in
the late afternoon. *405 Cordoba Rd., Box 5303, Taos 87571, tel.
505/758–4777. 2 rooms, 1 suite, all with baths and cable TV. No
smoking. Facilities: outdoor hot tub. MC, V.*

★ **Salsa del Salto.** Seven miles from the Taos Plaza, on the way to
the Taos Ski Valley, this large Western ranch–style home features a two-story common room with a massive stone fireplace,
heated outdoor pool, hot tub, and tennis court. Located at the
edge of the Sangre de Cristo Mountains, overlooking the Taos
mesa, it was designed for owners Mary Hockett and Dadou
Mayer by well-known architect Antoine Predock. Each of the
guest rooms is furnished with handcrafted, hand-painted New
Mexican furniture. All have king-size beds with goose-down
comforters and tiled bathrooms, and all have spectacular
views. The Master/Honeymoon Suite has a fireplace with copper detailing. Full gourmet breakfasts are served each morning. During the summer, the gentle clack of croquet balls can
be heard on the front lawn; everyone dresses in white to play.
In the winter, co-owner Dadou Mayer, a renowned French
chef, doubles as a ski instructor at Taos Ski Valley. *Hwy. 150,
Box 453, El Prado 87529, tel. 505/776–2422. 6 rooms with
baths. Facilities: heated pool, hot tub, tennis court. MC, V.*

Moderate **American Artists Gallery House.** Only minutes from the Taos Plaza, this bed-and-breakfast art gallery features work by local, regional, and nationally known artists, including such Indian and Southwest favorites as R. C. Gorman, Amado Pena, and Virgil Velroy. Each of the guestrooms has a gallery name and each is individually furnished in charming Southwest style. For example, the Garden Gallery room is set in a courtyard with brick and fieldstone areas abundant with flowers, while the Gallery Lilac room is in a separate guest house with high wood ceilings, a kiva fireplace, and a kitchen. Guests may also enjoy the main living room with its large fireplace, as well as a brick portico and side gardens. Owners Benjamin and Myra Carp are on hand to offer travel advice and information about Taos. Full breakfasts, cooked to order, include such specialties as French toast stuffed with nuts and soft cheese, along with fresh fruit, coffee, and bagels. *132 Frontier Rd. Box 584, Taos 87571, tel. 505/758–4446. 5 rooms, all with private bath. Facilities: hot tub. M.C.V.*

Brooks Street Inn. A large rambling adobe house with a circular drive and an adjoining guest house comprise the Brooks Street Inn, at one time an artist's residence. Although constructed in 1956, the house was built in the traditional manner with adobe bricks made on the property, beamed ceilings, polished wood floors, and a large stone fireplace. An elaborately carved corbel arch (the handiwork of Japanese carpenter Yaichikido) spans the entranceway, and alongside is a shaded, walled garden. The guest rooms show great attention to detail—the perfect basket; fresh-cut flowers; a decanter of sherry; plump, fluffy pillows. In the large living room, paintings by local artists share wall space with family photographs. The full breakfast features handed-down family recipes, such as Lithuanian bacon buns and Czech coffee cakes, along with muffins, breads, and other home-baked delights. When the weather is warm, breakfast is served at umbrella tables on the patio; in the winter, it's served by the fireplace. *119 Brooks St., Box 4954, Taos 87571, tel. 505/758–1489. 7 rooms, 2 with shared bath. No smoking. No credit cards.*

★ **Casa de Milagros.** A single-story, turn-of-the-century adobe house, a half-mile east of the Taos Plaza, Casa de Milagros (House of Miracles) offers the texture and flavor of the Taos of long ago, with all the conveniences of today, from hot tub to cable TV. Actually two buildings connected by a portal (where the hot tub is located), the inn is furnished in an eclectic style. Southwestern decor predominates—viga ceilings; Mexican tiled bathrooms; custom cabinets; and lots of pottery, tapestry, and weavings. American Indian art, particularly the work of Taos Pueblo artist Jonathan Warmday, hangs on the walls, along with the work of other local artists. Much of it is for sale, and some is commissionable—a portrait, a landscape, if you like. When available from the local Indians, breakfast includes breads baked in traditional Pueblo Horno ovens, as it has been baked for centuries. There are also fresh fruit, muffins, bread pudding, and homemade granola. *321 Kit Carson Rd., Box 2983, Taos 87571, tel. 505/758–8001. 4 rooms, plus a 2-bedroom suite, all with bath. No smoking indoors. MC, V.*

Chile Azul. Around the corner from the Millicent Rogers Museum, this former home of Taos artist Ray Vinella offers unobstructed views of the Taos Mountains and the Taos mesa. Owners Ginny and Larry Van Eaton have preserved the central area of the house as a gathering area, while creating guest rooms with privacy and dazzling views. Guests may choose from the artist's spacious studio, with private entrance and bath, or a smaller, less expensive room filled with antiques. Home-baked Continental breakfasts and snacks are included with the room rate. *Taos Mesa, Taos 87571, tel. 505/758–8841. 2 rooms with baths. No credit cards.*

Hacienda del Sol. This is a house with a history. Bordering the Taos Pueblo, it was acquired in the 1920s by art patron Mabel Dodge Luhan. She and her fourth husband, Pueblo Indian Tony Luhan, lived here while building their main house, Las Palomas (*see* below). After moving, they kept Hacienda del Sol as a private retreat and as a guest house for visiting notables; author Frank Waters wrote *People of the Valley* while staying here. Overlooking 95,000 acres of pueblo land and shaded by huge cottonwood, ponderosa pine, blue spruce, and willow trees, the site offers a majestic, uninterrupted view of the Taos Mountains, one particularly enjoyed by today's guests while soaking in the secluded outdoor hot tub. All guest rooms are constructed with thick adobe walls, and all are furnished with antiques, handcrafted furniture in the Southwestern style, and original art (much of it for sale). One room has a private Jacuzzi, another its own steam room. Almost all have kiva fireplaces. Breakfast is served in front of the dining-room fireplace or, weather permitting, on the patio. *109 Mabel Dodge La., Taos 87571, tel. 505/758–0287. 7 rooms, 2 with shared bath. Facilities: hot tub. Credit cards discouraged.*

★ **Las Palomas de Taos/The Mabel Dodge Luhan House.** Once called Los Gallos, or the Big House, this is the Pueblo Indian–style structure that heiress Mabel Dodge Luhan lived in until her death in 1962. She bought the 200-year-old three-room adobe and the 12 acres of land surrounding it in 1915. Then, with all the drive and determination of the Pharaohs building the Pyramids of Giza, she enlarged and expanded it, vaguely intent, some say, on duplicating her palatial villa in Italy. Three rooms grew to 17, with the main part of the house rising from one story to three. What it resembled, of course, was not an Italian villa but an Indian pueblo, built for and with her fourth husband, Tony Luhan, a Tewa Indian from the Taos Pueblo. As a bed-and-breakfast inn, Las Palomas de Taos is certainly one of the oldest, largest, and most distinguished of its kind. Past guests included such luminaries as D. H. Lawrence, Georgia O'Keeffe, Willa Cather, Mary Austin, John Collier, and John Marin. Current owner Kitty Harrison bought the house from actor Dennis Hopper 14 years ago. The 12 guest rooms in the main house are furnished with turn-of-the-century pieces; the 10 rooms in the newer guest house are styled with regional New Mexican handcarved beds and handmade, hand-painted desks, chairs, end tables, cabinets, and wardrobes. The work of local artists and craftspeople is displayed throughout, much of it for sale. Bordered on two sides by Taos Pueblo land, the grounds are spectacular. Huge birdhouses perched atop poles near the front gate recall the inn's name, Las Palomas de Taos, the Doves of Taos. Guests may not be enthralled by the organized tour groups that come trooping through the house (at $4 per person), but that's part of the price of sleeping with history. *Morada La., Taos 87571, tel. 505/758–9456. 22 rooms, 6 with shared bath. MC, V.*

La Posada de Taos. Within walking distance of the Taos Plaza, La Posada de Taos (*posada* means inn) is a provincial adobe with beamed ceilings, a portal, kiva fireplaces, and the intimacy of a private hacienda. Four of its five guest rooms are in the main house; the fifth is a separate cottage with a sky-lit double loft bed, its own sitting room, and fireplace—all cozy and pretty enough to be dubbed *La Casa de la Luna de Miel* (The Honeymoon House). Wood-burning stoves or adobe fireplaces can be found in all of the guestrooms, which have either mountain or flowered courtyard views. Innkeeper Sue Smoot, who proudly boasts the Posada as the first bed-and-breakfast inn in Taos, offers a full hearty breakfast, from traditional ham and country eggs to a spicy burrito. *309 Juanita La., Box 1118, Taos 87571, tel. 505/758–8164. 5 rooms with private baths. No credit cards.*

Orinda. Surrounded by open meadows and towering elm and cottonwood trees, Orinda is a dramatic adobe estate combining spectacular views and country privacy, all within walking distance of the Taos Plaza. Getting there is half the fun, off bustling Placitas Road, down a drive flanked by pastures and grazing horses to the grove of trees. Orinda's spacious one- and two-bedroom suites have kiva fireplaces and private entrances. Owners Carol and Dave Dondero, inveterate collectors, have filled the nooks, walls, and corners of their inn with black-and-white photographs and an ever-expanding collection of pottery. A prize Navajo rug came from Buffalo Bill Cody's ranch in Wyoming. Hearty, healthy breakfasts are served in the huge, art-filled sunroom, which has a 20-foot-high open-viga ceiling and tile floor. *Valverde St., Box 4451, Taos 87571, tel. 505/758–8581. 2 suites, each with private bath. No credit cards.*

The Ruby Slipper. Within easy walking distance of the Taos Plaza to the east, The Ruby Slipper is one of the few adobe structures in Taos with a gabled roof. A former farmhouse, the inn includes five guest rooms in the main house and two more in an adjoining building, also styled in adobe. All the rooms have private entrances and include kiva fireplaces, Mexican tile baths, and locally crafted furniture of the Santa Fe school—simple and practical, handmade and hand-painted in the brighter colors favored there. Owners Diane Fichtelbert and Beth Goldman envision Taos as a mythical land and have themed all their guest rooms after the movie classic *The Wizard of Oz* (thus the name, The Ruby Slipper). The Auntie Em room has a poster bed and oak floors. Dorothy has handcrafted willow furniture, a double bed, and a kiva fireplace. The Cowardly Lion offers a king-size water bed, a wood-burning stove, and beamed ceilings. The Good Witch has saltillo tile floors and a kiva fireplace. The Scarecrow shares a bath with The Tin Man. Breakfast offerings consist of all natural foods. *416 La Lomita, Box 2069, Taos 87571, tel. 505/758–0613. 7 rooms, 5 with baths. Facilities: outdoor hot tub. Smoking outside only. MC, V.*

San Geronimo Lodge. The historic San Geronimo Lodge is 2 miles east of the Taos Plaza in the peaceful valley of the Rio Don Fernando de Taos, with beautiful views of the mountains and the high desert valley of the Rio Grande. Built by the Witt family in 1925, it incorporated an existing farmhouse that predated the 1800s. Situated on 2½ secluded wooded acres, the two-story adobe lodge, built in traditional Pueblo-Mission style, is filled with art and antiques. Like many of the lodging facilities in Taos, this one also serves as an art gallery. The rooms, both public and guest, are styled with Southwestern furnishings, handmade and hand-painted, as well as Southwestern antiques in rugged, heavy woods. Some of the guest rooms have kiva fireplaces. Continental breakfast is served in the guest rooms;

near the fireplace in the main living room; or, weather permitting, outside on the patio. *1101 Witt Rd., Box 2491, Taos 87571, tel. 505/758–7117 or 800/828–TAOS. 18 rooms with bath. Facilities: covered heated pool, hot tub, sauna, art gallery. AE, D, DC, MC, V.*

The Suite Retreat. In historic La Loma Plaza, which predates the Taos Plaza 2½ blocks away, the Suite Retreat is an art-filled adobe that was once the home of Buck Dunton, one of the founders of the Taos Society of Artists. (Unwilling to take his turn at being secretary and arranging shows for the group, he was expelled from the society and left for Texas to pursue his favorite subject, cowboys). Current owners Greg Payton and Diane Enright restored the studio and home. The entrance sign is carved on the back of Dunton's old studio sign, which was uncovered during remodeling. The two bedrooms in the upstairs guest suite are decorated with regional Southwestern furniture, and each has a bedside kiva fireplace. The adjoining living room is filled with Mexican antiques and artwork (Greg Payton is a sculptor of note). An old-fashioned Victrola plays vintage '78s, including one called "Santa Fe Is a Long, Long Way from Broadway." Breakfast is served in the guest rooms or, weather permitting, on the walled garden patio. *110 La Loma Plaza, Box 85, Taos 87571, tel. 505/758–3960. 2-bedroom suite (accommodates 2–6) with bath. No credit cards.*

Two Pipe. This spacious 300-year-old hacienda, off NM 518 in historic Talpa (near the San Francisco de Asis Church), offers all the enchantment of New Mexico of old, plus a hot tub; cable TV; and a garden to die for, with hollyhocks 10 feet tall, irises, poppies, peonies, and daisies. The adobe portal in front of the hacienda is a favorite subject of visiting artists and photographers. Innkeepers Babs and Dusty Davis, artists who create lamps and decorative items from animal horns and antlers (all for sale on the premises), lavished their creative talents on the guest rooms as well. One is decorated with antique Victorian ranch furnishings, the other with Southwestern aspen. The main room, where Continental breakfast is served, has a huge kiva fireplace. The Davises raise and train horses; guests with riding experience may participate in trail rides into Carson National Forest. *Box 52, Talpa Rte., Ranchos de Taos 87557, tel. 505/758–4770. 2 rooms with bath. Two-day minimum stay. No smoking. No credit cards.*

Whistling Waters. Soft pink adobe walls, dark green trim, low doorways, dark beams, six fireplaces, old handcrafted painted cupboards, clay pots, homespun yarns, woven rugs, a quiet courtyard with rustling cottonwoods, and whistling waters of a nearby stream—all add to the charm of this large hacienda with an interior courtyard. Owners Al and Jo Hutson spent two years remodeling the property, which now serves as a bed-and-breakfast inn and art gallery. Rooms are decorated with regional Southwestern furnishings—handmade, handcarved headboards, chests, tables, and desks. *Box 9, Talpa Rte., Ranchos de Taos 87557, tel. 505/758–7798. 3 rooms with bath. No credit cards.*

Inexpensive **Harrison's Bed and Breakfast.** A large adobe home in a rural setting, 2½ miles north of the Taos Plaza and convenient for trips to the Taos Ski Area, Harrison's is the domain of Bob and Jean Harrison, who have lived in Taos for 25 years. The house overlooks a wooded area and the town from the foot of the west mesa and is beautifully set off by trees and bushes. The guest rooms are furnished with handmade and hand-painted desks, tables, and headboards crafted in northern New Mexico, less ornate than their Santa Fe–style counterparts. Breakfast— tailored to the guests' preference—is served in the rooms or, weather permitting, on the flower-bedecked patio. *Box 242, Taos 87571, tel. 505/758–2630. 3 rooms, 1 with private bath. No credit cards.*

★ **The Blue Door.** Located in the foothills between Taos and Ranchos de Taos, the Blue Door is a 100-year-old adobe farmhouse situated amid orchids, flower gardens, lawns, and patios. Nearby is the famous San Francisco de Asis Church, surrounded by colorful shops. Each of the bedrooms is decorated in country style, with viga ceilings, wood floors, handcarved beds, and Indian-drum end tables. Owner Bruce Allen makes and markets traditional Taos drums, crafted from carved tree trunks and covered with tautly stretched leather. His workshop and studio are located at the far end of the horse pasture, where his wife Pat raises Arabian horses. Breakfast at the Blue Door is a particular treat—green chili quiche, juice, fresh fruit, muffins, blueberry pancakes, bacon, waffles, coffee, and homemade jams from the orchard. *La Mirada Rd., Talpa, Box 1168, Taos 87571, tel. 505/758–8360. 2 rooms with bath. No credit cards.*

Camping Thousands of miles of unspoiled wilderness await campers in and around the Taos area. The **Orilla Verde Recreation Area** (Bureau of Land Management, Santa Cruz Rd., Taos 87571, tel. 505/758–8851), located 10 miles south of Taos along the banks of the Rio Grande, offers opportunities for camping, hiking, fishing, and picnicking. It's open year-round; camping fees are $7. The **Carson National Forest** (Box 558, Taos 87571, tel. 505/758–6200) has more than 30 campgrounds (and 400 miles of cool mountain trout streams), including those of the Wheeler Peak Recreational Area, the highest point in New Mexico at 13,120 feet. Most campgrounds are free; some charge a $5–$8 camping fee.

A number of commercial campgrounds can be found as well, among them the **Taos RV Park** (Hwy. 68, South Santa Fe Rd., Ranchos de Taos 87557, tel. 505/758–1667 or 800/323–6009), located next to the Taos Motel just off the intersection of NM 518. Now in its third year, the park has 29 spaces: 22 full hookups with cable TV capacity, and 7 tent sites with water and electricity. Hot showers are available. The trailer sites are $15 per night for two; the tent sites are $12 for two. Located in the Sangre de Cristo Mountains, 5 miles from the Rio Grande Gorge, the area is grassy, with a few small trees. Open year-round.

Taos Valley RV Park (Estes Rd., Box 200, Ranchos de Taos 87557, tel. 505/758–4469), a former KOA franchise, has complete campground facilities, with 60-foot pull-throughs and full hookups. Facilities for tenters are also available. In the Rio Grande valley, 2½ miles south of the Taos Plaza, the campground is at an elevation of 7,000 feet and has been in operation for over 20 years. It has 92 sites, with prices ranging from $11.75 to $17.75, depending on size and requirements. Local TV signals come in sharp and clear. Open March 1–Nov. 1.

Questa Lodge (Questa, Box 155, Questa 87556, tel. 505/586–0300) has 24 units on the banks of the Red River, two blocks from NM 522. Fees are $5 for the tent sites, $12 for full hookups. Open May–mid-Oct.

The Roadrunner Campground (Red River, Box 588, Red River 87558, tel. 505/754–2286 or 800/243–2286) has 155 units located at the end of Red River–NM 578 in a spectacular wooded mountain setting, with the Red River running right through the campground. Fees are $12 for water and electrical hookup or tent site. Hookups for cable TV and sewer are also available. Open year-round.

The Arts and Nightlife

Taos Magazine (Whitney Publishing, Box 1236, Santa Fe 87504, tel. 505/989–7603), published eight times a year, covers events, fashion, arts, and the general cultural beat in town.

The Arts

The **Taos Community Auditorium** (133 Paseo del Pueblo Norte, tel. 505/758–4677) offers performances of modern dance groups and the local theater group, concerts, movies, and even the sounds of Andean folk music. For a weekly entertainment listing, check the "Tempo" section of the *Taos News*. Contact the **Taos Art Association** (tel. 505/758–2052), which owns and operates the Taos Community Auditorium, for ticket information. The **Taos Spring Arts Celebration** (mid-May–early June) and the **Taos Arts Festival** (Sept. 18–Oct. 4) are the major arts gatherings in Taos. Both events highlight the visual, performing, and literary arts of the community and allow visitors to rub elbows with the many artists who call Taos home. For information about both events, call the office of the Taos Arts Celebrations (tel. 505/758–0516). The **Wool Festival** (late Sept.), held in Kit Carson Park, features everything from sheep to shawl, with demonstrations of shearing, spinning, and weaving, handmade woolen items for sale, and tastings of favorite lamb dishes.

Music From mid-June through early September, the Taos School of Music and the International Institute of Music fill the evenings with the sounds of chamber and symphonic orchestras at the **Taos Chamber Music Festival.** This is the oldest summer-camp music program in America and possibly the largest enclave of professional musicians in the Southwest. It has been furthering the artistic growth of young string and piano students for over 25 years. Concerts are presented every Saturday evening from June 21 through August at the Taos School of Music, Taos Community Auditorium (tel. 505/776–2388). The tickets are $10. Concerts and recitals are also presented at the **Hotel Saint Bernard** (tel. 505/776–2251) in the Taos Ski Valley. Admission is free. **Music from Angel Fire** is a series of classical and jazz concerts presented at the Community Auditorium from the middle of August to early September. Admission is free. For information, call 505/758–4667. *See also* Jazz clubs, below.

Nightlife

Bars and Lounges **Carl's French Quarter** (Quail Ridge Inn and Tennis Ranch, Ski Valley Rd., tel. 505/776–8319) has classical music on Thursdays. **Fernando's Hideaway** (Holiday Inn, Paseo del Pueblo Norte, tel. 505/758–4444) presents live entertainment nightly, alternating rock, jazz, vocals, and country music. Lavish complimentary Happy Hour buffets are offered on weekday evenings. The **Taos Park Inn International** (Paseo del Pueblo Sur, tel. 505/758–8610) features dancing and live entertainment nightly, usually of the rock or country variety. The **Adobe Bar** (Taos Inn, 125 Paseo del Pueblo Norte, tel. 505/758–2233), Taos's local meet-and-greet spot, offers a summer performing artist series showcasing local talent, from a flute choir to individual guitarists and small jazz, folk, and country bands.

Cabaret The **Kachina Lodge Cabaret** (413 N. Pueblo Rd., tel. 505/758–2275) brings in headline acts, such as Arlo Guthrie and the Kingston Trio, on a regular basis and is open for dancing.

Country and Western Clubs The **Sagebrush Inn** (S. Santa Fe Rd., tel. 505/758–2254) offers live entertainment—mostly of the country-western variety—nightly in its spacious lobby lounge. There's no cover charge.

Jazz Clubs During the ski season, **Thunderbird Lodge** in the Taos Ski Valley (3 Thunderbird Rd., tel. 505/776–2280) presents Jazz Legends, an annual series of concerts that brings world-famous jazz musicians to the intimate setting of the Thunderbird Bar. The concerts are popular and seating is limited, so early reservations are recommended.

5 Albuquerque

Introduction

A large city—its population is nearing the half-million mark—Albuquerque spreads out in all directions, with no apparent ground rules. No cohesive pattern, either architecturally or geographically, seems to hold it together; the city seems as free and free-spirited as all those hot-air balloons that take part in its annual October Balloon Festival. Even residents seem confused by the street system that, like the city itself, goes this way and that. Each main street and boulevard has a direction designation after it, NE, SW, or what have you, so people can find out where they are.

Once the code is broken, however, it's a marvelous city. Like all New Mexico, it blends its cultures well; its citizens are descendants of the Native Americans who first inhabited the land and defended it bravely, of the Spanish who came on horseback to conquer and settle, and of the Anglos who were trappers and hunters and traders and pioneers in a new and often inhospitable land. From the beginning, Albuquerque was a trade and transportation center. It was an important station on the Old Chihuahua Trail, an extension of the Santa Fe Trail winding down into Mexico.

Albuquerque's incredible sprawl can be explained in a number of ways. The city was founded in 1706 on the banks of the Rio Grande, near a bend in the river, an ideal location for crop irrigation, transportation, and protection. The settlement prospered, thanks to its strategic trade-route location and its proximity to several Native American pueblos that offered mutual support and commerce. The settlers built a chapel and then a church, the church of San Felipe de Neri (named after the patron saint of King Philip V of Spain). Their homes were built close together around a central plaza for protection, as were those in other early Spanish settlements in the hostile new land. Entrance to the fortresslike community could be gained only at the four corners, making it easier to defend.

That original four-block downtown area is now known as Old Town, the city's tourist hub, with all its galleries and trendy Mexican and New Mexican restaurants. Had the city simply continued to grow, progressively expanding from its central hub, that would have made sense. But something happened. First the Rio Grande gradually changed its course, moving farther and farther west. That caused a shift in the population. Then, in 1880, the railroad came to Albuquerque, its tracks skirting Old Town by a good two miles. The result was another population shift. Old Town wasn't exactly abandoned, but "New Town" began to sprout up along the train depot, and it grew until it eventually enveloped Old Town. Finally, there was Route 66. Designated in 1926, called the "Mother Road" by author John Steinbeck, it sparked much of Albuquerque's early economic development. During the 1930s and '40s it surged through town with as much impact as the railroad and the river combined, and the burgeoning city swelled around the asphalt pavement—motels, gas stations, diners, and truck stops, a sea of neon that celebrated America's new independent mobility.

Today Albuquerque is a thriving arts center, as are many other areas of New Mexico. From the moment visitors step off a plane at Albuquerque International Airport, they're surrounded by art. Throughout the terminal building, special display areas are devoted to the work of New Mexican artists—a collection assembled by the Albuquerque Arts Board as part of the city's 1% Art Program, in which 1% of Albuquerque's municipal budget is devoted to public art projects. Other projects are under way. In addition, the city has numerous privately funded museums and galleries and is a growing center for artists, writers, poets, filmmakers, and musicians.

Essential Information

Important Addresses and Numbers

Tourist Information The **Albuquerque Convention and Visitors Bureau** (Springer Center, 121 Tijeras Ave., NE, Box 26866, Albuquerque 87125, tel. 505/842–9918 or 800/284–2282) publishes a variety of informative materials, including quarterly calendars of events and brochures describing local and out-of-town driving tours. An after-hours tape-recorded bulletin on current local events in Albuquerque can be reached after 5 PM on weekdays and all day Saturday and Sunday by phoning 505/243–3696.

Emergencies **Fire, Medical, or Police** (tel. 911).

Police (non-emergency) (tel. 505/568–1986).

Hospital Emergency Rooms. University Hospital (2211 Lomas, NE, tel. 505/843–2411), **Presbyterian Hospital** (1100 Central Ave., SE, tel. 505/841–1234). Call either for locations of Urgent Care Centers around the city.

Dentists. Dental Society referrals (tel. 505/292–2620).

Late-night Pharmacies Walgreen's offers a 24-hour prescription-refill service at two locations (2950 Central Ave., SE, tel. 505/262–1743, and 5001 Montgomery, NE, tel. 505/881–5050).

Other Numbers **Time and temperature** (tel. 505/247–1611).

Weather and road conditions (tel. 800/432–4269).

Arriving and Departing by Plane

Airport The newly expanded and remodeled **Albuquerque International Airport** (Box 9022, Albuquerque 87119, tel. 505/842–4366), located 5 miles south of downtown Albuquerque, is the gateway to New Mexico. The Albuquerque Convention and Visitors Bureau maintains an information center on the lower level of the airport at the bottom of the escalator; it is open daily from 9:30 to 8. Car rentals, air taxis, and bus shuttles are readily available at the airport, which is 65 miles southwest of Santa Fe and 130 miles south of Taos.

Airlines Airlines serving Albuquerque International Airport are **America West** (tel. 800/247–5692), **American** (tel. 800/433–7300), **Continental** (tel. 800/525–0280), **Delta** (tel. 800/221–1212), **Mesa Air** (tel. 800/637–2247), **Southwest** (tel. 800/531–5601), **TWA** (tel. 800/221–2000), **United** (tel. 800/241–6522), and **USAir** (tel. 800/428–4322).

Air-shuttle service between Albuquerque and Santa Fe via **Mesa Airlines** operates up to seven times a day; the flying time is approximately 25 minutes.

Between the Airport and Downtown The trip into town from the airport takes about 10–15 minutes, and there is a variety of ground transportation to choose from. Taxis, available at clearly marked stands, charge about $7 (plus 35¢ for each additional rider); *see* the By Taxi section, below. Sun Tran buses, which cost 75¢, pick up at the sunburst signs every 15 minutes; the fare is 75¢; *see* the By Bus section in Getting Around Albuquerque, below. The following hotels provide shuttle service to and from the airport: Hilton, La Posada de Albuquerque, Marriott, Ramada, and Sheraton. If you like to go in high style, *see* the By Limousine section, below. For car rental companies that operate out of Albuquerque, *see* Chapter 1, Essential Information.

Arriving and Departing by Car, Train, and Bus

By Car The main routes into Albuquerque are I–25 from points north and south and I–44 from points east and west.

By Train **Amtrak's** (tel. 800/872–7245) Southwest Chief services Albuquerque daily from Los Angeles and Chicago. Built by the Santa Fe Railroad in 1901, **Albuquerque Station** (314 First St., tel. 505/842–9650), with its Spanish-style architecture, graceful domes, and archways, is typical of many of the railway stations constructed in the Southwest during the heyday of passenger railway service. It is located downtown near the intersection of US 66 and I–85, about 1½ miles from picturesque, historic Old Town. Red Cap service and handcarts are available. Facilities include a snack bar, vending machines, pay telephones, taxi stands, and the public Sun Tran bus service.

By Bus **Greyhound/Trailways** offers comprehensive daily service into **Albuquerque's Transportation Center** (200 Second St., SW, tel. 505/243–4435 or 800/531–5332).

Getting Around Albuquerque

Unlike more compact Taos and Santa Fe, Albuquerque sprawls out in all directions, so you'll need transportation to get wherever you're going.

By Bus The **Sun Tran** buses blanket the city with frequent connections (about every 30 minutes, less frequently in the more remote areas of the city and on weekends). The fare is 75¢. Bus stops are well marked with the line's sunburst signs. For information, call 505/843–9200, or write Sun Tran (City of Albuquerque, 601 Yale, SE, Albuquerque 87106).

By Taxi Taxis are metered in Albuquerque, service is around the clock, and rates run about $2.90 for the first mile and $1.40 for each additional mile. Contact **Albuquerque Cab** (tel. 505/883–4888), **Checker Cab** (tel. 505/243–7777), or **Yellow Cab** (tel. 505/247–8888) for service.

By Limousine Albuquerque has several limousine companies offering pampered service for those who require the best. Rates range from $25 to $35 per hour, with a two-hour minimum. Call for special airport shuttle rates. **American Limousine** (tel. 505/891–LIMO), **At Last, The Past,** Antique Limousine Service (tel. 505/298–9944), **Classic Limousine** (tel. 505/247–4000), **Dream Limousine** (tel. 505/884–6464), **Lucky's Limousine Service** (tel. 505/836–4035), **Luxury First Class Limousines** (tel. 505/269–5010 or 505/344–1985), **VIP Limousine Service** (tel. 505/883–4888).

Opening and Closing Times

General business hours in Albuquerque are 9–5; most shops, galleries, and museums are open 10–5 or 6, with limited hours on weekends. Banking hours are weekdays 9–4, and, in some cases, Saturday 10–2.

Guided Tours

Orientation **Gray Line of Albuquerque** offers several seasonal tours (May–Oct.). Among them is a three-hour Albuquerque city tour, including the University of New Mexico campus, historic landmarks, and Old Town. The tours, departing at 9, are given on Monday, Wednesday, and Friday. For reservations and information, call 505/764–9464.

Special-Interest Gray Line has a three-hour **Indian Heritage Tour,** including a visit to the Indian Pueblo Cultural Center in Albuquerque and to a living pueblo. This tour, departing at 1 PM, is offered on Monday, Wednesday, and Friday.

Shopper's Shuttle (1014 Dakota, NE, tel. 505/266–3698 or 505/298–2552) takes visitors to a variety of retailers in Albuquerque and nearby Santa Fe; tours include discounts, special fashion shows, and lunch.

Wild West Show & Tours (2430 Juan Talbo, NE, Suite 142, tel. 505/293–3326) schedules a variety of educational and adventure tours featuring Wild West reenactments, with visits to ranches, pueblos, and other historic sites in the heart of the Old West.

There are also many operators offering early morning **hot-air balloon tours** of Albuquerque (*see* Ballooning in Sports and Fitness, below).

Walking Tours The **Albuquerque Museum** (tel. 505/243–7255) leads hour-long historical walk through **Old Town** at 11 AM each Wednesday, Thursday, and Friday and at 1 PM on Saturday. There is no charge for the tour, which is available on a first-come basis and meets in the lobby of the Albuquerque Museum before setting out for Old Town.

A 30-minute walking tour of the **University of New Mexico** campus, available through the Public Affairs office (tel. 505/277–5813), emphasizes the university's cohesive Pueblo-style architecture.

Exploring Albuquerque

Orientation

Historic and colorful Route 66 is Albuquerque's Central Avenue, unifying, as nothing else, the diverse areas of the city— Old Town cradled at the bend of the Rio Grande, the University of New Mexico to the east, and Nob Hill (a lively strip of restaurants, boutiques, galleries, and shops farther east along Central Avenue). The river and the railroad tracks, running almost neck and neck and traversed by Central Avenue/Route 66, divide the city into quadrants, or quarters—SW, NW, SE, NE.

Because Albuquerque is so spread out, it covers a large geographical area, rendering its terrain rather diverse. Along the river in the north and south valleys, elevations hover at around 4,800 feet. To the northeast, land rises over mesas to the foothills of the Sandia Mountains at an elevation of 6,500 feet; the Sandia Crest is a grand spot to view the city spread below, and get a feel for its layout. West of the Rio Grande, where much of Albuquerque's growth is taking place, the mesa rises more abruptly than it does in the east—with a difference in elevation of 1,700 feet in the lowlands and highlands of the city. There are corresponding changes in temperature, as much as 10°F at any time; it's even been known to snow or rain in one part of town, while remaining dry and sunny in another.

Highlights for First-time Visitors

Indian Pueblo Cultural Center (*see* Tour 1)
New Mexico Museum of Natural History (*see* Tour 1)
Old Town (*see* Tour 1)
Petroglyph National Monument (*see* Parks and Monuments)
Sandia Peak Aerial Tramway (*see* Tour 3)
University of New Mexico Galleries (*see* Tour 2)

Tour 1: Old Town

Numbers in the margin correspond to points of interest on the Albuquerque and Albuquerque Old Town maps.

An exploration of Albuquerque begins where the city began, in Old Town. It was here on the plaza in 1706 that Don Francisco Cuervo y Valdez, a New Mexico provincial governor, decided to seal his mark in history by founding a town. No slouch when it came to political maneuvering, he named the new town, or *villa*, after the Duke of Alburquerque, Viceroy of New Spain, hoping that the flattery would cause the duke to overlook the fact that the newly formed community had only 15 families instead of the required 30 needed for a charter. The Duke of Albuquerque acquiesced, of course, but somewhere down the line the first "r" in his name was dropped. Don Francisco couldn't have made a better choice for the town's location. The new settlement was on the banks of the Rio Grande where the river made a wide curve, providing good irrigation for crops, and where several Indian pueblos already existed, meaning mutual aid, protection, and trade. The nearby mountains and the "bosque" offered ample wood—cottonwoods, willows, and olive trees. The weather was ideal.

❶ Today, Albuquerque's **Old Town Plaza** remains the heart of the city's heritage. While the modern city of 500,000 grew up all around it, the four-square-block area of Old Town hugs fiercely to the past, at least in spirit. The tree-shaded Plaza of today is much the Plaza of then, except that a graceful white gazebo and **❷** lacy wrought-iron benches have been added. The **San Felipe de Neri church** (2005 Plaza, NW, tel. 505/243–4628), enlarged and expanded several times over the years, still stands facing the Plaza, its massive adobe walls and other original sections intact. Most of the old adobe homes surrounding the church and the Plaza have been converted to shops, galleries, and restaurants, and many of the hidden *placitas*, or little plazas, offer more of the same. The best time to visit Old Town is early in the morning before the stores have opened and the daily rush of ac-

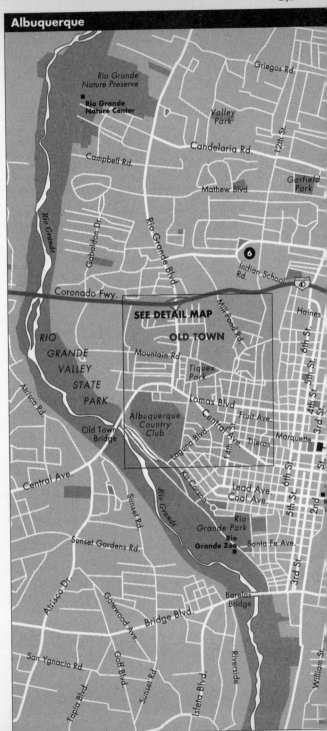

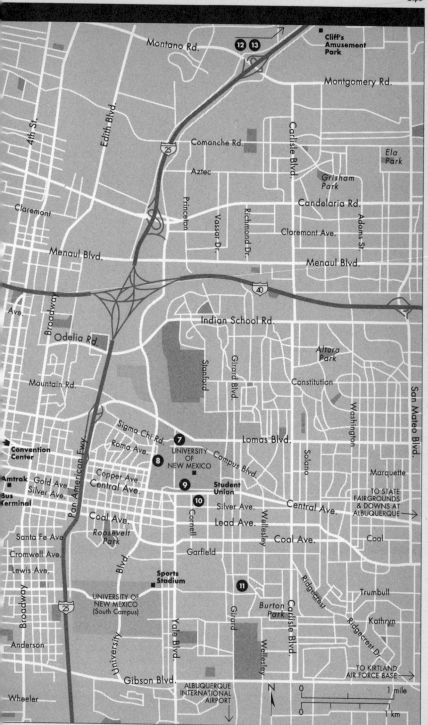

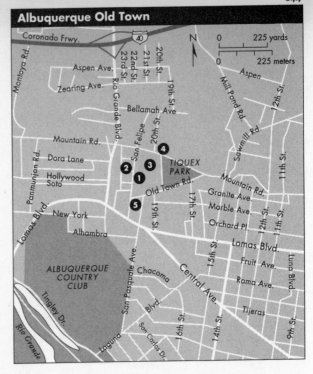

tivity begins. In the defused light of morning, you can almost hear the strum of a Spanish guitar and the click of heels, possibly a dancer, a conquistador, or a woman opening her shop.

The Plaza has not been without its share of controversy of late. In early 1991, the colorful 40-year tradition of Native Americans selling jewelry and crafts under the portals of a block-long section of Old Town shops was interrupted when a longstanding dispute between shop owners and Native American and non–Native American vendors came to a head. The non–Native American vendors complained that they were unfairly being denied the right to sell their wares. Shopkeepers complained that the Native American vendors were taking away their business. Quality control and sales taxes were also at issue. To put an end to the squabble, the City Council voted to ban sidewalk vending in Old Town, effective March 1991. There was a subsequent public uproar, and within three months the ban was lifted, and the Native American vendors were back, spreading their blankets on the sidewalk under the portals, their wares proudly on display.

Old Town, which is one block north of Central Avenue (the city's main street) at Rio Grande Boulevard, is a beehive of activity, with over 150 shops, restaurants, cafés, and delis. The scent of bubbling vats of green chili, enchiladas, and burritos hangs in the air. Gunfights are staged on Romero Street on Sunday afternoons, and during times of fiesta Old Town is alive with mariachi bands and dancing señoritas. You can pick up schedules of events and maps, which contain a list of public rest rooms, at the **Old Town Information Center** across the street from the San Felipe de Neri church. *305 Romero St., tel. 505/ 243–3215. Open Mon.–Sat. 10–5, Sun. 11–5.*

Adjacent to Old Town, just off the northeast corner on Mountain Road, are two of the city's major museums. The solar-heated **Albuquerque Museum** enshrines relics of the city's birth and development and is home to the largest collection of Spanish colonial artifacts in the nation. The centerpiece of the exhibit is two life-size models of Spanish conquistadores in chain mail and armor, one on horseback, they represent the arrival of Francisco Vasquez de Coronado and his soldiers on their quest for gold in 1540, the turning point of New Mexico's history. Among the museum's treasures are early maps—some from the 15th century showing California as an island and the Rio Grande River spilling into the Pacific—treasure chests once filled with pearls and gold coins, Colonial and contemporary paintings, and religious artifacts. A multimedia audiovisual presentation chronicles the development of the city since 1875. *2000 Mountain Rd., SW, tel. 505/243–7255. Admission free. Open Tues.–Sun. 9–5.*

New Mexico Museum of Natural History, just across the street from the Albuquerque Museum, is the city's newest showpiece. The striking glass-and-sand-colored building with slanted roofs opened in 1986. Its spectacular world of wonders, rumored to have been mounted, in part, with the help of Disney experts, includes an active volcano (its river of bubbling hot lava flows beneath museum visitors under a see-through glass floor), a frigid Ice Age cave, dinosaurs, and an Evolator (short for Evolution Elevator), a 6-minute high-tech ride through 35 million years of New Mexico's geological history via a mountain of video wizardry. An on-board video host on the large elevator escorts 25 passengers per ride, during which the floors and video-screen walls move, simulating a ride through the dimensions. The Dynax Theater makes viewers feel equally involved. An 85-foot-long replica of the Rio Grande flows from its source in Colorado, all the way down through Texas. A full-size replica of a 100-million-year-old Quetzalcoatlus, with a wingspan of 38 feet, hovers over the museum's central atrium, while visitors arriving via the front walkway outside share space with a giant brontosaurus. The museum has a Fossil Hot Line—505/841–8837—to assist amateurs in identifying paleontological finds. *1801 Mountain Rd., NW, tel. 505/841–8837. Admission: $4 adults, $3 senior citizens and students, $1 children 3–11, toddlers free. Tickets to the Dynamax Theater are the same. Combination tickets for the museum and Dynamax Theater are available at about a $1 saving. Open daily 9–5.*

For some more specialized natural history, go back down to Old Town, at the corner of San Felipe and Old Town Road: At the **American International Rattlesnake Museum,** the largest exhibit of rattlesnakes and rattlesnake memorabilia ever mounted can be viewed. Included are rare and unusual species, such as an albino rattlesnake. There are also rattlesnake artifacts, videos, and a Southwestern gift shop. *202 San Felipe, NW, tel. 505/242–6569. Admission: $1. Open Memorial Day– Labor Day, Mon.–Sat. 9–9, Sun. 1–9; Labor Day–Memorial Day, Mon.–Sat. 10–6, Sun. 1–9. Closed major holidays.*

Numbers in the margin correspond to points of interest on the Albuquerque map.

6 A short drive north of Old Town brings you to the **Indian Pueblo Cultural Center.** Its unique multilevel semicircular design was inspired by that of Pueblo Bonito, the famous prehistoric ruin in Chaco Canyon in the northwestern section of New Mexico. The cultural center is owned and operated by the 19 Pueblo tribes of New Mexico, each of which has an upper-level alcove devoted to its particular arts and crafts. Lower-level exhibits trace the history of the Pueblo Indians from prehistoric times to the present. Original paintings and sculpture of the highest quality, jewelry, leather crafts, rugs, souvenir items, drums, beaded necklaces, painted bowls, and fetishes on display are for sale. It's the largest collection of Indian arts and crafts in the Southwest and the richest resource for the study of America's first inhabitants of the region. Indian ceremonial dances are performed during the summer and on special holidays, free to the public. *2401 12th St., NW, tel. 505/843-7270. Admission: $2.50 adults, $1.50 senior citizens, $1 students. Open daily 9– 5:30; restaurant open 7:30-3. Closed major holidays.*

Time Out The Indian Pueblo Cultural Center has a restaurant, open for lunch, that serves Native American food exclusively, including blue-corn enchiladas; posole; Indian bread pudding; and, of course, fry bread, that almost addictive popoverlike creation topped with honey, beans, chili, or powdered sugar or gobbled up plain. In Old Town, a sidewalk café at **Forget-Me-Not** (308 San Felipe, NW, tel. 505/247-8901), a toy shop and bookstore for children, is a delightful spot for lunch or refreshments. A good alternative is the **Owl Cafe** (800 Eubank Blvd., NE, tel. 505/291-4900), a nostalgic 1950s-style diner with a soda fountain, jukebox, pictures of Marilyn Monroe, and milk shakes and green chili cheeseburgers.

Tour 2: The University of New Mexico

Just east of I–25 on Central Avenue is Albuquerque's 103-year-old **University of New Mexico,** the state's largest university, internationally recognized for its programs in anthropology, biology, Latin American studies, and medicine. It's also noted for its Pueblo-style architecture and superb landscaping. A central oasis within its 700 acres contains knolls, a duck pond, fountains, waterfalls, and benches. Throughout the campus are large-scale sculptures by internationally known artists and murals by famous New Mexican painters. The central information number for the university is 505/277-0111.

The university is a mainstay of Albuquerque's cultural and educational life, and its many outstanding galleries and museums, open to the public free of charge, shouldn't be missed. Included **7** among them is the **Jonson Gallery,** containing the works of the late modernistic painter Raymond Jonson (1891–1982), as well as those of contemporary artists. This intimate gallery is Jonson's former home and studio. A special retrospective exhibit of his work is presented each summer. *1909 Las Lomas, NE (University of New Mexico campus), tel. 505/277-4967. Admission free. Open Tues. 9-4 and 5-9, Wed.-Fri. 9-4; closed Sat.-Mon. and all major holidays.*

8 The **Maxwell Museum of Anthropology,** in the university's Anthropology Building, one block north of Grand Avenue on University Boulevard, has two permanent galleries. In one, the

"Ancestors" exhibit chronicles four million years of human emergence. In the other, "Peoples of the Southwest" explores the lifeways, art, and cultures of 10,000 years of human occupation in the Southwest. The museum shop offers a wide selection of traditional and contemporary Southwestern Indian jewelry, rugs, pottery, basketry, beadwork, and folk art from around the world. It also has a children's section with inexpensive books, kits, and handmade tribal artifacts. *Maxwell Museum of Anthropology (University of New Mexico campus), tel. 505/ 277–4404. Admission free. Open weekdays 9–4, Sat. 10–4, Sun. noon–4.*

❾ The **University Art Museum,** located in the Fine Arts Center just northwest of the entrance on Stanford Drive and Central Avenue, features permanent and changing displays of contemporary and historical art. Its fine-art collection is the largest in the state and includes the work of such old masters as Rembrandt and such newer ones as Picasso and (of course) Georgia O'Keeffe. The museum also has one of the largest holdings of prints and photographs in the country, including contemporary leaders and early pioneers in the field. *Fine Arts Center (University of New Mexico campus), tel. 505/277–4001. Admission free. Open Tues. and Wed. 9–4 and 5–9, Thurs. and Fri. 9–4, Sun. 1–4; closed Mon. and Sat.*

❿ At the corner of Central Avenue and Cornell is the sales and exhibit gallery of the **Tamarind Institute,** an internationally renowned school and workshop for lithographers where fine-art prints pulled from stones and metal plates are created. A Tamarind Master Printer certification is to an artist what a degree from Juilliard is to a musician. Tamarind maintains a gallery where prints and lithographs done by professionals, as well as those recently produced by students, are on display. Special guided tours are conducted on the first Friday of each month at 1 PM. *108 Cornell, SE, tel. 505/277–3901. Admission free. Open weekdays 9–5 and by appointment.*

⑪ Two blocks south of the university on Girard Boulevard, SE, you'll find the **Ernie Pyle Memorial Library,** the memorabilia-filled home of the beloved Pulitzer Prize–winning war correspondent, now the smallest branch of the Albuquerque Public Library. Pyle bought the house in 1940 after several visits to New Mexico with his wife, Jerry. On display are photos, handwritten articles by Pyle, and news clippings of his career and of his death by a sniper's bullet on April 18, 1945, on the tiny Pacific island of Ie Shima; he's buried in the National Cemetery of the Pacific in Punchbowl Crater, near Honolulu. "There are really two wars," wrote John Steinbeck. "One is the war of maps, logistics, campaigns, ballistics, divisions. . . . Then there is the war of the homesick, the weary, the wounded and dying, the common man . . . that is Ernie Pyle's war." *900 Girard Blvd., SE, tel. 505/256–2065. Admission free. Open Tues. and Thurs. 12:30–8, Wed., Fri., and Sat. 9–5:30. Closed Sun. and Mon.*

Time Out The university's **Student Union Building** (tel. 505/277–2331) on Central Avenue, just north of the visitors parking area, is a good spot to grab a burger or just rest your feet for a while. Here you'll also find changing exhibits and students' showings in three exhibit spaces—the Centennial (on the main level),

Union (north end, lower level), and ASA (south end, lower level) galleries.

Tour 3: Sandia

For a view of Albuquerque on high—and of half of New Mexico for that matter—head for **Sandia Crest,** the 10,678-foot summit of the Sandia Mountains. The road to the Crest, the Sandia Crest National Scenic Highway (east on I–40 to NM 14, north to NM 536), is well paved and carefully maintained year-round. Of course, there's more than one way to get to the top. The ⑫ **Sandia Peak Aerial Tramway,** the world's longest single-span tramway, takes visitors from a point outside Albuquerque's city limits on an awesome 2.7-mile climb to the top of Sandia Peak, where at sunset the desert skies produce a kaleidoscope of changing colors. From its lower terminal the tram car glides across a terrain of jagged boulders and clawing peaks, causing deer or perhaps a family of Rocky Mountain bighorn sheep to scamper away from the strange sight. The tram cars are new, custom made in Switzerland with expanded window space. From the sky-top observation deck at the summit, you can see Santa Fe to the northeast and Los Alamos to the northwest. And isn't that Tucson over there? Heading back, you can go the way you came or take the double-chair skiers' chairlift 7,500 feet down the other side. To reach the tramway's base, take I–25 north to the Tramway Road exit, then east on Tramway Road, or take Tramway Boulevard north from I–40 and Central Avenue for 8.5 miles to the stop sign, then head right on Tramway Road. *Sandia Peak Tramway, 10 Tramway Loop, NE, tel. 505/296–9585. Open Memorial Day–Labor Day, daily 9–10; slightly varied hours during the rest of the year. Weekends only during the second and fourth weeks of April. Tickets for the 18-minute ride are $10 adults, $7.50 senior citizens and children 5–12.*

Time Out There's a pricey restaurant atop the tramway called, appropriately, **High Finance** (Sandia Crest, tel. 505/243–9742). Needless to say, the view is outstanding. An alternative is the **Sandia Crest House Gift Shop and Restaurant** (Sandia Crest, tel. 505/243–0605), which provides family dining and more spectacular views.

⑬ A few miles farther north, the **Sandia Pueblo** is one of the most industrious of the Rio Grande pueblos, even though its residents are not particularly well versed in traditional arts and crafts; although its Bien Mur Indian Market Center (on I–25) features authentic American Indian wares, virtually all of them come from other pueblos and reservations. In fairness, the Sandia Pueblo does produce a variety of small, rough pottery pieces and some flat, traditional paintings. Yet another enterprise of the pueblo is the Los Amigos Stables, which offers horseback riding and caters Western-style banquets for large groups. The pueblo's original American Indian name was *Nafiat*, which means "a dusty place." Francisco Coronado, the first European to visit the pueblo (1540), named it "Sandia," which is Spanish for watermelon. The patron saint of the Sandias is St. Anthony, whose feast day is June 13. Traditionally, on that day mothers bring their unmarried daughters to church in the hope that Saint Anthony will find them husbands.

Recently opened on the reservation is the Sandia Lakes Recreation Area, where picnicking and fishing are offered. The pueblo's tribal bingo hall is open seven nights a week, 24 hours a day. *Sandia Pueblo, Bernalillo, tel. 505/867–3317. Admission free, but permission to tour the pueblo is required from the Sandia Pueblo Governor's Office. Open daily 8 AM–sundown (except on religious holidays). No photography or sketching is permitted.*

Albuquerque for Free

Among the city's free attractions are the **Albuquerque Museum** (*see* Tour 1, above), the numerous galleries at the **University of New Mexico** (*see* Tour 2, above), and the **National Atomic Museum** (Kirtland Air Force Base, Wyoming Gate, tel. 505/844–8443), which is devoted to an exploration of atomic energy and the role New Mexico played in nuclear technology. Exhibits include replicas of Little Boy and Fat Man, the atomic bombs dropped on Japan. In the Missile Park section you can examine a B-52 bomber and an F-105D fighter bomber, touch the rocket that was used to boost Alan Shepard into space, and see an array of historic flying machines with names like *Hound Dog, Bomarc, Mace,* and *Snark.* David Wolper's film *Ten Seconds That Shook the World* can also be seen here; call ahead for movie times. The charming **Old Town** area (*see* Tour 1, above), marking the site of Albuquerque's original Spanish settlement, is filled with colorful shops, galleries, and restaurants. It's ideal for browsing, shopping, or relaxing over coffee or a cool drink in the shade of a cottonwood tree that has stood tall since before the time of the conquistadores.

What to See and Do with Children

Cliff's Amusement Park, on Osuna Road at San Mateo Boulevard, includes 23 thrill rides, live entertainment, games, an arcade room, and private picnic areas. *4800 Osuna Rd., tel. 505/883–9063. General admission $3.25. Special ride passes are available Mon.–Thurs., $9.45; Fri., Sat., and Sun., $11.55. Open April 1–Oct. 14.*

The Hands-on Corner at the **Indian Pueblo Cultural Center** (*see* Tour 1, above) allows youngsters to touch Native American pottery, jewelry, dried corn, weaving, and tools. Children can draw their own petroglyphs or design pots. Colorful Native American dances in the museum's courtyard will impress the entire family.

Go about 30 miles north of Albuquerque on NM 14, which runs between Albuquerque and Santa Fe, you can visit the **Old Coal Mine Museum** in the quasi ghost town of **Madrid,** now populated with writers, artists, potters, poets, and home to a sprinkling of unusual shops and galleries. Children love exploring the old coal mine tunnel, with its vein of coal; climbing aboard a 1906 steam train; and nosing through a variety of antique buildings full of marvelous old relics, including 1920s movie projectors, early hospital and dental equipment, antique cars, and even a 1928 International dump truck. Tickets for the museum are available at the Mine Shaft Tavern out front. If you're there on a weekend during the summer (between Memorial Day and Labor Day), catch the museum's old-fashioned melodrama, staged in a former roundhouse machine shop that's been converted

into the **Engine House Theater.** It's probably the only theater
anywhere with a full-size steam train that comes chugging onto
the stage; the rear of the theater opens onto the tracks. In this
production, when the pretty heroine gets tied onto the tracks,
she's really got something to worry about. *Old Coal Mine Museum, Madrid, tel. 505/473–0743. Daily, weather permitting.
Admission: $2 adults, 75¢ children. Tickets for the melodra-
ma: $6.50 adults, $3.25 children 12 and under.*

New Mexico Museum of Natural History (*see* Tour 1, above) is
particularly appealing to kids, with a number of interesting
programs and exhibits designed just for them. A big favorite is
the Evolator, which takes visitors through 35 million years,
back to a seacoast where dinosaurs roamed. The naturalist center lets children touch snakes and frogs, see objects through
microscopes, and make animal tracks in a sand box. The museum also arranges camp-ins, when groups of children can sleep
overnight—if they dare close their eyes—with dinosaurs, giant
flying reptiles, and an active volcano.

What child doesn't love the zoo? Albuquerque's **Rio Grande Zo-
ological Park** is home to more than 1,000 animals from around
the world, from pink flamingos to chest-thumping gorillas.
Don't miss Moonshadow, the snow leopard, one of the rarest of
its kind. Sprawled over 60 acres, the zoo is especially well
known for its spacious naturalistic exhibits and lush landscaping, including a half dozen waterfalls. *903 10th St., SW, tel. 505/
843–7413. Admission: $4 adults, $2 children and senior citizens. Open daily 9–5, closed major holidays.*

While in the Sandia Mountains, you'll find lots to do with the
kids. A quick stop at the **Sandia Ranger Station** (tel. 505/281–
3304), off NM 14 South, offers a variety of pamphlets and maps
on the many outdoor recreational attractions and trails in the
park. The ranger station has a fire prevention program with a
Smokey the Bear movie and occasional tours to the nearby fire
station; call to reserve a time. You might also take a couple of
hours to see **Sierra Goat Farms,** 15 miles south of NM 14. Here
you and your little ones will meet Carmen Sanchez, the Goat
Lady, who owns the farm and delights in teaching children
about goats and mother nature. Ms. Sanchez shows children
how to milk the animals and how to care for them. The baby
goats are the biggest attraction on the farm, blurting a nasal
"wa, wa, wa, wa" in unison. The farm has plenty of outdoor
grills and picnic tables. A variety of goat cheeses, cheesecake,
and chocolate are for sale. *Sierra Goat Farms, Hwy. NM 40,
Tijeras, tel. 505/281–5061. Admission free. Open Tues.–Sun.
8–8.*

There are plenty of interesting attractions for small-fry travelers in Albuquerque, but perhaps none more so than the
Tinkertown Museum in Sandia Park on the way to Sandia
Crest. Run by Ross and Carla Ward, the museum houses a
world of miniature carved-wood characters. It contains the results of more than 30 years of carving and collecting by its owners, including an animated, miniature Western village. The
latest addition is a circus exhibit with wooden merry-go-round
horses from the 1940s and original circus emblems. Tiny vendors sell cotton candy, pink lemonade, and popcorn; other figures include trapeze artists, a bear act, a fire eater, a tiger
trainer, and an animated fat lady. Visitors entering the roadside attraction, passing through the building's colorful glass

bottle facade, are greeted by ragtime piano music. There's a
general store (life size) where deliveries arrive by horse-drawn
wagon. Put a quarter in a slot and Boot Hill Cemetery comes to
life, as lightning crackles and the devil and an angel do battle
over a poor lost soul. Tinkertown and most of its delightful creations represent a lifetime of carving for Ross Ward, whose
dream was hatched in the late 1950s. Today, more than 900 figures populate the tiny village. *Tinkertown Museum, Hwy. 536,
Sandia Park, tel. 505/281–5233. Admission: $2 adults, 50¢
children 15 and under. Open Apr. 1–Oct. 31, daily 9–6.*

The Children's Guide to Albuquerque, a book published by A
Child's Garden preschool, contains over 250 local listings of fun
things to do with kids. The guide is available at local bookstores or may be obtained by sending a check or money order
for $6 to A Child's Garden (215 Locust St., NE, 87105).

Off the Beaten Track

The Turquoise Trail. A scenic drive initiated nearly a quarter-
century ago and still popular, the Turquoise Trail departs from
freeway travel and ventures into backroad country, where the
pace is slow, talk is all about weather and crops, donkeys have
the right of way, and Albuquerque seems like another planet.
It's the old route between Albuquerque and Santa Fe, now full
of ghost towns that are being restored, thanks to writers, artists, and travelers who come through.

Heading east on I–40, the NM 14 North exit takes you to the
back road of Sandia Crest (NM 44), snaking up through a portion of Cibola National Forest and on to the 10,678-foot crest.
Stop to enjoy the view. Back on NM 14, again heading north,
you'll hit **Golden,** site of the first gold rush (1825) west of the
Mississippi. Golden has a rock shop and a mercantile store, and
its rustic adobe church and graveyard send photographers into
a state of euphoria. La Casita, a shop at the north end of the
village, serves as a kind of unofficial Chamber of Commerce, in
case you've got any questions.

Ten miles past Golden, you'll come to **Madrid** (*see* What to See
and Do with Children, above), where coal was once king. Long
abandoned, Madrid has been rebuilding, but slowly. Weathered old houses have been repaired and a shop opens here, and
another one there, mostly converted company stores or old
homes. Some of the shops are definitely worth a visit—
Carmen's Purple Palace (tel. 505/471–8393), for Southwestern
fashions, blankets, coats, and such; **Madrid Earthenware Pottery** (tel. 505/471–3450); the **Turquoise Trail Trading Post** (tel.
505/471–3450); the **Tapestry Gallery** (tel. 505/471–0194), for
hand-loomed knits and rugs; and **Maya Jones** (tel. 505/471–
4840), for Guatemalan imports. You'll probably also want to
visit the **Old Coal Mine Museum** and its **Engine House Theater,**
remnants of a once-flourishing coal mining business. During
melodramas staged here on weekends during the summer, you
can cheer the hero and hiss the villain.

A few miles farther north on NM 14, **Cerrillos** comes into view,
yet another echo of bygone days. A boom town in the 1880s, its
mines brimmed with gold, silver, and turquoise; it had eight
newspapers, four hotels, and 21 taverns flourishing. Then the
mines went dry, and the town went bust. The location site for a
number of television and Hollywood Westerns (*Young Guns,*

Lonesome Dove), Cerrillos today has a number of interesting shops along its tree-shaded streets, including **Why Not Shop** (tel. 505/471–2744), which carries a little bit of just about everything. The **Casa Grand** (tel. 505/438–3008), a sprawling 21-room adobe, offers early mining exhibits, a gift shop, a petting zoo, and a scenic overlook.

When you're ready to return to Albuquerque, you can turn around and drive back the way you came, or head west when you reach NM 22 and drive to the **Santo Domingo Reservation and Trading Post** (*see* Pueblos Near Albuquerque, below), then drive south to town.

Parks and Monuments

Aztec Ruins National Monument
So-named because early 19th-century settlers believed they had stumbled upon the Halls of Montezuma, Aztec contains 500 rooms laid out in an E-shape plan around a plaza. Archaeologists recently restored the kiva here to mint condition, complete with a timbered roof packed with mud. The site even offers mood music; stereophonic Navajo chants can be summoned by the mere push of a button. There's a visitors center and a museum (ancient pottery, clothes, tools, and artifacts). A complete tour of the site takes about 90 minutes. *Aztec Ruins National Monument, Box 640, Aztec 87410, tel. 505/334–6174. I–25 north from Albuquerque to Bernalillo, NM 44 north another 140 mi to Aztec. Total driving time is 3½–4 hrs one way. Admission: $5 per car, $2 per bus passenger. The Golden Age Passport, issued to U.S. citizens 62 or older, allows free admission to all occupants of the same car, regardless of age. Open Memorial Day weekend–Labor Day weekend, daily 8–6:30; rest of the year, daily 8–5; closed Christmas and New Year's Day.*

Coronado State Monument
Coronado State Monument is named in honor of the first Spanish expedition into the Southwest (1540–42). This prehistoric Kuaua pueblo, on a bluff overlooking the Rio Grande, is believed to have been the headquarters of Francisco Vasquez de Coronado's army of 1,200, who came seeking the legendary Seven Cities of Gold. The pueblo's restored kiva contains copies of magnificent frescos done in black, yellow, red, blue, green, and white, depicting fertility rites, rain dances, and hunting rituals; the original frescos are preserved in a small, nearby museum next to the visitor's center. The area is lovely. The Sandia Mountains rise abruptly from 5,280 to 10,678 feet a mere 6 miles away. The small community of Bernalillo, settled by Spanish colonists before Albuquerque was founded in 1706, is nearby. In the autumn, the views are especially breathtaking, with the trees turning russet and gold. Coronado State Monument is part of Coronado State Park, which has campsites and picnic grounds. *Coronado State Park, Box 853, Bernalillo 87004, tel. 505/867–5589. 1 mi northeast of Bernalillo on NM 44, off I–25. From Albuquerque's Old Town, travel 20 mi north on I–25 and take either the first turnoff (Bernalillo) or the second directly to the monument on NM 44. Admission: $2 adults, $1 children 6–16. Admission free for holders of Museums of New Mexico $6 2-day combination passes. Open daily 9–5 except holidays.*

Fort Sumner State Monument
Established in 1862, Fort Sumner is located in De Baca County, 2 miles east of the town of Fort Sumner and 4 miles south of

U.S. 60 on Billy the Kid Road along the east bank of the Pecos River. Artifacts and photographs on display—the Soldiers, the Indians, and Billy—relate to Fort Sumner and the Bosque Redondo Reservation, where 9,000 Navajos were interred from 1863 to 1868. Forced to make the infamous "Long Walk," they were brought to the site by Colonel Kit Carson from their original homeland in Canyon de Chelly, Arizona. The land was far from hospitable. Natural disasters destroyed crops, wood was scarce, and even the water from the Pecos proved unhealthy. Those who survived the harsh treatment and wretched living conditions (3,000 didn't) were allowed to return to Arizona in 1868. When the garrison left, the post was sold at auction and eventually converted into a large ranch. It's the same ranch where, in 1881, Sheriff Pat Garrett gunned down Billy the Kid, who's buried in a cemetery just off nearby NM 212. Adjacent is the Billy the Kid museum. *Fort Sumner State Monument, 2 mi east and 2 mi south of the town of Fort Sumner on NM 212, tel. 505/355–2573. I–40 east from Albuquerque to Santa Rosa, then NM 84 south for 45 mi and look for signs. Total distance from Albuquerque: about 180 mi. Admission: $2 adults, $1 children 6–16; admission free for holders of Museums of New Mexico $6 2-day passes. Open May 1–Sept. 15, daily 9–6, Sept. 16–Apr. 30, daily 8–5. Closed all state holidays except July 4, Memorial Day, and Labor Day.*

Fort Selden State Monument Established in 1865 to protect settlers of the Mesilla Valley and pioneers who were traveling through, this fort was typical of frontier posts in the Southwest, consisting of flat-roofed adobe brick buildings arranged around a drill field. In the early 1880s, Captain Arthur McArthur was appointed post commander. With him was his young son Douglas, who spent several years on the post. He grew up to become World War II hero General Douglas McArthur. A permanent exhibit called "Fort Selden: An Adobe Post on the Rio Grande" depicts the roles of officers, enlisted men, and women on the American frontier during the Indian Wars. Food and gas are available locally, and there are camping facilities at the adjacent Leasburg State Park. *Fort Selden State Monument, 13 miles north of Las Cruces at the Radium Springs exit, off I–25, tel. 505/526–8911. I–25 south from Albuquerque to Exit 19, about 225 mi. Admission: $2 adults, $1 children 6–16. Admission free for holders of Museums of New Mexico $6 2-day passes. Open May 1–Sept. 15, daily 9–6, Sept. 16–Apr. 30, daily 8–5. Closed all state holidays except July 4, Memorial Day, and Labor Day.*

Petroglyph National Monument Located 8 miles west of Albuquerque in the West Mesa area, at the site of five extinct volcanoes, the Petroglyph National Monument contains nearly 15,000 ancient American Indian rock drawings (petroglyphs) inscribed on the 17-mile-long West Mesa escarpment. American Indian hunting parties camped at the base of the lava flows for thousands of years, chipping and scribbling away. Archaeologists believe the petroglyphs were carved on the lava formations between AD 1100 and 1600. Viewers can see many of the drawings—there are four walking trails—at this former state park. *Petroglyph National Monument, 6900 Unser Blvd., NW, Albuquerque 87120, tel. 505/897–8814 or 505/823–4016. Admission free; $1 for parking. Open Memorial Day–Labor Day, daily 9–6, rest of the year, daily 8–5.*

Rio Grande Nature Center State Park
On the east bank of the Rio Grande in a cottonwood forest known as the "bosque," the Rio Grande Nature Center State Park is home to all manner of birds and migratory fowl that can be viewed year-round. Its unique visitors' center is constructed half above and half below ground; viewing windows provide a look at what's going on at both levels as birds, frogs, ducks, and turtles do their thing. *2901 Candelaria Rd., NW, Albuquerque 87107, tel. 505/344–7240. Admission: adults 25¢, children under 6 free. Open daily 10–5, closed major holidays.*

Pueblos Near Albuquerque

Acoma
Acoma Pueblo, 40 miles west of Albuquerque (12 miles off I–40), deserves its name, Sky City. Situated atop a 357-foot mesa that rises abruptly from the valley floor, it was built more than a thousand years before the Spanish conquistadores discovered it while searching for the Seven Cities of Cibola. It's still inhabited, although its onetime population of 6,000 has dwindled to a mere 50 who live in the village without electricity or running water. (Acoma people from neighboring Acomita, Anzac, and McCarty return to their ancestral home during feast days and celebrations, the most important of which is on September 2.) A series of terraced adobe pueblos, dominated by the massive mission church of San Estevan del Rey, Acoma is by far the most spectacular of the pueblo communities. Although a widened road takes you there today, the pueblo was originally accessible only by a narrow path carved into the face of the rock; food and water had to be hauled up the sides of the cliffs. When the early Spanish soldiers arrived, they were welcomed with gifts and hospitality, but their take-charge attitude quickly drew disfavor. The Spanish visitors were bludgeoned and thrown off the cliffs to their deaths. A similar fate befell a later group of Franciscan missionaries. Eventually, about 1700, the Acoma Pueblo Indians accepted the Spanish monks and their bearded Christ, and work began on the incredible mission at Sky City, with walls 60 feet high and 10 feet thick. The Acoma Indians are known for their fine, thin-walled pottery, characterized by "Op Art" patterns and mimbres (small animal and godlike figures) designs. Acoma may be visited by guided tours only. A shuttle accommodating 16 passengers leaves every hour from the visitors' center just below the mesa and drives to the top where the tours are conducted on foot. At the visitors' center there is also a museum, a restaurant, and a crafts shop. Nearby is the ubiquitous bingo hall. *Acoma Tourist Center, Box 309, Acoma 87034, tel. 505/252–1139. Admission: $6 adults, $5 senior citizens, $4 children 6–18. Open spring and summer, daily 8–7, tours daily 8–6; fall and winter, daily 8–4, tours daily 8–3:30. There is a $5 charge per camera for still photos. Movie and video cameras are prohibited.*

Isleta
The original pueblo was abandoned during the Pueblo Revolt in 1680, when many of the Tiwa-speaking Isleta Indians fled to Hopi; they returned and built a new village in 1693, which stands where it did then, 13 miles south of Albuquerque off I–25. Isleta now consists of several communities spread out across the reservation, the largest of which is Shiawiba to the west of the Rio Grande. Visitors will find a bingo hall on the reservation, as well as picnicking and camping facilities and fishing at the Isleta Lakes and Recreation Area (*see* Camping,

below). Polychrome pottery with red-and-black designs on a white background is the specialty here. The pueblo celebrates with a Harvest Dance on its feast day, September 4, in honor of St. Augustine. *Box 317, Isleta 87022, tel. 505/869–3111. Open year-round. Admission free. Cameras prohibited. Camping, fishing, and picnicking permits available at Isleta Lakes.*

Laguna The Laguna Pueblo, 46 miles west of Albuquerque on old Route 66, consists of six scattered villages. It is one of the youngest and largest of the New Mexican pueblos, and one of the most enterprising, with businesses like Laguna Industries (manufacturer of U.S. Army communications shelters). A large uranium field located on Laguna lands provided mining jobs for many of its members for years and is now the site of ongoing restoration through the Laguna Reclamation Project. The 1970s brought about a resurgence of interest in traditional crafts, so an abundance of fine pottery, decorated in geometric designs, is to be found in the area. The pueblo celebrates many feast days and dances (March 19, San José Feast Day; September 8, Virgin Mary Feast Day; October 17, St. Margaret and Mary Feast Day), since each of the six villages hosts its own ceremony, but all join at Old Laguna on September 19 to honor St. Joseph with Buffalo, Corn, and Eagle dances and a fair. Permits for fishing the pueblo's Paguate Reservoir can be obtained in Paguate village. *Box 194, Laguna Pueblo 87026, tel. 505/552–6654 or 505/243–7616. Open year-round. Admission free. Photography regulations vary in each village; contact the governor's office for information.*

San Felipe Located off I–25, between Albuquerque and Santa Fe, about 10 miles north of Bernalillo, San Felipe is one of the most traditional and conservative of the pueblo communities. Ceremonial dances are performed several times a year. The most notable is the Green Corn Dance on May 1, celebrating the Feast of Saint Philip, the pueblo's patron saint. Wearing symbolic costumes, hundreds of men, women, and children participate in the singing and dancing rituals that continue throughout the day. The plaza on the pueblo has been worn deep, like a rounded-out bowl, 3 feet below the surface of the surrounding ground, by years of dancing feet. *Box A, San Felipe Pueblo 87001, tel. 505/867–3381. Admission free. Open daily 9–6 except special feast days; closed days of religious celebrations. Cameras, sketching, and recording are prohibited.*

Santa Ana Except for ceremonial feast days, the Santa Ana Pueblo, located 8 miles northwest of Bernalillo on NM 44, appears to be empty most of the time because many members live in houses off the grounds. However, life returns to the pueblo with a passion on Santa Ana Feast Day, July 26, when the Corn Dance is held. Craftspeople of the pueblo are noted for their woven belts and headbands, paintings, and pottery, all of which can be purchased through the pueblo's Cooperative Association (open Tues. and Thurs. 10–4:30). Tribal lands are currently being redeveloped, with agricultural projects and a new 27-hole golf course in the works. Since the pueblo is not always open to visitors, check with the tribal governor's office before making the trip. *Santa Ana, Star Rte., Box 37, Bernalillo 87004, tel. 505/867–3301. Admission free. Open Jan. 1 and 6, Easter Day, June 24 and 29, July 25 and 26, Dec. 25–28, and by appointment. Check with the governor's office for tribal rules regarding photography and recordings.*

Santo Domingo Located off I–25 at the Santo Domingo exit between Albuquerque and Santa Fe, the Santo Domingo Pueblo operates a Tribal Cultural Center, where its outstanding *heishi* (shell) jewelry is sold, along with other traditional arts and crafts. Sales are also made from roadside ramadas leading into the pueblo. Long a farming community, the Santo Domingo Pueblo is now developing commercial property along the interstate. It is the Santo Domingo Indians who are most often seen selling their wares beneath the portal of the Palace of the Governors on the Santa Fe Plaza. The August 4 Corn Dance is one of the most colorful and dramatic of all the pueblo ceremonial dances, often with more than 500 dancers, clowns, singers, and drummers participating. *Box 99, Santo Domingo 87052, tel. 505/465–2214 or 505/465–2645. Open daily sunrise–sunset. Admission free, but donations are encouraged. Cameras, recorders, and sketching materials prohibited.*

Zia The Zia Pueblo has existed at its present site, 17 miles northwest of Bernalillo on NM 44, since the early 1300s. The sun symbol appearing on the New Mexican flag was adopted from this ancient pueblo. Bird motifs, another easily recognized pueblo marking, adorn the fine polychrome ware produced by the skillful Zia potters. The tribe's painters are equally skilled, producing outstanding watercolors that are highly prized. A colorful Corn Dance is held on August 15, the pueblo's annual feast day honoring Saint Anthony. Permits for fishing in Zia Lake, about 2 miles west of the pueblo, may be purchased on the site. *Zia Pueblo, San Ysidro 87053, tel. 505/867–3304. Cameras, recorders, and sketching materials prohibited.*

Shopping

Shopping anywhere in northern New Mexico brings on a feeling of déjà vu: after a while, one shop looks like the next. Still the prowl, shopping bag in hand, is well worth the effort. The tourist trail in New Mexico is paved with Native American arts and crafts (handsome turquoise and silver jewelry, baskets, blankets, pottery, etc.), Spanish Colonial handmade furniture, leather goods, textiles, colorful items from South of the Border, trendy Taos and Santa Fe designs in interior furnishings, and antique mementos of the early West, everything from Billy the Kid's gunbelt (of dubious authenticity) to Kit Carson's hat (well, maybe). Tourist demand has forced prices up, but if you diligently stalk the fairs and powwows, the back-street shops, flea markets, and second-hand stores, you'll surely come away with a treasure or two.

When it comes to art, buy what you like and let the experts hiss and howl. But unless you're really knowledgeable, beware of those high-priced, once-in-a-lifetime purchases. You'll also find some funky, good-natured souvenir art and merchandise that's always worth a few dollars, if only as a keepsake of happy days visiting dusty pueblos or flea markets in the sun.

As with most large, sprawling Western cities, Albuquerque's main shopping areas are malls and shopping centers scattered throughout the community. Hours are generally 10 AM–9 PM weekdays, Saturdays 10–6, and Sundays noon–6.

Shopping Malls

Among the major shopping centers are **Coronado Center** (Louisiana Blvd. and Menaul Blvd., tel. 505/881–2700), New Mexico's largest shopping center, with over 160 stores including Broadway, Sears, and J.C. Penney; **Fashion Square** (San Mateo Blvd. and Lomas Blvd., tel. 505/265–6931), anchored by Kistler Collister department store, but mostly filled with boutiques selling jewelry, shoes, home furnishings, children's clothes, and beauty products; **First Plaza Galeria** (20 First Plaza, tel. 505/242–3446), with a variety of small shops and restaurants; and **Winrock Center** (Louisiana Blvd. exit off I–40, tel. 505/883–6132), with 120 stores, including Dillard's, Montgomery Ward, and Marshall's, and 17 restaurants, from fast food to upscale fare.

Specialty Stores

Antiques The **Antique Specialty Mall** (4516 Central Ave., SE, tel. 505/268–8080, and 330 Washington St., SE, tel. 505/256–9653) is Albuquerque's most prestigious center for collectibles and fine antiques, with special emphasis on memorabilia from the early 1880s to the 1950s. When the set designers for the hit television miniseries *Lonesome Dove* needed special props to establish authenticity, they came here. At the mall's two locations, collectors will find Art Deco and Art Nouveau items, Depression glass, pottery, American Indian arts and crafts, quilts and linens, vintage clothes, cherrywood furniture, antique jewelry, and Western memorabilia.

Books **Book Fare** (56901 Wyoming Blvd., NE, tel. 505/821–6758) handles books on such subjects as horses, children, travel, cooking, the Southwest, and nature and hiking guides. Also available are large-print books, gift books, and books by local authors. The store it also features a wide selection of domestic and foreign maps.
Little Professor Book Center (6001 Lomas Blvd., NE, tel. 505/266–3110), located in the Fair Plaza Shopping Center, offers a wide range of general books and has a large stock of autographed volumes, among them store owner Norman Zollinger's *Riders to Cibola*. The shop specializes in Southwestern reading matter and is frequently the scene of book signings with leading Southwestern authors.
Page One (11200 Montgomery Blvd., NE, tel. 505/294–2026), voted the best bookstore in Albuquerque by *Albuquerque Monthly Magazine*, is certainly one of the biggest, claiming the largest selection of titles in New Mexico. It also handles computer software, technical and professional books, maps, globes, racing forms, and 150 out-of-state and foreign newspapers.

Home Furnishings **Ernest Thompson Furniture** (2618 Coors Rd., SW, tel. 505/266–7751) showcases handcrafted and handcarved New Mexican pieces.
Mariposa Gallery (113 Romero St., NW, tel. 505/842–9658) is a six-room Old Town space handling contemporary American crafts, including jewelry, sculptural art glass, mixed media, clay works, and painted wooden coyotes in the tradition of New Mexican folk art.
Ortega's de Chimayo (324-C San Filipe Ave., NW, tel. 505/842–5624) is the Old Town showcase of the Ortega family's famous

weaving and arts and crafts shop in Chimayo, the tiny village located on the High Road between Santa Fe and Taos (*see* Chapter 3, Santa Fe). One of the original families to settle Chimayo, the Ortegas have been weavers for eight generations, from Gabriel de Ortega in the early 1700s to 13-year-old Katherine Ortega, the youngest weaver in the family today. Also featured are Southwestern paintings, *santos* (saints) and other wood carvings, kachina dolls, and Navajo and contemporary rugs and blankets.

Native American Arts and Crafts

Adobe Gallery (413 Romero Rd., NW, tel. 505/243–8485) specializes in historic and contemporary art of the Southwestern Indians: Pueblo pottery, Hopi kachinas, Navajo rugs, blankets, and paintings. Founded in 1978, the shop is housed in a historic *terrones adobe* (bricks are cut from the ground, rather than formed from mud and dried) homestead that dates back to 1878. Owned and managed by Alexander E. Anthony, Jr., the shop also has an extensive stock of books about Southwestern Indians.

Andrews Pueblo Pottery (Suite 8, 400 S. Felipe Ave., NW, tel. 505/243–0414) handles Pueblo Indian pottery, fetishes, kachinas, and Southwestern graphics.

Penfield Gallery of Indian Arts (2043 S. Plaza Ave., NW, tel. 505/242–9696) is owned by Julia Reidy, who specializes in Pueblo pottery, storytellers, Hopi jewelry, kachinas, Zuni fetishes, and sand paintings.

Sam English Gallery (400 San Felipe Ave., NW, tel. 505/843–9332), a half block north off the Plaza in Old Town, features traditional and contemporary Native American works, plus oils, watercolors, prints, and lithographs by Sam English and his son, Sam Jr.

Tanner Channey Gallery (410 Romero St., NW, tel. 505/247–2242) is housed in a beautiful old pre–Civil War adobe hacienda in Old Town. On display in several showrooms is an extensive collection of jewelry, sculpture, contemporary and historic pottery, and weaving by Native Americans. Huge handcarved wooden doors lead from the showrooms to a flagstone patio, shaded by old *letias* (strips of wood laid in a herringbone pattern); bougainvilleas and hibiscus tumble this way and that; and the famous Angel of Old Town fountain bubbles forth. It's one of the prettiest courtyards in town. The main showroom, the Great Gallery, is filled with Navajo rugs (some dating back to the early 1800s), pottery, baskets, and an extensive selection of books on the Southwest. The shop also has a branch at the Hyatt Regency.

Weyrich Gallery (2935D Louisiana Blvd. E, tel. 505/883–7410) features contemporary and traditional fine crafts, jewelry, sculpture, etchings, clay, paintings, and clothing.

Wright's Collection of Indian Arts (6000 Indian School Rd., tel. 505/883–6122), one block north of the Marriott in Park Square, was founded as a trading post in 1907. Considerably more upscale these days, Wright's offers authentic Native American arts and crafts, from the traditional to the contemporary. Shoppers may also visit the unique museum on the premises, with its impressive display of Southwestern art and pottery.

Art Galleries

Amapola Gallery (2045 S. Plaza St., NW, tel. 505/242–4311), just west off the Plaza near Rio Grand Boulevard, has a lovely cobbled courtyard and an indoor space, both of which are overflowing with pottery, paintings, textiles, carvings, baskets, jewelry, and more. It's worth a visit just to see the handsome displays. Amapola is one of the largest co-op galleries in New Mexico.

Concetta D. Gallery (Suite 29, 20 First Pl., NW, tel. 505/243–5066) features multimedia, traditional, and contemporary art by Southwestern artists.

Dartmouth Street Gallery (206 Dartmouth Dr., NE, tel. 505/266–7751) is owned by John Cacciatore, who handles paintings and tapestries by regional artists.

Navajo Gallery (333 Romero St., NW, tel. 505/843–7666) is the Albuquerque branch of famed Navajo artist R. C. Gorman's trend-setting Taos space. The first American Indian painter to open his own fine arts gallery, Gorman now has outlets in Hawaii, New York, and Tokyo that represent his work exclusively.

Reynolds Gallery (324-C San Felipe Ave., NW, tel. 505/843–7373) focuses on Southwestern and contemporary sculpture, paintings, and drawings by national and local artists.

Russell's Gallery (7720 Central Ave., SE, tel. 505/255–1918) features works from several area painters and a select group of signed and numbered prints by internationally acclaimed Southwestern artists, including Bill Rabbit and Robert Redbird. Also featured are the paintings and ceramics of co-owner Vera Russell. The latter are handcast pottery pieces accented with American Indian figures and scenes of Southwestern landscapes.

Weems Gallery (2801-M Eubank Blvd., NE, tel. 505/293–6133) represents over 150 artists, with emphasis on originality and quality. Featured are paintings, pottery, sculpture, jewelry, weaving, stained glass, and original-designed clothes. Gift items and a framing service are also available. The **Weems Winrock Gallery** (129 Winrock Center, tel. 505/881–3794) also owned by Mary Ann Weems, carries Southwestern art in all media and all price ranges.

Sports and Fitness

Participant Sports

The **Albuquerque Parks and Recreation Department** (Box 1293, Albuquerque 87103, tel. 505/768–3490) maintains a widely diversified network of parks and recreational programs, encompassing over 20,000 acres of open space, four golf courses, 200 parks, six paved tracks for biking and jogging, as well as numerous recreational facilities, such as swimming pools, tennis courts, ball fields, playgrounds, and even a shooting range.

Ballooning Known for its International Balloon Fiesta (*see* Spectator Sports, below), Albuquerque also offers myriad opportunities to those who want to take to the skies themselves. If you'd like to give it a try, contact any of the following:

A & R Sky Voyages (4600 Quartz Dr., tel. 505/8991–9529).
Ad Venture Balloons (31232 San Mateo, NE, tel. 505/298–8887).
Aerco Balloon Port (523 Rankin Rd., tel. 505/344–5844).
Balloon Fiesta (8309 Washington Pl., NE, tel. 505/821–1000).
Ceron Balloons New Mexico (2950 San Joaquin Ave., SE, tel. 505/265–4007).
Delta Yankee Balloons (800 Park Ave., SW, tel. 505/842–6171).

Duke City Balloonport (12100 Anaheim Ave., NE, tel. 505/299–5481).

Rainbow Riders (430 Montclaire Dr., SE, tel. 505/268–3401).

Southwest Aviation Management (2730 San Pedro Dr., NE, tel. 505/889–6318).

Tours of Enchantment (5801 Jones Pl., NW, tel. 505/831–4285).

World Balloon Corporation (4800 Eubank Blvd., NE, tel. 505/293–6800).

Bicycling　Albuquerque is big on biking, both as a recreational sport and as a means of cutting down on automobile traffic and its resulting emissions. In 1973, the city established a network of bikeways, recommending existing streets and roadways as bike routes, lanes, and trails. Since then, many new ones have been added, and the program continues to expand. On designated bike routes, bicycles share lanes of traffic with automobiles, with no separation between car and bicycle; the bicyclist has the same right to use the street as does the motorist and must obey the same traffic laws and signals. Bike lanes, on the other hand, are designated exclusively for bike riders. Designated Recreational Trails are shared with pedestrians and provide the safest off-road area for both (*see* Jogging, below, for a list of these routes). An elaborately detailed **Metropolitan Albuquerque Bicycle Map** can be obtained free of charge by calling 505/768–3550. The foldout map also includes rules and regulations concerning biking in the city, as well as safety tips. For information about mountain biking in the adjacent national forest, call the Sandia Ranger Station (tel. 505/281–3304).

Golf　The Albuquerque Parks and Recreation Department maintains four public golf courses. Greens fees range from $6.50 for nine holes to $10.50 for 18 holes, with special discount rates for Early Bird and Sundown play. (The courses are open from sunup to sundown.) Each has a clubhouse and pro shop, where clubs and equipment can be rented. Weekday play is on a first-come basis, but reservations are advised for weekend use. The city's **Golf Management Office** (6401 Osuna Rd., NE, tel. 505/888–8115) can provide more information.

Arroyo del Oso (7001 Osuna Rd., NE, tel. 505/884–7505) has an 18- and a 9-hole regulation course and practice facilities. Selected as one of the top 50 27-hole public golf courses in the country by *Golf Digest*, **Puerto del Sol** offers a driving range, a full-service restaurant, and an up-to-the-hour information line for tee-off status (tel. 505/889–3699).

At **Ladera** (3401 Ladera Dr., NW, tel. 505/836–4449), 10 miles west of downtown, there are an 18-hole regulation course, practice facilities, a 9-hole executive course, a large driving range, a restaurant, and a full-service pro shop.

Los Altos (9717 Cooper Ave., NE, tel. 505/298–1897) includes an 18-hole regulation course, a short 9-hole course, and practice facilities. One of the Southwest's most popular facilities, Los Altos has a driving range, grass tees, a restaurant (mainly Mexican food), instructors for individuals or groups, and a large selection of rental equipment.

Located near the Albuquerque airport, **Puerto del Sol** (1800 Girard Blvd., SE, tel. 505/265–5636) has a 9-hole regulation course, a lighted driving range, and a full-service pro shop. There are no reserved tee times.

The University of New Mexico also maintains two public golf courses. One, **UNM North** (on Yale, tel. 505/277–4149) is a first-class nine-hole course on campus; the other, **UNM South** (on Rio Bravo, tel. 505/277–4546) is an 18-hole championship course, including an excellent beginners' three-hole regulation course. Both are open daily (except Christmas) and have full-service pro shops, instruction, and snack bars offering New Mexican favorites.

Health Clubs Most of the large hotel health clubs are reserved for the guests' use only. However, keeping fit in Albuquerque is easy, with numerous health clubs, gyms, and fitness centers from which to choose in virtually every neighborhood.

Academy Court Club (5555 McLeod Rd., NE, tel. 505/884–5555) features 16 regulation racquetball/handball courts, a weight room with free weights, separate sauna and whirlpool facilities, and an on-premise nursery. It's open to nonmembers at a $4.50 walk-in fee.

Albuquerque Rock Gym (3300 Princeton Dr., NE, tel. 505/881–3073) has a complete indoor climbing facility, with a pro shop and equipment rentals. It's one block east of I–25, one block north of Candelaria Road.

Body Elite (640 Coors Blvd., NW, No. 15, tel. 505/831–2934) offers complete body management, with free weights, specialized machines, aerobics, personalized training programs, sauna, whirlpool, karate lessons, tanning, and day-care facilities. The walk-in fee for nonmembers is $5.

Executive Sports Club (40 First Plaza, tel. 505/842–9428) has free weights, handball/racquetball courts, a heated swimming pool, rowing machines, treadmills, aerobicycles, Nautilus equipment, sauna, whirlpools, massages, tanning—and a fine downtown location. Nonmembers pay $10.50 per day.

Gold's Gym (5001 Montgomery, NE, Suite 147, tel. 505/881–8500) is a state-of-the-art fitness complex, part of the national chain. It offers free weights, a cardiovascular deck, aerobics, sportswear, and Pro-line supplements. Nonmembers pay $8 per day.

The facilities at **Liberty Gym** (2525 Jefferson St., NE, tel. 505/884–8012), one of the largest body-building and fitness centers in the Southwest, include specialized machines (including Stairmasters), free weights, personalized instruction, and nutritional counseling. The nonmembers' walk-in fee is $5.

Jogging The **Albuquerque Parks and Recreation Department** maintains an extensive network of Designated Recreational Trails that joggers share with bicyclists, as follows:

Bear Canyon, a 1-mile trail along the Bear Arroyo, extends east from Eubank Boulevard to Juan Tabo Boulevard, going through El Oso Grande Park.

Embudo, a 1½-mile trail, connects to the Las Montanas trail at Morris Street, NE, then runs east along the Embudo Channel to Tramway Boulevard. A bicycle-pedestrian bridge at Tramway Boulevard links this to the Tramway Trail.

Jefferson-Osuna, a 4-mile trail, runs along the Bear Arroyo between Jefferson Street and Osuna Road, NE.

Paseo del Bosque, a 5-mile trail, is parallel to the irrigation ditch on the east side of the Rio Grande. Trail users may enter at Candelaria, Campbell, and Mountain roads or at Central Avenue, SW.

Paseo de las Montanas, a 4.2-mile trail, goes from east of Winrock at Pennsylvania Street to Tramway Boulevard, NE.

Paseo de Nordeste, a 6.13-mile asphalt trail, begins at Tucker Avenue (University of New Mexico campus) and ends at Sandia High School, Pennsylvania Street, NE.

Pino, a 1.5-mile trail, starts at Wyoming Boulevard near Harper Road at the Albuquerque Academy and proceeds west along the South Pino Channel to San Pedro Drive, NE.

Tramway, a 4-mile-long trail, runs along the east side of Tramway Road from Montgomery Boulevard to I–40.

Swimming   The City of Albuquerque has a number of year-round pools that are open to both lap and recreational swimming. (Admission: children 6 and under 35¢, children 7–12 $1, children 13–19 $1.50, adults $1.75, and senior citizens 25¢. Special monthly and yearly rates are available. A number of pools have swim-for-25¢ Friday-night specials.)

Highland Pool (400 Jackson, SE, tel. 505/256–2096) is open for lap swimming 6–8 AM and 11:45 AM–12:30 PM for adults only on weekdays, and for recreational swimming at all other times.

Los Altos Pool (10100 Lomas Blvd., NE, tel. 505/291–6290) has lap-swim hours for adults only 6–9 AM weekdays, and recreational-swimming hours at all other times.

Sandia Pool (7801 Candelaria Rd., NE, tel. 505/291–6279) is open for lap swimming 6–8 AM and 4:30–6 PM for adults weekdays only and for recreational swimming at all other times.

Valley Pool (1505 Candelaria Rd., NW, tel. 505/761–4086) is reserved for lap swimming for adults only 6–8 AM and 4:30–6 PM weekdays, and for recreational swimming at all other times.

A number of public swimming pools are open only from June 1 to August 18:

East San José (2015 Galena, SE, tel. 505/848–1396), weekdays noon–4 and weekends noon–5.

Eisenhower (11001 Cino Cuatro, NE, tel. 505/291–6292), weekdays 12:30–5 and weekends noon–5.

Montgomery (5301 Palo Duro Ave., NE, tel. 505/888–8123), weekdays 12:30–5 and weekends noon–5.

Rio Grande (1410 Iron Ave., SW, tel. 505/848–1397), weekdays 12:30–5 and weekends noon–5; lap swimming only weekdays noon–1.

Sierra Vista (1410 Iron Ave., SW, tel. 505/897–8819), weekdays 12:30–5 and weekends noon–5; reserved for lap swimming weekdays 5:15–6:15.

Sunport (5301 Palo Duro Ave., NE, tel. 505/848–1398), weekdays 12:30–5 and weekends noon–5.

West Mesa (5301 Palo Duro Ave., tel. 505/836–8718), weekdays 12:30–5 and weekends noon–5.

Wilson (6000 Anderson Ave., SE, tel. 505/256–2095), weekdays 12:30–5 and weekends noon–5.

Tennis Albuquerque's wide-ranging network of public parks contains nearly three dozen public tennis facilities that generally have one to six courts. Lessons are available at some; others are lighted for night play (until 10 PM). For information call the Albuquerque Parks and Recreation Department (tel. 505/848–1381). In addition, the city maintains three tennis complexes.

Albuquerque Tennis Complex (1903 Stadium Blvd., SE, tel. 505/848–1381) consists of 16 Laykold tennis courts and 4 racquetball/handball courts, which may be reserved by phone or in person; reservations are taken two days in advance at 10 AM. The rate is $2 per hour.

The **Jerry Cline Tennis Complex** (Louisiana Blvd. and Constitution Ave., tel. 505/256–2032) has 12 Laykold courts, 3 of which are lighted. There is no charge, and no reservations are needed to play here.

Sierra Vista Tennis Complex (5001 Montano Rd., NW, tel. 505/848–1381) consists of 10 tennis courts (2 Omni courts), 2 platform tennis courts, and a swimming-pool area. The reservation policy and charge for courts are the same as at the Albuquerque Tennis Complex. No racquetball facilities are available.

Along with the numerous tennis courts located in the city's various hotels and resorts (*see* Lodging, below), a number of private clubs have excellent facilities and generally allow guest privileges at a member's invitation or honor memberships from out-of-town clubs with reciprocal arrangements or equal status. Among these are the **Highpoint Racquet and Swim Club** (43001 Landau Dr., NE, tel. 505/293–5820), **Tanoan Country Club** (10801 Academy Rd., NE, tel. 505/822–0455), and the **Tennis Club of Albuquerque** (2901 Indian School Rd., NE, tel. 505/262–1691).

Spectator Sports

The **Albuquerque Dukes** are the Triple-A farm team of the Los Angeles Dodgers and members of the Pacific Coast League; Orel Hershiser is a Dukes alumnus. Exciting professional baseball can be seen from April through September at the city-owned Albuquerque Sports Stadium, located at Stadium and University Boulevard, the only stadium anywhere with a drive-in spectator area. Admission varies from $1 to $4. Call or write the Albuquerque Dukes (1601 Stadium, SE, Albuquerque 87125, tel. 505/243–1791) for schedules and information.

The **New Mexico Chiles** are the professional men's outdoor soccer team, representing New Mexico in the American Professional Soccer League. The Chiles, who made their APSL debut in the 1990 season, bring their exciting pro-soccer action to Wilson Stadium (on Lomas Blvd. east of Juan Tabo Blvd.) from April through August. Call or write the New Mexico Chiles (2512 San Mateo Pl., Albuquerque 87110, tel. 505/883–1025) for schedules and further information.

The **University of New Mexico's** Lobo football and basketball games are also a major draw. The University Arena has a 17,000-seat capacity to accommodate the city's intensely loyal UNM basketball fans. Across the street is the 30,000-seat Lobo football stadium. For schedules and ticket information call 505/277–3901 (basketball) and 505/277–2116 (football).

Downs at Albuquerque is a glass-enclosed, climate-controlled racing facility located in the center of Albuquerque at the State Fairgrounds. Quarter-horse and thoroughbred racing begins in January and runs through June 10. Admission is $2, with preferred seating tickets from $4 to $6. Afternoon racing takes place on Friday, Saturday, Sunday, and holidays. Call 505/262–1188 for post times.

Albuquerque International Raceway (4520 Montgomery Blvd., NE, tel. 505/884–0323) is a state-of-the-art motor-sports facility scheduled to open in 1992. Featured events will include the NASCAR Winston Cup, CART Indy cars SCCA TransAM, AMA Motorcycle Grand Prix, and the IMSA Camel GT.

Ballooning Mention hot-air ballooning to an enthusiast, and Albuquerque automatically comes to mind. The city's high altitude, few obstructions, and steady but manageable winds make it especially suitable. Albuquerque's long history of ballooning dates back to 1882, when Professor Park A. Van Tassel, a saloon keeper, made the first balloon ascent at the Territorial Fair. Van Tassel's vehicle was destroyed during a subsequent flight, but that didn't dampen his enthusiasm. He bought another balloon; went on a world flight; and, during the trip, fell into the Pacific Ocean, where, it was rumored, he was eaten by sharks.

Since those colorful early beginnings, Albuquerque has become the hot-air-balloon capital of the world, partly because of the success of the annual **Albuquerque International Balloon Fiesta,** the first one of which took place in 1972 when 16 balloons participated. Today the nine-day event, held in early October, is the largest hot-air-balloon gathering in the world, attracting more than 500 registered hot-air balloons and entrants from as far away as Australia and Japan.

A special feature of the annual gathering is the "balloon glow," when hundreds of balloons are inflated after the sun sets. Propane burners send heat into the colorful envelopes, the balloons light up like giant light bulbs, and the magical glow can be seen for miles. The balloons remain grounded, or tethered; ballooning at night, when balloonists can't see telephone wires or other obstacles, is forbidden.

An estimated 800,000 people attend the nine-day program, and thousands more glimpse the balloons as they float over Albuquerque's backyards, setting off a serenade of barking dogs. Most spectacular are the Saturday- and Sunday-morning ascensions on the opening and closing weekends of the fiesta. In the early hours of dawn 500 massive, candy-color balloons are inflated and, shortly after, lift off, silently caressing the sky with fantasy and brilliance. It is one of New Mexico's biggest draws for out-of-state visitors and a delight for those who live here. For additional information, contact Albuquerque International Hot Air Balloon Fiesta (8309 Washington Pl., NW, 87113, tel. 505/821–1000).

Dining

Albuquerque, like many cities in the West, loves to eat out. The choice is almost limitless, as diverse and revealing as restaurants with such names as High Noon Saloon, Ciao!, and Chardonnay's. Many of the city's favorite dining spots specialize in northern New Mexico–style cooking, with flavorful Spanish recipes that have been handed down for generations. (*See* Dining in Essential Information, Chapter 1, for an explanation of Mexican food terms.) French, Continental, Mediterranean, and Italian fare are also readily available, as are standard American favorites of seafood, steaks, and burgers. The clientele is folksy for the most part. You can dress as casual as you like and order wine by color instead of label. Restaurants in the major business hotels tend to be a bit more formal, of course, but as the evening wears down, so do the restrictions.

Highly recommended restaurants are indicated by a star ★.

Category	Cost*
Very Expensive	over $30
Expensive	$21–$30
Moderate	$16–$20
Inexpensive	under $16

per person, excluding tax (5.75%), service, or drinks

Expensive

★ **Chardonnay's.** Chardonnay's, in the Ramada Hotel Classic, offers a Continental-French–style menu, specializing in lamb chops Madagascar, braised with green peppercorns, burgundy, and cream; beef tenderloin filet; Mediterranean saffron scallops; and veal Florentine, milk-fed veal served in butter and topped with mozzarella and *merchard de vin* sauce. Chef Randolph Valdez is one of Albuquerque's most lauded. His creations, many prepared tableside, are served in an English country home atmosphere. The main dining room has dark, elegant alcoves; walnut paneling; stained-glass windows; and brass fixtures and trim. Napkins, chairs, and carpets are all deep blue and burgundy. Fresh flowers grace the tables in tiny silver vases. Even the recorded background music is lush. *Ramada Hotel Classic, 6815 Menaul Blvd., tel. 505/881–0000. Reservations suggested. Jacket and tie advised. No lunch Sat. Closed Sun. AE, D, DC, MC, V.*

High Noon Restaurant and Saloon. Located two blocks north of the Plaza in one of Old Town's original 200-year-old adobe buildings, this former woodworking shop now offers fine dining in a territorial setting, with viga ceilings, brick floors, and handmade Southwestern tables and chairs. A skylight offers cool, defused lighting during the day and a glimpse of the sky at night. Native American rugs and New Mexican art decorate the walls, and antique pots rest on ledges and sills. White tablecloths and well-appointed table settings offer an upscale accent. A Flamenco guitarist plays here on weekends. Topping the menu offerings are pepper steak, steak Diane, seafood specials, and Southwestern dishes, along with veal, chicken, and

Albuquerque Dining

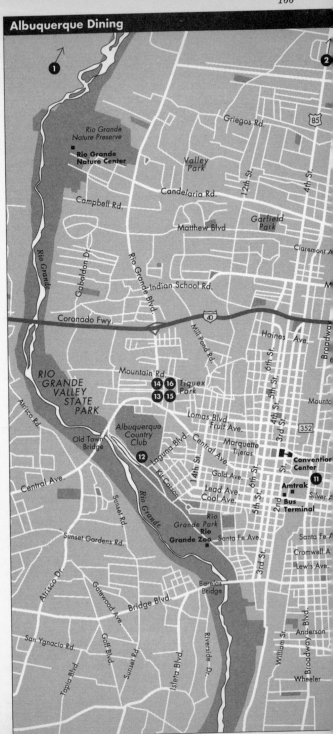

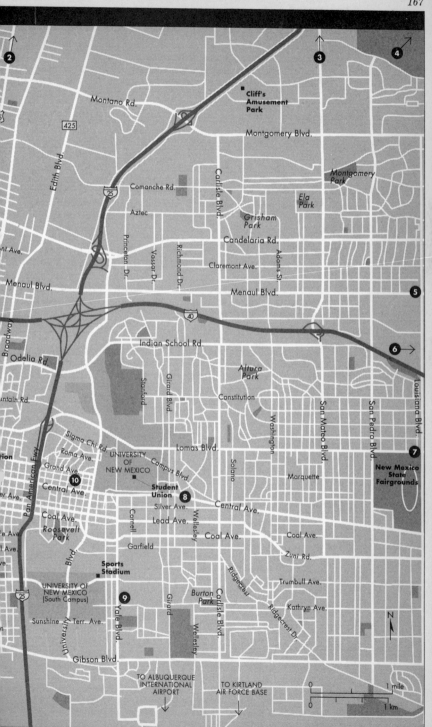

beef entrées. *425 San Felipe Ave., NW, tel. 505/765–1455. Reservations suggested. Jacket and tie advised. AE, D, DC, MC, V.*

Monte Vista Fire Station. Located on Central Avenue at the base of the Sandia Peak Tramway, this spacious, airy restaurant was once an actual working fire station—it even has a brass pole. The adobe-style building, built in 1936, was used as a fire station until 1972; it's listed on Albuquerque's National Register of Historic Places. Well-prepared grilled steaks and seafood highlight the menu, at higher than fire-sale prices. The bar is upstairs in what was once the station's sleeping quarters. During the evening hours, the piano player plays "Smoke Gets in Your Eyes" over and over and over. *3201 Central Ave., NE, tel. 505/255–2424. Reservations suggested. Dress: casual. AE, MC, V. No lunch weekends*.

The Rio Grande Yacht Club. This restaurant, located two blocks north of the airport, offers fresh seafood and traditional American entrées—baby-back ribs, smoked pork loin, steaks, and chicken—in a nautical atmosphere. The dining room has lots of wood and brass, accented with hanging greenery; vintage prints and paintings of clipper ships, fish, and foaming seas hang on the walls. Other yachty touches include an ornate steering wheel looking fresh from the South Pacific and a colored sailcloth hanging from one section of the dining room, which is built in levels. The floors are carpeted; the tables are of wood with black inlay designs; and the chairs are captain's, of course. The full-service bar is nautical as well. There are also background music, patio dining in warmer weather, and a fireplace for cooler evenings. *2500 Yale Blvd., SE, tel. 505/243–6111. Reservations required. Jacket and tie advised. AE, D, DC, MC, V.*

Moderate

Antiquity Restaurant. This secluded restaurant is in the heart of Old Town, with adobe walls as old as time (thus the name). Two separate dining areas face an open kitchen with a charcoal grill, where the chef performs his wonders for all to see. The floors are brick, and local art is featured on the walls, along with framed posters touting the glories of Albuquerque, its balloon rallies and art festivals. The restaurant was originally built as a honeymoon cottage, and the aura of romance remains. This Old Town favorite features chateaubriand and charcoal-grilled steaks, fresh seafood, veal, and excellent homemade desserts in an intimate setting. *1112 Romero, NW, tel. 505/247–3545. Reservations suggested. Dress: casual. AE, D, DC, MC, V. No lunch. Closed Sun.*

★ **Artichoke Cafe.** Located in a turn-of-the-century brick building just east of downtown on Central Avenue, the Artichoke Cafe offers a variety of cuisines—New American, Italian, and some French—and specializes in broiled salmon, veal, and lamb. Founded and operated by Terry Keene since August 1989, the restaurant, which does all its own baking, has gotten high local acclaim. The building is old, but the decor is modern; one large dining room on three broad levels spills onto a small courtyard, where seven tables are located. Exhibited on the dining room walls, and rotated every two months, is the work of local artists, some established, others up and coming. All the paintings are for sale. *424 Central Ave., SE, tel. 505/243–0200.*

Reservations suggested. Dress: casual. AE, MC, V. Closed Sun.

Bella Vista. Set on a tree-covered hill in Cedar Crest, about 20 miles east of town, this restaurant specializes in steaks and seafood; lobster tails are particularly popular. Preparations are Italian, American, and Mexican style, but the red tablecloths and taped background music will bring you quickly back to Sorrento. The restaurant is in a huge, rambling building with 12 dining rooms, six of which have gas-log fireplaces. The Bella Vista has a seating capacity of 1,200, making it one of the few restaurants anywhere where any number of people could turn up without reservations and barely fluster the maître d'. The full bar holds almost as many people as does the restaurant itself. Founded in 1961 as an "all-you-can-eat" restaurant, one of the first anywhere to establish this policy, it still offers all-you-can-eat chicken, fish, spaghetti, and Mexican dishes, but draws the line on lobster and steak. Bella Vista also has a packaged liquor store, deli, and seafood mart. *N. Hwy. 14, Cedar Crest, tel. 505/281–3370 or 505/281–3914. Reservations suggested. Dress: casual. AE, MC, V.*

Casa Vieja. Casa Vieja, in Corrales about 13 miles northwest of Albuquerque, offers Continental dining in a charming 280-year-old adobe that has a history almost as long as its menu. The oldest building in Corrales, it was originally a homestead, then became a church, the territorial governor's home, and a military outpost. A restaurant since 1970, it has two large dining rooms, a smaller one, and a patio for outdoor dining in the summer. With beamed viga ceilings, regional paintings, Native American rugs on the walls, and handsome tinwork on the handcarved doors, it has a rich frontier flavor without straining to achieve it. Owner-chef Jean Pierre Gozard specializes in French and Northern Italian cuisine, with wild game, quail, duck, and pheasant offered in season. *4541 Corrales Rd., tel. 505/898–7489. Reservations suggested. Jacket and tie required. AE, D, DC, MC, V. Dinner only. Closed Mon.*

Ciao! This tastefully decorated northern Italian restaurant, in the modern new Skyview Center on the northeast side of town, offers spectacular views of the city lights and of the nearby Sandia Mountains. The dining room is decorated in soft shades of pink and gray, with muted neon lighting in pale pastels and sculptured glass. The floors are imported marble, and there are three outdoor decks. The menu's specialties include veal *saltimbocca*, fettuccine Alfredo, deftly prepared seafood, homemade pasta, and steak, along with 14 premium wines served by the glass. The upstairs bar has a large-screen TV. *Tramway Blvd. and Indian School Rd., NE, tel. 505/293–2426. Reservations suggested. Jacket and tie advised. AE, DC, MC, V. Closed for lunch Sat.*

Cooperage Restaurant and Lounge. As the name suggests—cooperage means barrel maker—the one-story restaurant is built to resemble an enormous barrel. The top of the barrel is a skylight, offering atrium dining below. The main dining room is dominated by a huge lightning-shaped salad bar, surrounded by circular rooms with intimate nooks and booths. The decor is bright and cheerful, with light tan walls, green carpeting, and bay windows that afford diners a good view of the world outside. Featured on the menu are prime rib, lobster, and steaks. On weekends there's dancing in the lounge to blues and jazz (*see* Nightlife, below). *7220 Lomas Blvd., NE, tel. 505/255–1657. Reservations suggested. Dress: casual. AE, D, DC, MC, V.*

El Pinto. This family-owned Mexican restaurant has been in business since 1962. Located in an adobe-style hacienda, with shade trees and a year-round heated dining patio (the largest in New Mexico), its specialties include chile rellenos, hot or mild Hatch (a breed apart in the world of chili), *sopa de pollo* (chicken soup), fajitas, tamales, and frijoles. There's a full bar and soft Mexican background music. *10500 4th St., NW, tel. 505/898–1771. Reservations suggested. Dress: casual. AE, MC, V.*

★ **La Hacienda Cantina.** Ted Garcia, chef-owner of this newly opened restaurant, also owns and operates La Hacienda restaurant in Old Town (only blocks away), and seems to manage to be in both places at once, meeting and greeting customers and dashing into the kitchen to see what's cooking. The menu here features a wide range of Mexican specialties—fajitas, enchiladas New Mexico, sopaipillas, chile rellenos, and chimichangas—as well as a number of fine Northern Italian dishes, to placate longtime customers of the site's former occupant, Al Monte's, whose owner and namesake died in 1990 after more than 40 years in business. The decor of the new restaurant is bright and colorfully Mexican throughout, while retaining some of the furnishings from the previous establishment, including the handsome wooden tables with copper tops and the five fireplaces that glow cozily in wintertime. In the full bar the margaritas flow and happy hour reigns from 5 to 7 on weekdays and from 8 to 10 on Saturday. Sunday brunch lasts from 11 to 4. Weather permitting, there's dining al fresco on the patio. *1306 Rio Grande Blvd., tel. 505/243–3709. Reservations suggested. Dress: casual. AE, DC, MC, V.*

La Placita. Housed in a historic hacienda on Old Town Plaza, La Placita offers traditional New Mexican dishes, such as chile rellenos, enchiladas, tacos, and sopaipillas, plus a wide selection of American entrées. The building dates from 1706. For years it housed Ambrosio Armijo's mercantile store, where ladies' lace gloves sold for 10¢ a pair and gents' linen underdrawers could be purchased for $1. The adobe walls are 3 feet thick in places. La Placita has six dining rooms, and since it's an art gallery as well, patrons dine surrounded by outstanding examples of Native American and Southwestern painting. *302 San Felipe, NW, tel. 505/247–2204. Reservations suggested. Dress: casual. AE, D, DC, MC, V.*

Maria Teresa. This nationally preserved landmark in historic Old Town, next to the Sheraton, offers aged beef, seafood, poultry, and New Mexican specialties; recommended entrées include chicken Acapulco (breast of chicken stuffed with avocado and crab, topped with a delicate lemon-lime sauce) and *carne adovado* (cubed, marinated pork, rolled in a flour tortilla and covered with red chiles and cheese). The restored 1840s adobe, its 32-inch-thick brick adobe walls plastered with straw and more adobe, is entered through an attractive courtyard, a cool oasis even during the hottest days of summer. Maria Teresa's has early Spanish American furnishings—chests, carvings, and tables—Southwestern paintings, fireplaces, and walled gardens. In the summer, everyone wants to eat in the Plum Tree Courtyard. *618 Rio Grande Blvd., NW, tel. 505/242–3900. Reservations suggested. Jacket and tie advised. AE, D, DC, MC, V.*

Seagull Street. Seagull Street is a little bit of Cape Cod, clapboard shingles and all, set down in Albuquerque, where fresh fish is grilled over mesquite fires. The restaurant features an average of 20 seafood entrées flown in daily from Pacific, Atlantic, and Gulf waters. Choice cuts of steak are also offered. Tables set up on the dock outside (a little bit of Cape Cod, remember?) are the perfect place to enjoy cocktails and oysters on the half shell. The decor is nautical, outside and in, with starfish, fish nets, and pictures of boats and sea captains on the walls. *5410 Academy Rd., NE, tel. 505/821–0020. Reservations suggested. Dress: casual. AE, DC, MC, V. No lunch Sat.*

Inexpensive

★ **66 Diner.** Once a transmission shop on old Route 66, the 66 Diner is now a glitzy Art Deco establishment with neon lights outside, black-and-white tile floors, and turquoise-and-pink vinyl seats (rarely an empty one) inside. Burgers, blue-plate specials—spaghetti and meat balls, pot roast, chicken-fried steak, grilled liver and onions, and beef stew—and a separate soda fountain all add to the pervasive tone of 1950s nostalgia, as do the framed photos of old Route 66 on the wall. The soda fountain's milk shakes were voted the best in town by a local publication, but you might want to try the 35¢ hot fudge sundae (small but yummy). *1405 Central Ave., NE, tel. 505/247–1421. No reservations. Dress: casual. AE, MC, V.*

Lodging

As is typical of many large cities in the Southwest today, Albuquerque's hotels offer a comfortable mix of modern conveniences and technology and Old West flavor. The city's accommodations range from budget motels to bed-and-breakfast inns to soaring hotel skyscrapers. All are uniformly friendly and folksy, and include much of the Southwest heritage in their decor and design. A waitress sitting down to chat with customers having dinner in a restaurant may be the stuff of TV sitcoms, but in the West—and cities come no more "Western" than Albuquerque—it really happens. This informality rubs off on guests as well. Ties come off, boots come on, and the streets outside are littered with briefcases.

Highly recommended lodgings in each price category are indicated by a star ★.

Category	Cost*
Very Expensive	over $150
Expensive	$100–$150
Moderate	$65–$100
Inexpensive	under $65

All prices are for a standard double room, excluding 5% room tax, 5.75% sales tax, and service charges.

Hotels

Expensive **Albuquerque Hilton.** Located just 2 miles from downtown, the Albuquerque Hilton blends the charm and decor of the colorful Southwest—Native American rugs, arched doorways, and high ceilings—with the sophistication and elegance of a contemporary hotel. The guest rooms are done in Southwestern

172

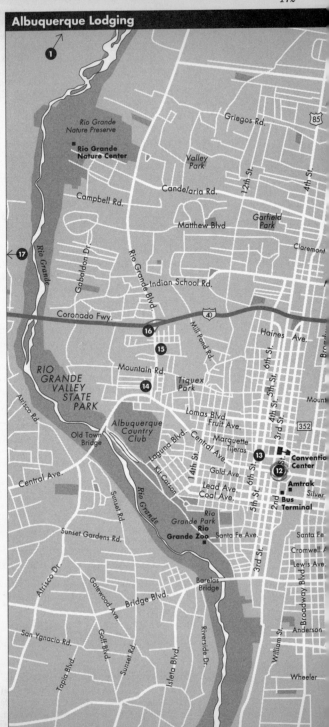

Albuquerque Lodging

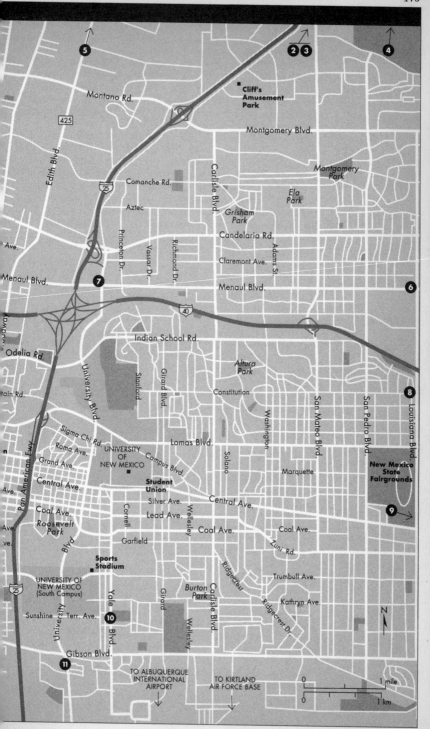

pastels, with Santa Fe–style wooden furniture and bleached wood bedsteads; many have balconies. Original American Indian and Western art is featured throughout, including numerous works by famed Taos painter R. C. Gorman. The elegant Ranchers Club restaurant has high beamed ceilings and a roaring fireplace on the wall over which a mounted buffalo head stares down benevolently. Its authentic grill room—you almost expect to find J. R. Ewing here—features prime meats and fresh seafood prepared over a selection of aromatic woods (patrons select the flavor—piñon, mesquite, and so on—themselves). The Casa Chaco, the hotel's other restaurant, serves typical coffee-shop breakfast and lunch fare, but is transformed at night, when nouvelle Southwestern cuisine is served in considerably more elegant style: candlelit tables, waiters in tuxedos, crisp linens, and sparkling crystal. *1901 University Blvd., N.E., Box 25525, Albuquerque 87102, tel. 505/884–2500 or 800/HILTONS, fax 505/889–9118. 428 rooms. Facilities: indoor pool, outdoor pool, whirlpool, sauna, free transportation to and from the airport and bus and train stations, 2 "Luxury Level" floors, bar, lounge, café, dining room. AE, D, DC, MC, V.*

Albuquerque Marriott. This luxury property is located uptown at the junction of I–40 and Louisiana Boulevard, near some of the city's best shopping areas (Winrock and Coronado malls). Geared to the executive traveler with its special 28-room Concierge Level, complete with faxes and computer hookups, it also has the vacationer in mind. The 17-story hotel with its elegantly decorated lobby (the glowing hues of the furnishings reflect the region's natural colors) has Southwestern touches throughout—kachina dolls, American Indian art, and native pottery. Nicole's Restaurant is the hotel's upscale dining room, with soft lighting, pink napkins and tablecloths, and tableside service; Herbs & Roses, open for breakfast, lunch, and dinner, is more informal. Guest rooms feature walk-in closets, free in-room movies, and modern furnishings, all in those pleasing Southwestern tones. *2101 Louisiana Blvd., NE, Albuquerque 87110, tel. 505/881–6800 or 800/228–9290, fax 505/888–2982. 412 rooms. Facilities: 2 restaurants, lounge, gift shop, health club, indoor-outdoor pool, exclusive concierge level with 28 rooms, free limousine service to and from Albuquerque Airport. AE, D, DC, MC, V.*

Amfac. The 14-story Amfac at the Albuquerque Airport is 3 minutes from the freeway. Its modern decor is embellished with a Southwestern flair. The spacious guest rooms feature cool earth-tones, with large framed abstract and impressionistic watercolors on the walls. Bathrooms have a separate vanity. The upscale family-style restaurant, Lil's, serves Continental cuisine in a Southwestern setting—Mexican tiles on the floors, and viga ceilings. With its airport location, it's not surprising that the hotel is geared toward the traveling businessperson. *2910 Yale, NE, Albuquerque 87119, tel. 505/843–7000 or 800/227–1117, fax 505/843–6307. 266 rooms. Facilities: heated pool, lighted tennis courts, fitness center, nearby golf. AE, DC, MC, V.*

Hyatt Regency Albuquerque. Adjacent to the Convention Center in the heart of downtown is the city's newest major hotel addition, and a beauty it is, with two soaring desert-colored towers climbing high above the city skyline. A private forest and a splashing fountain outside, a shopping promenade inside—it's all totally modern and luxurious. The spacious guest rooms are finished in contemporary Southwestern style with a mauve, burgundy, and tan color scheme and all the standard Hyatt amenities. The Presidential Suite has a canopy bed, as though Abe Lincoln himself might stop by. McGrath's, the hotel's award-winning restaurant, offers steaks, chops, chicken, and seafood in an intimate atmosphere of levels and alcoves, with rich-color wood furnishing. It's open for breakfast, lunch, and dinner. *330 Tijeras Ave., Albuquerque 87102, tel. 505/842–1234 or 800/233–1234, fax 505/766–6710. 391 rooms, 14 suites. Facilities: restaurant, 3 lounges, health club, spa, outdoor pool, special Regency Club accommodations. AE, D, DC, MC, V.*

★ **La Posada de Albuquerque.** This historic, highly lauded hotel in the heart of downtown Albuquerque oozes Southwestern charm, with its tiled lobby fountain, massive vigas, encircling balcony, fixtures of etched glass and tin, and American Indian war-dance murals behind the reception desk. The guest rooms, many with fireplaces, are large and decorated throughout with Southwestern and Native American themes, from the designs on couches, slipcovers, and drapes to incidental pieces of Hopi pottery and R. C. Gorman prints on the walls. In 1939, Conrad Hilton opened the hotel, then called the Albuquerque Hilton, as his first lodging venture outside Texas; it was also the first air-conditioned building in New Mexico, Hilton's native state. The hotel mogul honeymooned here with his bride, Zsa Zsa Gabor. La Posada has been carefully restored and is listed in the National Register of Historic Places. Its dining room, the popular Eulalia's Restaurant, features waiters and waitresses singing snippets from the latest Broadway hits. The cuisine is Continental, with veal, duck, and salmon topping the list of specialties. There's live jazz and a good happy-hour buffet in the Lobby Lounge (*see* Nightlife, below). *125 2nd St., NW, Albuquerque 87102, tel. 505/242–9090 or 800/777–5732, fax 505/242–8664. 114 rooms. Facilities: bar, restaurant, gift shop, exercise room, free airport pickups by limousine. AE, D, DC, MC, V.*

Radisson. This two- and three-story motor hotel at the Albuquerque Airport has a Southwestern Spanish flavor throughout, with arched balconies, tan desert colors, a year-round courtyard pool, and indoor and outdoor dining. The guest rooms are comfortable enough, but not outstanding. Diamondback's Café and Coyote's Cantina offer a Western setting and regional Northern New Mexican cuisine. This property also caters to traveling business executives. *1901 University Blvd., Albuquerque 87106, tel. 505/247–0512 or 800/333–3333, fax 505/843–7148. 148 rooms. Facilities: restaurant, lounge, year-round outdoor pool and spa, and complimentary airport and train and bus-station transfers. AE, D, DC, MC, V.*

Ramada Hotel Classic. Set in the heart of Albuquerque's uptown business and financial district, across from the Coronado Shopping Mall, this modern, eight-story hotel has convention facilities and enough bars, restaurants, and space to keep all the delegates happy. Each of the hotel's recently refurbished, oversized guest rooms and suites is equipped with a refrigerator and boasts a grand view of the majestic Sandia Mountains or the desert West Mesa and the downtown skyline. Southwestern colors (mauve and light green) predominate in the rooms, complementing the Southwestern-style bedspreads and curtains. The bed lamps have pottery bases, and the ceiling lamps are brass. (One wonders why the featured artworks are primarily bland florals and European landscapes when so much good local art is available.) The Café Fennel is open for breakfast, lunch, and dinner, and Chardonnay's (*see* Dining, above) features fine Continental dining in oak-paneled elegance. *6815 Menaul Blvd. NE, Albuquerque 87110, tel. 505/881–0000 or 800/228–2828, fax 505/881–3736. 287 rooms. Facilities: heated indoor pool, whirlpool and sauna, American Airlines ticket counter in lobby, 2 restaurants, 2 lounges, courtesy transportation to and from the airport. AE, D, DC, MC, V.*

Sheraton Old Town. In the heart of Albuquerque's historical district, the Sheraton Old Town is a modern, 11-story structure that gracefully sits among the region's 400 years of culture and history with no overly jarring effects. The guest rooms are large and modern, with tan desert-color appointments and hand-wrought furnishings. The large bathrooms have vanities with lighted makeup mirrors. The Rio Grande Customs House Restaurant offers prime rib, steaks, seafood, and poultry specialties, while the casual Café del Sol has a varied menu, with lots of Southwestern favorites for breakfast, lunch, and dinner. *800 Rio Grande Blvd., NW, Albuquerque 87104, tel. 505/843–6300 or 800/325–3535, fax 505/842–9863. 190 rooms. Facilities: 2 restaurants, 2 lounges, heated pool, whirlpool, shopping arcade, free airport and train and bus-depot pickups. AE, D, DC, MC, V.*

Bed-and-Breakfasts

Moderate   **Apple Tree Bed and Breakfast.** This bed-and-breakfast in Cedar Crest is 15 miles and a world away from downtown Albuquerque. Nestled in the Sandia Mountains, at 7,000 feet, where hummingbirds feed outside the guest-room windows, the Apple Tree offers two large units, accommodating one to four people. "The Casita" is a rustic adobe room with white walls, red brick floors, a viga ceiling, and a kiva fireplace. It's filled with country antiques, a Victorian desk and bookcase, and a deluxe king-size bed. The bright and sunny "Hummingbird Suite" has antique furnishings, with comfortable chairs and sofa, and a wood-burning stove. Blue-corn waffles, apple pancakes, and honey-glazed whole wheat cinnamon rolls are typical of the breakfasts that are served in the guest rooms. *12050 Hwy. 14 N, Box 287, Cedar Crest 87008, tel. 505/281–3597 or 800/648–4262. 1 casita and 1 suite, both with private bath. No credit cards.*

Casa del Granjero. Casa del Granjero (The Farmer's House), 10 miles from the airport, is a sprawling old Territorial adobe with a land grant that goes back to 1740. The 5,000-square-foot dwelling is decorated throughout with Southwestern and Mexican furnishings. Even the dishes are Mexican—"Old, old Mexican"—says owner Victoria Farmer, who also runs a catering service. Full breakfasts feature Mexican, French, or American specialties and are served in the guest rooms or in the living room in front of the two-story-high adobe fireplace. There's also a garden room with a sunken hot tub and miles of nature trails outside. Casa del Granjero shares its grounds with horses, goats, and other ranch animals. Experienced riders are occasionally permitted to saddle up. *9213 4th Ce De Baca La., NW, Albuquerque 87114, tel. 505/897–4144. 3 rooms, all with private baths and sitting area. No credit cards.*

★ **Casas de Suenos** (Houses of Dreams), adjacent to Old Town on Rio Grande Boulevard, SW, is a 2-acre garden compound, with 10 attractively decorated casitas that have beehive fireplaces, pigskin furniture, bleached cattle skulls on the wall, regional paintings, and American Indian rugs. Long a historic gathering spot for artists, Casas de Suenos provides a uniquely New Mexican setting. Breakfasts start with decadent french toast or savory eggs, a fruit platter, and a selection of fresh breads and muffins. *310 Grande Blvd., SW, Albuquerque 87104, tel. 505/247–4560. 9 suites, 3 rooms, all with private bath. AE, MC, V.*

Casita Chamisa. Located in Los Ranchos, 12 miles from the Albuquerque Airport and about 15 minutes north of Old Town, this two-bedroom guest house, set in a cottonwood-shaded valley, sleeps one to six and is rented to one party at a time. The furnishings are Southwestern, with American Indian blankets, pottery, and artifacts adding authenticity. Owners Kit and Arnold Sargeant opened their guest house in 1974, the first bed-and-breakfast in Albuquerque. The property is also an archaeological site, with remnants of a prehistoric American Indian dwelling still visible. Kit Sargeant, an archaeologist, supervised the dig herself. Also for guest use, even at 2 AM if the urge strikes, is an enclosed 15- by 33-foot swimming pool. The solar-heated pool house has a hot tub and full bath. Breakfast is Country Continental, which translates into waffles, pancakes, and lots of seasonal fruits (14 of Casita Chamisa's more than 200 trees are fruit bearing). Arnold Sargeant is famous for his sourdough bread, "with a starter," he says, "that's 110 years old." *850 Chamisal Rd., NW, Albuquerque 87107, tel. 505/897–4644. 2-bedroom guesthouse sleeps 1–6. Facilities: enclosed pool, hot tub. AE, MC, V.*

Corrales Inn. Located 14 miles north of Albuquerque in picturesque Corrales, this Territorial adobe–style, solar-heated home was built to serve as a bed-and-breakfast in 1987. Each of the guest rooms is theme decorated—Oriental, Native American, Victorian, Corrales (Southwestern), and Balloon (in honor of the hot-air-balloon festivals held nearby). Each room has an individual temperature control, as well as a sitting and dressing area. Full gourmet French Country breakfasts—quiche, soufflés, omelets, crêpes, croissants—are served in the guest rooms or in the inn's common room. Outside is a courtyard with a hot tub. *Plaza San Ysidro, Box 1361, Corrales 87048, tel. 505/897–4422. 6 rooms, all with full private baths. Facilities: hot tub. MC, V.*

★ **Elaine's, A Bed and Breakfast.** This beautiful three-story log home, located in the evergreen folds of the Sandia Peaks, is tastefully furnished throughout with European antiques and a sprinkling of early regional pieces. The top two floors are for guest rooms, with balconies and big picture windows bringing the lush mountain views indoors. The third-floor room has cathedral ceilings and a brass bed, while the second-floor accommodations share a massive stone fireplace, as well as a bath. A well-stocked library and big fireplaces invite cerebral pursuits while 4 acres of wooded grounds beckon just outside the back door. Full ham-and-egg–style breakfasts are served, with all the accompaniments. *72 Snowline Rd., Snowline Estate, Box 444, Cedar Crest 87008, tel. 505/281–2467. 3 rooms, 2 with shared bath. No credit cards.*

Turquoise Inn Bed and Breakfast. Nestled on 2¼ acres adjacent to Cibola National Forest (25 miles northeast of the Albuquerque Airport on the road to Sandia Crest), the Turquoise Inn Bed and Breakfast is surrounded by cedars, and ponderosa and piñon pines. The house was originally a four-bedroom private home that was remodeled and modified to become a bed-and-breakfast. One guest room, formerly the master bedroom, is furnished in Colonial antiques, with Southwestern touches. The large upstairs suite, with a private outside entrance, fireplace, and wet bar, showcases modern Scandinavian furnishings. A Continental breakfast served in the rooms helps guests get a good start on the day. *142 Sandia Crest Rd., Sandia Park 87047, tel. 505/281–4745. 1 room and 1 suite, both with private bath. D, MC, V.*

William E. Mauger Estate. Centrally located downtown, 12 blocks from historic Old Town, is an elegant 1897 Queen Anne residence with comfortable accommodations. Four of the guest rooms are Victorian style, with either a brass bed, a cherrywood sleigh bed, an iron bed, or a standard Victorian bed with a large, ornate headboard. The other two rooms are Art Deco in design, with tinted mirrors and fluted vases. Full breakfasts— egg dishes, home-baked pastries, juice, and coffee—are served in the guest rooms or in the downstairs parlor or common room. *701 Roma Ave., NW, Albuquerque 87102, tel. 505/242–8755. 6 rooms, all with private bath. AE, D, DC, MC, V.*

Windmill Ranch Bed and Breakfast. Located on the west side in the heart of the bosque (4 miles west of I–40, Exit 155), with a spectacular view of the Sandia Mountains, this bed-and-breakfast was recently remodeled and spruced up under new management. Guest rooms and public areas are furnished with antiques, including a player piano (with often-played tunes such as "Red River Valley"), a roller-type Edison, and a Victrola. (For the benefit of guests who are trying to sleep, not all of them get cranked up at the same time.) There's also a large-screen VCR with a film library of over 200 titles. The Windmill is only 100 yards from the Rio Grande, where ancient elms and cottonwoods grow in profusion. Paths along the river are ideal for biking, jogging, or walking. The 5,000-acre spread is a working ranch, so there are horses, ducks, and chickens about. Freshly laid eggs are served for breakfast, with all the country trimmings. From the Windmill's balcony, visitors can overdose on scenery, watch the hot-air balloons glide by during seasonal balloon rallies, or just breathe the good air. *6400 Coors Blvd., NW, Albuquerque 87102, tel. 505/898–6864. 4 rooms, each with private bath, 2 with fireplaces. MC, V.*

Camping

Isleta Lakes and Recreation Area. Fifteen minutes south of Albuquerque on I–25 (take Exit 215 to NM 47), the Isleta Lakes and Recreation Area has complete campground facilities and tent sites. There are also three fishing lakes on the property. *Box 383, Isleta 87022, tel. 505/877–0370. Over 100 tent sites. 40 RV hookups (water and electricity). Tent site $9 per night, RV site $12 per night. Showers and flush toilets in central bathhouse. D, MC, V.*

KOA Albuquerque Central. Within the city limits (Exit 166 of I–40), the KOA Albuquerque Central has full hookups, Kamping Kabins, a swimming pool and spa, hot showers, flush toilets, LP gas refills, and laundry facilities. There is also a shuttle between the campground and Old Town. *12400 Skyline*

Rd., Albuquerque 87123, tel. 505/296–2729. 200 sites, 101 full hookups. Water and electric hookup $17.95 per night, full hookup $19.95 per night. D, MC, V.

KOA has two other properties in Albuquerque with similar services, the **Albuquerque North KOA** (1021 Hill Rd. in Bernalillo, tel. 505/867–5227) and the **Albuquerque West KOA** (5730 Ouray Rd., NW, tel. 505/831–1911).

Turquoise Trail Campgrounds. Located in the Sandia Mountains, 15 minutes east of Albuquerque (east on I–40, Exit 175, 4 miles north on I–14), the Turquoise Trail Campgrounds has full hookups, hot showers, laundry, and a wooded tent area. *22 Calvary Rd., Cedar Crest 87008, tel. 505/281–2005. Camping space for 2 is $10.50; a full hookup is $15.*

The Arts and Nightlife

The Arts

Dance **The Southwest Ballet** (tel. 505/294–1423), under the direction of Edward Androse and now in its 13th season, is in the forefront of regional ballet companies and presents a wide variety of classical and contemporary performances.

Music The conductor of the **New Mexico Symphony Orchestra** (220 Gold, SW, tel. 505/842–8565), now in its 60th year, swings a wide baton, with presentations of pops, Beethoven, and Handel's *Messiah* at Christmas. Performances are frequently scheduled under the stars at the Rio Grande Zoo Bandshell and at Popejoy Hall on the University of New Mexico campus.

Opera **Albuquerque Civic Light Opera Association** is one of the largest community-based producers of musical theater in the country. Its five annual productions are seen by a total audience of 75,000. Performances are held in the 2,000-seat Popejoy Hall at the University of New Mexico campus. For information or tickets, call the box office, tel. 505/345–6577.

Theater **The KiMo Theater** (419 Central Ave., NW; box office, tel. 505/764–1700; business office, tel. 505/848–1370), an old movie palace on Central Avenue restored to its original design—Pueblo Deco–style architecture painted in bright colors—offers a varied menu, everything from traveling road shows to local song-and-dance acts. The KiMo is also where the **New Mexico Repertory Theatre** (tel. 505/243–4500), the state's only resident professional theater group, stages its seasonal offerings of comedies, dramas, musicals, and mysteries. The Rep's season runs from October through May, alternating two-week productions in Albuquerque and Santa Fe. The **Albuquerque Little Theater** (224 San Pasquale, SW, tel. 505/242–4750), a nonprofit community troupe, combines local volunteer talent with a staff of professionals to present an annual series of comedies, dramas, musicals, and mysteries of the highest caliber. The company theater, located across the street from historic Old Town, was built in 1936 and was designed by famed Southwestern architect John Gaw Meen. It contains an art gallery; a large, comfortable lobby; and a cocktail lounge. **La Compania de Teatro de Albuquerque** (518 First Ave., NW, tel. 505/242–7929), New Mexico's largest bilingual theater, performs classic and contemporary plays in English and Spanish during April, June, October, and December.

Nightlife

Bars and Lounges You'll find live entertainment of the jazz, blues, folk, and rock variety in the lounge of the **Cooperage Restaurant and Lounge** (*see* Dining, above). **Fat Chance Bar and Grill** (2216 Central Ave., SE, tel. 505/265–7531), across the street from the University of New Mexico, is a hangout for boisterous college students. It's got booths, a bar, tables, a dance floor, and live entertainment, from rock to reggae, Wednesday through Sunday nights.

Comedy Clubs **Laff's** (3100 Juan Tabo, NE, tel. 505/296–5653) is the place to go for live comedy in Albuquerque.

Country-and-Western Clubs **Caravan East** (7605 Central Ave., NE, tel. 505/265–7877) is a country-and-western nightclub offering free dance lessons and partners galore. Two live bands play nightly. There are a free buffet and half-price drinks during the 4:30–7 happy hour. **Midnight Rodeo** (4901 McLeod, NE, tel. 505/888–0100) is an enormous country-and-western complex, with a huge race track–style dance floor, several bars, and even boutiques. The happy-hour buffet spread is incredible. The **Sundance Saloon** (12000 Candelaria, NE, tel. 505/296–6761) is another C&W favorite in Albuquerque.

Jazz Clubs **La Posada Lobby Lounge** (La Posada de Albuquerque Hotel, tel. 505/242–9090) offers live jazz performances and a happy-hour buffet that's very popular among the locals.

6 Carlsbad

Carlsbad Caverns National Park, in the southeastern part of the state, contains one of the largest and most spectacular cave systems in the world. As such, it is the area's main lure, but the town of Carlsbad and such nearby attractions as Living Desert State Park are also well worth visiting.

Essential Information

Important Addresses and Numbers

Visitor Information
Carlsbad Caverns National Park (3225 National Parks Hwy., Carlsbad 88220, tel. 505/785–2232 or 505/885–CAVE for 24-hour recorded information).

Carlsbad Chamber of Commerce (302 S. Canal St., Carlsbad 88220, tel. 505/887–6516).

Living Desert State Park (Box 100, Carlsbad 88220, tel. 505/887–5516).

Arriving and Departing

By Car
Driving south from Albuquerque on I–25 for about 77 miles, exit on U.S. 380 East and continue for 165 miles to Roswell. There switch to U.S. 285 and continue directly to Carlsbad, about 75 miles from Roswell (a total of 320 miles from Albuquerque). The drive is a bit monotonous, with dry rolling hills and nothing to see but brown wooden roadsigns heralding "Carlsbad Caverns" along the way. From El Paso, Texas, going east on U.S. 180, the distance to Carlsbad is 167 miles. From Pecos, Carlsbad can be reached via U.S. 285 (off I–10 at Van Horn).

By Plane
The newly expanded and remodeled **Albuquerque International Airport,** 380 miles north of Carlsbad, is the gateway to New Mexico and is served by most major airlines (*see* Chapter 1, Essential Information). Air-shuttle service via **Mesa Airlines** (tel. 800/637–2247 or, in Carlsbad, 505/885–0245) connects four times daily to and from Cavern City Air Terminal in Carlsbad. Flying time aboard the nine-passenger Cessna Caravan is about 90 minutes. The fare is $104 one way, $208 round-trip. Interline buses at Albuquerque International Airport connect Mesa Airlines with all Albuquerque connections.

Carlsbad car-rental agencies include **Hertz Car Rental** (tel. 505/887–1500) at Cavern City Air Terminal and **Independent Auto Rental** (tel. 505/887–1469) at Park Inn International. Taxi transfers from the Carlsbad airport are also available via **Cavern City Cab Company** (tel. 505/887–0994).

By Bus
TNM&O Greyhound (tel. 505/887–1108) provides transcontinental bus service and connects Carlsbad and White's City. **Sun-Country Tours** (tel. 505/785–2291) offers van service between Carlsbad Caverns National Park and White's City. The buses leave from the gift shop at White's City (where you can purchase tickets, tel. 505/785–2291) and from the visitors' center at the caverns. The round-trip fare is $14 for two, $5 per additional person.

Festivals and Seasonal Events

Bat Breakfast. It's not exactly the swallows returning to Capistrano, but on the second Thursday of August each year, early risers—would you believe 5 AM?—gather for a sit-down breakfast at the entrance to Carlsbad Cavern. Last year over 600 bat fanciers showed up to watch tens of thousands of bats, who had just been out for the night feeding on insects, fly back into a black hole descending steeply into the ground. Park rangers are on hand for a lecture and to answer questions. The bats' homecoming may be viewed each morning from mid-May through October, but the breakfast is a once-a-year affair. For additional information, contact Superintendent, Carlsbad Caverns National Park (3225 National Parks Hwy., Carlsbad 88220, tel. 505/785–2232).

Guided Tours

While explorations of the main cavern are designed to be self-guided, park rangers frequently conduct guided tours during the low visitation winter months when the crowds are more manageable.

Children's Nursery

Because the long trek through the cavern is a bit much for young children—baby strollers are not permitted on the narrow cave trails because of safety considerations—visitors' center concessioners offer a well-equipped nursery, staffed by trained personnel. The charge is $5 per child for four hours.

Pets

Not even leashed pets are allowed into the cavern, and park rangers advise not to leave animals in parked cars, even with the windows open. Suffocating heat can build up quickly in the desert. Clean, air-conditioned kennels are available at the visitors' center. Inquire at the gift shop. The cost is $2.50 for four hours.

A Note of Caution

Be aware that motor homes and RVs are frequently the target of thieves in national parks and forests. Don't leave vehicle doors unlocked or windows open. And don't leave behind valuables, such as cameras and traveler's checks, whether hidden under seats or in blankets or towels; they're the first places thieves will look. The visitors' center has safe coin-operated lockers. If you are the victim of a crime or see someone tampering with a car, call the park rangers (tel. 505/.785–2232) or the Eddy County sheriff (tel. 505/887–7551).

Exploring Carlsbad

Carlsbad Caverns National Park

The huge, subterranean chambers, fantastic rock formations, and delicate mineral sculptures of Carlsbad Caverns National Park draw about three-quarters of a million people each year to a remote corner of southeast New Mexico. Although the park is in the Chihauhuan desert, near the rugged canyons and peaks of the Guadalupe mountain range and the piñon and ponderosa pines of Lincoln National Forest, the most spectacular sights here are all below the earth's surface, with such evocative names as the Green Lake Room, the King's Palace, the Devil's Den, the Sequoia Room, the Hooded Klansman, the China Wall, Iceberg Rock.

This cave system, hundreds of million years in the making, is one of the largest and most impressive in the world, but it was discovered relatively recently. Pictographs near the cave entrance tell us that prehistoric Indians took shelter in Carlsbad Caverns more than 1,000 years ago, but archaeologists doubt they ventured in very far; access to the depths was limited and the tribe may have believed that the dwellings of the dead lay below.

It wasn't until the 19th century that nearby settlers, curious about the huge groups of bats they saw in the area, rediscovered the caves. They were mined for bat guano (dung), which was used as fertilizer, for a number of years, but no one was interested in the caves for any other reason until the early 20th century, when one of the guano miners, Jim White, began exploring and telling people about this amazing underground universe.

White brought a photographer, Ray Davis, to bear witness to his extravagent claims for the place. Displayed in the nearby town of Carlsbad in 1915, Davis's black-and-white pictures astounded people and started a rush of interest in the caverns. White turned tour operator, taking people down 170 feet in a bucket left over from the days of mining bat guano and lighting their way with kerosene lamps.

Washington got wind of this natural wonder in the early 1920s, and in 1923 inspector Robert Holley was dispatched by the U.S. Department of Interior to investigate. His report was instrumental in getting Carlsbad Caverns declared a national monument later that year by President Calvin Coolidge. The area was designated a national park in 1930.

Carlsbad Caverns National Park was much in the news early in 1991 when Emily Davis Mobley, an expert caver, broke her left leg some 1,000 feet underground while mapping one of the system's rugged caves. It took rescuers four days to carry, lift, and pull her over gaping pits and narrow passageways to safety. Of course, unless you're an expert, you won't be allowed to go exploring the same route or even anything like it. Of the 77 caves in the park, only two, Carlsbad Cavern and New Cave, are open to the public.

Carlsbad Caverns owes it existence as much to slow drips and accretions as to cataclysmic events. Its origins go back some 250 million years, when Capitan Reef, 400 miles long, formed around the edge of the warm, shallow sea that once covered this region. The sea evaporated and the reef was buried until a few million years ago when a combination of erosion and convulsions that also created the Guadalupe mountains brought it partly back above ground. Rain water seeping down through the reef's cracks gradually enlarged them into cavities, which eventually collapsed, forming huge rooms. Over millenia, evap-

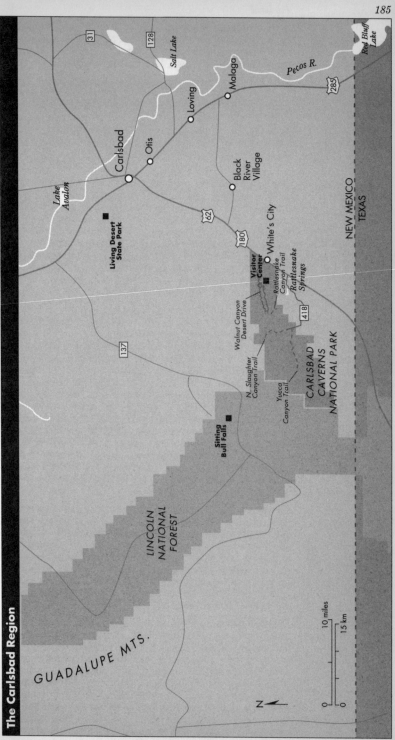

The Carlsbad Region

orated limestone deposited on the ceilings grew into great hanging stalactites, which in turn dripped the crystals that over time rose into massive stalagmites and other, more delicate formations—cave pearls, draperies, popcorn, and lilipads.

Whether you take the long route or the elevator shortcut, the trek through Carlsbad Cavern is long and you may find yourself getting a bit disoriented. The sheer vastness of the interior is overwhelming, and the proportions seem to change as one goes along. In places where pools of water have formed beside the walkway, reflections and reality merge; you may have to pause for a moment to regain your equilibrium.

Although you may be tempted to touch the cave's walls and jutting rock formations, heed the ranger's warning against doing so. Oil from the human hand forms a type of waterproofing that inhibits the natural water seepage. One or two people pawing at the rocks wouldn't make much of a difference, but thousands tour the cavern daily. Visitors are also warned not to leave the guided pathways. They're not told, however, that if they wander astray, silent alarms will quickly summon park rangers. The interior of Carlsbad Cavern is well lighted, but many people seem more concerned about where they're stepping than what's ahead, and make most of the trip looking down at their feet.

The two routes into Carlsbad Cavern are designated the Blue Tour and the Red Tour. If you take the former, you'll proceed on foot along the paved walkway that winds down into the cavern's depths for about 1¾ miles, passing through a series of underground rooms and descending slowly to a depth of about 830 feet. The trek takes about two hours; the trail can be slick in parts and the grades are fairly steep. The other way is to take a high-speed elevator from the visitors center down 750 feet to an underground lunchroom, and then begin your exploration from there; it should take another hour. (The elevator makes a portion of the main cavern accessible to visitors in wheelchairs.) In both cases you'll visit the Big Room, so called because it's large enough to hold 14 Houston Astrodomes; one corner could contain the White House. The ceiling's highest from the floor is 256 feet.

The temperature inside Carlsbad Cavern remains at a constant 56°F, and it's damp, so a sweater or warm clothes are recommended. So are comfortable shoes with rubber soles—because of the moisture, the underground walkways are slippery. But the cavern is well lighted and numerous park rangers are stationed about to offer assistance and information. Radio-tour guides are also available; small radio receivers can be rented for 50¢ each. Hold them to your ear as you walk through the cavern and you'll be enlightened.

Apart from the cave itself, one of the great attractions at Carlsbad Cavern is the **nightly bat flights.** Each evening between late May and mid-October at about sunset, bats by the tens of thousands exit from the natural entrance of the cavern and go flying about the countryside scouting for flying insects. They consume the insects in flight, collectively more than three tons of yummy bugs per night. (No scientist has yet figured out how a bat hanging upside down in a dark cave knows when the sun has set outside.) Because bats, albeit less lovable than furry kittens, are among the most maligned and misunderstood creatures, park rangers give informative talks about them each evening prior to the mass exodus, at about 7 PM. The time of the bat flights varies over the course of the season, so ranger lectures are flexible as well; the time is usually posted, but if not, check at the visitors' center. Lectures are suspended during the winter months, when the bats leave for Mexico.

New Cave, 25 miles from the main cavern, is much less accessible. You'll have to provide your own transportation to get there, and reservations (tel. 505/785–2232) are required a day in advance. The last few miles of the roadway there are gravel, and the mouth of the cave is a half-mile climb up a 500-foot rise. The name "New Cave" is a misnomer, of course, since the cave is actually millions of years old. New Cave was discovered by Tom Tucker, a local goatherd, in 1937. Guided tours have been available only during the past few years. The cave consists primarily of a single corridor, 1,140 feet long, with numerous side passages. The total extent of the surveyed passage is 1¾ miles, and the lowest point is 250 feet below the surface. Outstanding formations are the Christmas Tree, the Monarch, the Hooded Klansman, the Tear Drop, and the China Wall. Rangers lead groups of 25 on a two-hour lantern tour. Children under 6 aren't permitted. The cave temperature is a constant 62°, and the humidity is a clammy 90%. You'll need to bring along your own flashlight, hiking boots or good walking shoes (sneakers aren't recommended), and drinking water. Photographs are permitted, but no tripod setups are allowed, since the group moves along at a relatively brisk pace and you *really* wouldn't want to be left behind. Unless you're in great physical shape, with a long attention span, New Cave may be more cave peeping than you bargained for.

While you're exploring Carlsbad Cavern, you can pretty much set your own pace, either walking, which takes about three hours, or using the elevators up and down, for a total of perhaps 1½ hours. Add another hour or two if you have lunch at the cavern and peruse the museum exhibits and the gift- and book shops. That means a half day would certainly cover all the highlights. Then you can relax and enjoy the natural wonders of the park itself. Box lunches are available at the cavern's underground lunchroom, so you may want to have lunch at **Rattlesnake Springs.** (Don't let the name scare you. No one's seen a rattlesnake there in years.) A pleasant picnic area, with shade trees, grass, picnic tables, water, grills, and toilets, it's also a favorite spot for bird-watchers. Located near the Black River, Rattlesnake Springs was a source of water for American Indians hundreds of years ago. Army troops exploring the area used it as well, and today it's the main water source for all the park facilities.

Another option is to take the scenic 9½-mile **Walnut Canyon Drive.** This loop begins a half mile from the visitors' center and travels along the top of the ridge to the edge of Rattlesnake Canyon and back down through upper Walnut Canyon to the main entrance road. It's a one-way gravel road, and the backcountry scenery is stunning; go late in the afternoon or early in the morning to enjoy the full spectrum of changing light and dancing colors. There's also a self-guided **Desert Nature Walk,** about a half-mile long, which begins near the cavern's entrance. Experienced hikers might enjoy taking advantage of more than 50 miles of primitive trails that meander through the backcountry. On the other hand, if all or any of that sounds like a bit more of the Great Outdoors than you care to experience in one day, you could head into the town of Carlsbad and enjoy any number of the attractions there. *Carlsbad Caverns National Park, 3225 National Parks Hwy., Carlsbad 88220, tel. 505/ 785–2232. Cavern admission: $5 adults, $3 children 6–15, children 5 and under free for entry into the cavern; New Cave admission: $6 adults, $3 children 6–15, children 5 and under not permitted; fees for periodic, special guided trips into other undeveloped caves cost $10 a person; holders of Golden Age Passports get a 50% discount on all admission fees. Open June– Aug., daily 8–7; Sept.–May, daily 8–5:30. Facilities include a nursery, kennel, bookstore, gift shop, and 2 restaurants, 1 above ground and 1 750 feet below.*

Carlsbad and Environs

With the world-famous caverns nearby, the town of Carlsbad is among the most popular tourist destinations in New Mexico. Originally named Eddy after pioneer cattleman Charles B. Eddy, the town's name was changed to Carlsbad in 1889 because its spring-water mineral content was discovered to be similar to that found in Karlsbad, Czechoslovakia, a famous health spa. Situated along the Pecos River, which affords it 27 miles of beaches and picturesque pathways, Carlsbad is an attractive town of 30,000 that seems pleasantly suspended between the past and the present. Only a block from the river, its territorial town square encircles a Pueblo-style country courthouse designed by the famed New Mexican architect John Gaw Meed, who also designed many of the buildings on the University of New Mexico campus in Albuquerque. Surprisingly for a city its size, Carlsbad has 30 parks, more than any other city in New Mexico. It also has more than its share of hokey attractions—miniature train rides, riverboat paddlewheelers, an amusement village with carnival thrill rides—but somehow it all seems to work.

Carlsbad Museum and Arts Center, on the town square, contains the bones of prehistoric animals that once roamed the region—mammoths, camels, and ancient horses. It also has pioneer Apache relics, Pueblo pottery, American Indian art, early cowboy memorabilia, and remains of meteorites. The prize, however, is the McAdoo Collection, with its excellent sculptures by Frederic Remington and Charles Russell's paintings of the Old West, as well as works by painters of the Taos Society of Artists. *Fox St., Carlsbad, tel. 505/887–0276. Admission free. Open Mon.–Sat. 10–6; closed Sun. and major holidays.*

Living Desert State Park, atop Ocotillo Hills, about 1½ miles northwest of Carlsbad (off U.S. 285; look for the signs), contains an impressive collection of plants and animals native to the Chihuahuan Desert, which extends north from Mexico into southwestern Texas and southeastern New Mexico. Like many deserts, it's surprisingly rich in animal and plant life, as the park reveals. The Desert Arboretum has hundreds of exotic cacti and succulents. The Living Desert Zoo, more a reserve than a traditional zoo, is home to mountain lions, deer, elk, wolves, buffalo, rattlesnakes, and other indigenous species. Creatures of the night can be viewed below ground through special glass panels. The park has numerous shaded rest areas, rest rooms, and water fountains. *Living Desert State Park, Carlsbad, tel. 505/887–5516. Admission: $3, children 6 and under free. Open May 15–Labor Day, daily 8–8, 9–5 the rest of the year. Last tour takes place one hour before closing.*

Million Dollar Museum, 20 miles southeast of Carlsbad in the desert resort town of White's City (take U.S. 62/180 to White's City, then head west on NM 7), has 11 big rooms on two levels filled with early American memorabilia and artifacts—antique dolls and dollhouses, guns and rifles, music boxes, old cars, and a 6,000-year-old mummified Indian. There's an arcade and shooting gallery next door. *1 Carlsbad Caverns Hwy., White's City, tel. 505/785–2291. Admission: $2.50 adults, $2 senior citizens, $1.50 children 6–12, children under 6 free. Open daily 9–5.*

Sports and Outdoor Activities

Bird-watching

From turkey vultures to golden eagles, more than 200 species of birds have been identified in Carlsbad Cavern National Park. The best place to go birding in the park, if not the entire state, is Rattlesnake Springs, a desert oasis (*see* Carlsbad Caverns National Park in Exploring Carlsbad, above). Ask for a checklist at the visitors' center, and then start checking: red-tailed hawk, red-winged blackbird, white-throated swift, northern flicker, pygmy nuthatches, yellow-billed cuckoo, roadrunner, mallard, American coot, green-winged and blue-winged teal—over 200 in all.

Hiking

More than 50 miles of trails provide access to the 46,000 acres of scenic desert, plunging canyons, steep rocky ridges, and mountain wilderness of Carlsbad Caverns National Park. An hour's drive to the southwest is the rugged 76,293-acre Guadalupe Mountains National Park, containing eight of Texas's highest peaks.

Black walnut, oak, desert willow, and hackberry proliferate along the canyons' bottoms. The ridges and walls of the canyons contain a variety of desert plants—yucca, agave, sotol, sticklike branches of ocotillo, and clusters of sparse desert grass. Higher up, piñon pine, juniper, ponderosa, pine, and Douglas fir dominate. Animals that scamper about or roam the area at a more leisurely pace include raccoon; skunk; rabbits; fox; gopher; woodrat; mice; porcupine; mule deer; coyote; and the ever-elusive badger, bobcat, and mountain lions. There are plenty of snakes in the area, but because they're both nocturnal and shy, visitors rarely see them.

Backcountry hiking in Carlsbad Caverns National Park can be exhilarating—the desert terrain is stark and awesome—but few trails are marked as in other national parks, and there is no water (bring plenty). A topographical map, available at the visitors' center, will be helpful in defining some of the old ranch trails. Permits aren't required, except for overnight backpacking expeditions, but all hikers are requested to register at the information desk at the visitors' center. Bring plenty of water. No pets or guns are permitted. The following is a sampling of some of the most interesting and most accessible trails.

Guadalupe Ridge Trail, also known as the Jeep Road, starts at Walnut Canyon Loop Road and covers 13 miles, mostly along ridge tops, to Putnam Cabin. The 2,000-foot ascent is a gradual climb to the highest point in the park.

The Guano Trail, a little more than 3½ miles, was originally the truck and wagon route that miners used to transport guano from Carlsbad Caverns to White's City. The trail starts from the Bat Flight Amphitheater and affords good views on mostly flat terrain.

Take the short (¼ mile) **Rattlesnake Canyon Overlook Trail** to get superlative views of Rattlesnake Canyon. You can pick it up along the Walnut Canyon Loop Drive (*see* Carlsbad Caverns National Park in Exploring Carlsbad, above), a few hundred yards north of the Rattlesnake Canyon Trailhead.

Rattlesnake Canyon Trail covers close to 3 miles and descends from 4,570 to 3,900 feet as it goes down into the canyon. This trail, which is well-defined and marked with rock cairns, starts from the Walnut Canyon Loop Drive.

Yucca Canyon Trail, about 6 miles long, begins at the mouth of Yucca canyon and climbs up to the junction of Double Canyon Trail (the elevation ranges from 4,300 to 6,150 feet); at the top of the ridge, a level, well-marked route offers wonderful views of the Guadalupe escarpment. Much of the trail leads through a lovely forested area.

Dining and Lodging

Dining

Lunches may be purchased at the Carlsbad Caverns National Park's unique restaurant, located 750 feet underground, or at the full-service restaurant on the surface. There are numerous places to eat in White's City and Carlsbad as well.

Category	Cost*
Expensive	Over $25
Moderate	$10–25
Inexpensive	under $10

per person, excluding tax (5.8%), service, and drinks

Carlsbad   **Cortez.** This charming family-owned Mexican restaurant, with an all-brick interior and photo murals of Old Mexico, has been in business for more than half a century. Most people choose the all-you-can-eat option: for $7 you can fill up on almost anything on the menu. Try the combination plate, fajitas (tortillas stuffed with sizzling chunks of beef or pork), or sour-cream enchiladas. *506 S. Canal St., tel. 505/885–4747. Reservations accepted. Dress: casual. No credit cards. Inexpensive.*

Lucy's. Another family-owned (Lucy and Justo Yanez) oasis of great Mexican food, this one doesn't have much in the way of atmosphere. A large-screen TV blares accompaniment to meals, which are served in the restaurant and, when it gets crowded, the adjoining lounge. But the food is fresh and fabulous. When the waitress asks you "smoking or nonsmoking?" she's not referring to your nicotine habit but to the degree of fire you want in your food. All the New Mexican standards are available, along with some not-so-standard items such as chapa chicken chacos and Tucson-style chimichangas. *701 S. Canal St., tel. 505/887–7714. No reservations. Dress: casual. MC, V. Moderate.*

White's City

Fast Jack's. This fast-food favorite shares an adobe-style building with the Velvet Garter Restaurant and Saloon. Seated at one of the booths or at the counter, you can order great burgers; 32 flavors of homemade ice cream; and fresh baked pies, along with standard breakfast, lunch, and dinner fare, including Mexican specialties and some seafood selections. This is a good spot to chow down for a hearty breakfast before heading off into the caverns. Owner Jack White, whose father founded White's City, graduated from Stanford with an electrical engineering degree. He makes sure the bank of video games and souvenir token slot machine are all in good working order. *26 Carlsbad Caverns Hwy., White's City, tel. 505/785–2291. No reservations. Dress: casual. D, DC, MC, V. Inexpensive.*

The Velvet Garter Restaurant and Saloon. Come here for steak, chicken, catfish, shrimp, and Mexican food in a whoopee Wild West atmosphere, with bawdy paintings on the wall, the Carlsbad Caverns in stained glass, and rinky-dink background music. Food prices are old-style, too—a 12-ounce rib-eye steak costs $9.95—but a shot of tequila in the saloon will set you back $3. *26 Carlsbad Caverns Hwy., White's City, tel. 505/785–2291. No reservations. Dress: casual. D, DC, MC, V. Moderate.*

Lodging

Since tourism is a major industry in Carlsbad, the area offers a wide choice of motels and other services. Most of them are strung out along the highway going to the caverns, appropriately called National Parks Highway. At the turnoff from the highway to the caverns, White's City is a honky-tonk tourist complex, with three motels, a tent and RV campground, restaurants, a post office, souvenir shops, a small amusement park and museum, a miniature golf course, and a saloon.

The most highly recommended establishments are indicated by a star ★.

Category	Cost*
Expensive	$100–$150
Moderate	$65–$100
Inexpensive	under $65

Prices are for a double room, excluding 5.8% tax.

Carlsbad
Hotels and Motels
★

Best Western Stevens Motel. An old favorite, both locally and with tour groups, this is a reliable, well-operated place. The guest rooms have been recently redone, featuring bright desert colors, mirrored vanities, and modern furnishings; some have kitchenettes, some have private patios, and some have both. Buildings are scattered over a landscaped area covering more than a city block. The motel's Flume Room, an elegant local favorite dining spot, features steaks, prime rib, and tableside service. There's also a coffee shop offering regional and Mexican specialties. The hotel is owned by Carlsbad's mayor, Bob Forrest, but even knowing him won't get you a table at its Silver Spur bar and lounge on Saturday night when the Chaparrals are playing. *1829 S. Canal St., Box 580, Carlsbad 88220, tel. 505/887–2851 or 800/528–1234 for reservations. 202 rooms. Facilities: restaurant, café, lounge, pool, wading pool, playground. AE, D, DC, MC, V. Inexpensive.*

Carlsbad Travelodge South. One mile from the airport and one block from the Convention Center in Carlsbad, this three-story motel has rooms decorated in cheerful Southwestern tones, although the furnishings are generic. There is no restaurant on the premises, but Jerry's, in the immediate vicinity, serves Denny's-style fare 24 hours a day. *3817 National Parks Hwy., Carlsbad 88220, tel. 505/887–8888 or 800/255–3050 for reservations. 64 rooms. Facilities: pool, Jacuzzi, free airport transfers, complimentary full breakfast for each paying adult. AE, D, DC, MC, V. Inexpensive.*

Continental Inn. South of Carlsbad, on National Parks Highway, 30 minutes from Carlsbad Caverns, Continental Inn has simple rooms with matching curtains and bedspreads in colorful Southwestern patterns. The small grounds are pretty and well kept. *3820 National Parks Hwy., Carlsbad 88220, tel. 505/887–0341. 60 rooms. Facilities: heated pool in season, available airport pickups, truck parking. AE, D, DC, MC, V. Inexpensive.*

Park Inn International. This two-story, stone-facaded property encloses a landscaped patio with a pool and a sun deck about as large as an aircraft hanger. Rooms are comfortable, with undistinguished modern furnishings and king-size or two double beds with bright Native American–design bedspreads. The Cafe in the Park serves breakfast and lunch, and the Chaparral Grill Room, a more formal dining room, is open for dinner. Scott's Archery Range is next door. *3706 National Parks Hwy., Carlsbad 88220, tel. 505/887–2861 or 800/437–PARK for reservations. 124 rooms. Facilities: hot tub, pool, 2 restaurants, bar, game room, guest laundry, gift shop, free airport and bus-terminal transfers. AE, D, DC, MC, V. Inexpensive.*

Stagecoach Inn. Close to many of the major Carlsbad attractions, this family-style motor inn offers basic, household-variety rooms at affordable rates. *1819 S. Canal St., Carlsbad 88220, tel. 505/887–1148. 57 rooms. Facilities: restaurant, pool, wading pool, tree-shaded park with playground and picnic area, guest laundry, truck parking. AE, D, MC, V. Inexpensive.*

Bed-and-Breakfasts

La Casa Muneca Bed and Breakfast. One of the first of its kind in Carlsbad, La Casa Muneca is Southwestern through and through, from its red-tile roof and stucco exterior to the many paintings of Carlsbad scenery by local artists and the living room's colorful wicker furniture. The name Casa Muneca, which means "dollhouse" in Spanish, reflects the owner's hobby: her handmade dolls and teddy bears are displayed throughout the house. The guest rooms are large and filled with sunlight, and the Continental breakfast fare is fresh baked and bountiful. *231 N. Alameda, Carlsbad 88220, tel. 505/887–1891 or 505/887–5738. 4 rooms, 2 with bath, 2 with a shared bath. Facilities: cable TV and VCR in living room, croquet set. No smoking. MC, V. Inexpensive–Moderate.*

White's City   **Best Western Cavern Inn.** A two-story motor inn with Southwestern-style rooms, this hotel offers the closest accommodations to Carlsbad Caverns and is an immediate neighbor of the popular Velvet Garter Restaurant (*see* Dining, above). It's a pleasant, friendly place, determined to make you have a good time. Lots of tour groups are booked here, as well as families. *12 Carlsbad Caverns Hwy., White's City 88266, tel. 505/785–2291. 62 rooms. Facilities: 2 pools, spa, in-room whirlpool tubs, café, playground. AE, DC, MC, V.*

Campgrounds and RV Parks   Backcountry camping is by permit only in Carlsbad Caverns National Park; free permits can be obtained at the visitors center, where you can also pick up a map of areas closed to camping. You'll need to hike to campsites, which may not be seen from established roadways. There are no vehicle or RV camping areas in the park.

Nearby Brantley Lake State Park, the newest state park in New Mexico, and Lincoln National Forest both have camping facilities. In addition, a number of commercial sites are available at White's City, 7 miles northeast of the Caverns, and in Carlsbad, 27 miles northeast.

The AAA Park Entrance RV Park has full hookups, a swimming pool, pull-through spaces, and shades. *31 Carlsbad Caverns Hwy. (Box 128), White's City 88268, tel. 800/CAVERNS. 93 full hookups, 20 water and electric. $15 per night ($13.50 for AAA members). Reservations required 2 weeks in advance. AE, D, DC, MC, V.*

Brantley Lake State Park. Twelve miles north of Carlsbad via Highway 285, this facility has a playground, boat ramps, picnic areas, grills, bathhouse with running water and flush toilets, overnight camping spaces, and a visitors' center. Fishing (bass, trout, and crappie), boating, and other water sports are offered. *Box 2288, Carlsbad 88221, tel. 505/457–2384. 49 water and electric hookups. Primitive-area camping (no immediate facilities) $6 per night, developed-area camping (with facilities) $7 per night, hookup sites $11 per night. No reservations. No credit cards.*

KOA Kampgrounds. This shaded, full-service campground has level gravel sites and canopied tables, trees, year-round grass for tenters, a swimming pool, laundry, public phone and phone hookups, hot showers, flush toilets, a grocery store, grills, and sewage disposal. A professional RV service is located next door. *4301 National Parks Hwy., Star Rte. 1, Box 34, Carlsbad 88220, tel. 505/885–6333. 170 sites, 46 full hookups, 68 water and electric. $8.50–$11.50 for 2 persons. Reservations recommended during the summer months. D, MC, V.*

Park Entrance RV Park. In the heart of White's City, 7 miles from Carlsbad Caverns, this popular RV park offers natural desert sites with canopied shaded tables. Included are flush toilets, hot showers, sewage disposal, gasoline, grocery store, grills, parking control gates, and nearby recreational facilities (recreation hall, arcade, playground, tennis court, and two heated swimming pools). *13 Carlsbad Caverns Hwy. (Box 128), White's City 88268, tel. 505/785-2291 or 800/CAVERNS for reservations. 150 sites. 60 full hookups, 48 pull-throughs. $14 per vehicle. Reservations suggested during the summer. AE, D, MC, V.*

Windmill RV Park. Facilities for swimming, boating, and fishing, as well as laundry, hot showers, and flush toilets, are available at this RV park located on National Parks Highway (accessed by NM 180/62 South). *3624 National Parks Hwy., Carlsbad 88220, tel. 505/885-9761. 61 RV sites, water, flush toilets, hot showers. AE, D, MC, V.*

Nightlife

Carlsbad Caverns closes at 7 PM during the summer, 5:30 PM during the winter; between late May and mid-October you can hang around until sunset to watch thousands of bats leave the caves en masse to forage for food (*see* Carlsbad Caverns National Park in Exploring Carlsbad, above). For more conventional types of nighttime activities, you're pretty much limited to the Carlsbad lounge circuit. You can dance to country-and-western music at the **Silver Spur Lounge** in the Best Western Stevens Motel (tel. 505/887-2851), where live bands play Monday–Saturday 9 PM–1:30 AM. (If you want to start early, happy hour is 4–7 PM.) The **Park Inn International's lounge** (tel. 505/887-2861) has a big-screen TV and a jukebox and live country-and-western bands on Friday and Saturday nights. It's open Monday–Saturday from 4 PM until around 2 AM. Also operating during those hours is **My Way Lounge** (203 S. Central St., tel. 505/887-0212), a popular place to shoot some pool, play video games, and (you guessed it) dance to live country-and-western music; bands play from around 9 PM until 2 AM on Fridays and Saturdays only.

Index

Personal Itinerary

Departure *Date*

Time

Transportation

Arrival *Date*   *Time*

Departure *Date*   *Time*

Transportation

Accommodations

Arrival *Date*   *Time*

Departure *Date*   *Time*

Transportation

Accommodations

Arrival *Date*   *Time*

Departure *Date*   *Time*

Transportation

Accommodations

Personal Itinerary

Arrival *Date*   *Time*

Departure *Date*   *Time*

Transportation

Accommodations

Arrival *Date*   *Time*

Departure *Date*   *Time*

Transportation

Accommodations

Arrival *Date*   *Time*

Departure *Date*   *Time*

Transportation

Accommodations

Arrival *Date*   *Time*

Departure *Date*   *Time*

Transportation

Accommodations

Personal Itinerary

Arrival *Date*   *Time*

Departure *Date*   *Time*

Transportation

Accommodations

Arrival *Date*   *Time*

Departure *Date*   *Time*

Transportation

Accommodations

Arrival *Date*   *Time*

Departure *Date*   *Time*

Transportation

Accommodations

Arrival *Date*   *Time*

Departure *Date*   *Time*

Transportation

Accommodations

Personal Itinerary

Arrival *Date*   *Time*

Departure *Date*   *Time*

Transportation

Accommodations

Arrival *Date*   *Time*

Departure *Date*   *Time*

Transportation

Accommodations

Arrival *Date*   *Time*

Departure *Date*   *Time*

Transportation

Accommodations

Arrival *Date*   *Time*

Departure *Date*   *Time*

Transportation

Accommodations

Addresses

Name

Address

Telephone

Name

Address

Telephone

Name

Address

Telephone

Name

Address

Telephone

Name

Address

Telephone

Name

Address

Telephone

Name

Address

Telephone

Name

Address

Telephone

Name

Address

Telephone

Name

Address

Telephone

Name

Address

Telephone

Name

Address

Telephone

Name

Address

Telephone

Name

Address

Telephone

Name

Address

Telephone

Name

Address

Telephone

Addresses

Name	*Name*
Address	*Address*
Telephone	*Telephone*
Name	*Name*
Address	*Address*
Telephone	*Telephone*
Name	*Name*
Address	*Address*
Telephone	*Telephone*
Name	*Name*
Address	*Address*
Telephone	*Telephone*
Name	*Name*
Address	*Address*
Telephone	*Telephone*
Name	*Name*
Address	*Address*
Telephone	*Telephone*
Name	*Name*
Address	*Address*
Telephone	*Telephone*
Name	*Name*
Address	*Address*
Telephone	*Telephone*

Fodor's Travel Guides

U.S. Guides

Alaska
Arizona
Boston
California
Cape Cod, Martha's
  Vineyard, Nantucket
The Carolinas & the
  Georgia Coast
The Chesapeake
  Region
Chicago
Colorado
Disney World & the
  Orlando Area
Florida
Hawaii

Las Vegas, Reno,
  Tahoe
Los Angeles
Maine, Vermont,
  New Hampshire
Maui
Miami & the
  Keys
National Parks
  of the West
New England
New Mexico
New Orleans
New York City
New York City
  (Pocket Guide)

Pacific North Coast
Philadelphia & the
  Pennsylvania
  Dutch Country
Puerto Rico
  (Pocket Guide)
The Rockies
San Diego
San Francisco
San Francisco
  (Pocket Guide)
The South
Santa Fe, Taos,
  Albuquerque
Seattle &
  Vancouver

Texas
USA
The U. S. & British
  Virgin Islands
The Upper Great
  Lakes Region
Vacations in
  New York State
Vacations on the
  Jersey Shore
Virginia & Maryland
Waikiki
Washington, D.C.
Washington, D.C.
  (Pocket Guide)

Foreign Guides

Acapulco
Amsterdam
Australia
Austria
The Bahamas
The Bahamas
  (Pocket Guide)
Baja & Mexico's Pacific
  Coast Resorts
Barbados
Barcelona, Madrid,
  Seville
Belgium &
  Luxembourg
Berlin
Bermuda
Brazil
Budapest
Budget Europe
Canada
Canada's Atlantic
  Provinces

Cancun, Cozumel,
  Yucatan Peninsula
Caribbean
Central America
China
Czechoslovakia
Eastern Europe
Egypt
Europe
Europe's Great Cities
France
Germany
Great Britain
Greece
The Himalayan
  Countries
Holland
Hong Kong
India
Ireland
Israel
Italy

Italy 's Great Cities
Jamaica
Japan
Kenya, Tanzania,
  Seychelles
Korea
London
London
  (Pocket Guide)
London Companion
Mexico
Mexico City
Montreal &
  Quebec City
Morocco
New Zealand
Norway
Nova Scotia,
  New Brunswick,
  Prince Edward
  Island
Paris

Paris (Pocket Guide)
Portugal
Rome
Scandinavia
Scandinavian Cities
Scotland
Singapore
South America
South Pacific
Southeast Asia
Soviet Union
Spain
Sweden
Switzerland
Sydney
Thailand
Tokyo
Toronto
Turkey
Vienna & the Danube
  Valley
Yugoslavia

Wall Street Journal Guides to Business Travel

Europe   International Cities   Pacific Rim   USA & Canada

Special-Interest Guides

Bed & Breakfast and
  Country Inn Guides:
  Mid-Atlantic Region
  New England
  The South
  The West

Cruises and Ports
  of Call
Healthy Escapes
Fodor's Flashmaps
  New York

Fodor's Flashmaps
  Washington, D.C.
Shopping in Europe
Skiing in the USA &
  Canada

Smart Shopper's
  Guide to London
Sunday in New York
Touring Europe
Touring USA